Praise for

"Award-winning author Paul D. Marks hits it out of the park with his latest, *The Blues Don't Care*. On one level it's a mystery where a white musician, Bobby Saxon, in an all-black jazz band, works to solve a murder and clear his name under extraordinary racially-tinged circumstances. But this finely-written novel takes place in World War II-era Los Angeles, and Marks brings that long-gone era alive with memorable characters, scents, descriptions, and most of all, jazz. Highly recommended."

—Brendan DuBois, award-winning
and *New York Times* bestselling author

"Paul D. Marks finds new gold in '40s L.A. noir while explor-ing prejudices in race, culture, and sexual identity. Marks has an eye for the telling detail, and an ear that captures the music in the dialogue of the times. He is one helluva writer."

—Michael Sears, award-winning author
of *Tower of Babel*, and the Jason Stafford series

"In *The Blues Don't Care*, Paul D. Marks deftly portrays the colors and contradictions of World War II era L.A. as navi-gated by unlikely sleuth Bobby Saxon whose disparate worlds collide in this impressive series debut."

—Dianne Emley, *L.A. Times* bestselling author
of the Nan Vining mysteries

THE BLUES DON'T CARE

OTHER TITLES BY PAUL D. MARKS

The Duke Rogers P.I. Thrillers
White Heat
Broken Windows

Other Novels
Vortex

Short Story Collection
L.A. Late @ Night

Anthologies (Editor w/ Andrew McAleer)
Coast to Coast: Murder from Sea to Shining Sea
Coast to Coast: Private Eyes from Sea to Shining Sea

PAUL D. MARKS

THE BLUES DON'T CARE

Down & Out Books
3959 Van Dyke Road, Suite 265
Lutz, FL 33558
DownAndOutBooks.com

Cover design by JT Lindroos

ISBN: 1-64396-050-4
ISBN-13: 978-1-64396-050-0

It might sound corny, but I want to dedicate this book to all the jazz and swing musicians who've brought so much music and joy into my life and others' lives. All the folks who made Central Avenue what it was. I only wish I could have seen it in its heyday. The best part about writing this book was doing the research, listening to the music and watching old movies.

AUTHOR'S NOTE

Some of the language and attitudes in the novel may be offensive. But please consider them in the context of the time, place and characters. I've taken liberties with the timelines of some things such as Dick Tracy's wrist radio and particularly with songs and music. If I thought a song would work for this story, I used it, even though it may not have come out at that exact moment.

All the world's a stage,
And all the men and women merely players;
They have their exits and their entrances;
And one man in his time plays many parts.
—William Shakespeare

Once you eliminate the impossible, whatever remains,
no matter how improbable, must be the truth.
—Sir Arthur Conan Doyle

I don't mind a reasonable amount of trouble.
—Sam Spade, *The Maltese Falcon*

Everybody has something to conceal.
—Sam Spade, *The Maltese Falcon*

PROLOGUE

San Francisco—The Eve of the Millennium

The late-night phone call jangled Diane awake.

"Diane Saxon?" the officious voice on the other end said.

"Yes." She tried to shake the sleep out of her voice.

"This is the Los Angeles County Coroner's office—"

In those few words, any leftover sleepiness Diane had escaped, replaced by dread.

She pressed the phone tighter against her ear. Squeezed the receiver until it nearly cracked in her hand. As soon as the phone rang, she knew it couldn't be good news.

"Are you related to, um—" papers rattling "—Robert Saxon?"

"Yes, I'm his daughter. Did he—"

"I'm sorry to call you so late, but I'm afraid your, uh, father has passed away. Can you come down to L.A. to identify him?"

Diane looked at the clock. Midnight. Bobby would have appreciated that.

Los Angeles—The Next Morning

Diane walked the musty halls of Bobby's house, killing time before her appointment at the coroner's office. Bobby, so meticulous all his life—sometimes to the point of driving her crazy—had let things go in the last year or so.

1

She returned to the scrapbook she'd left on the dining table, turned the yellowing pages in the fragile book. A pristine shellac seventy-eight rpm record spun on an ancient but near-mint condition record player. This record had only been removed from its sleeve a handful of times over the years for fear of breaking the delicate material. "La Tempesta," an allegro tune for two pianos—Bobby on one of them—spun its satiny web from the player's speaker. The tune reverberated in Diane's head; she'd heard it many times. She could picture Bobby wailing on the piano like a possessed demon.

The brittle scrapbook paper nearly crumbled in her fingers. Faded photographs, brown with age, stared up at her. Bobby from the forties, sitting at a grand piano in a snazzy wide-lapelled pinstriped suit. Bobby in a white jacket and bow tie in the fifties. Bobby in black tie and jacket in the sixties. Bobby in shirt sleeves barbequing in the backyard of the rented duplex on Edinburgh. Diane as a baby, on her stomach, feet in the air—cheesecake pose. Her sister Mindy on their favorite red rocking horse with painted on black saddle. Diane's mom and Mindy's mom—Diane and Mindy, sisters with different mothers. She sipped the Bubble Up she'd gotten from the fridge. Who knew if they even made that anymore? She wanted to keep turning pages but had an appointment to keep. She gently closed the cover on the scrapbook.

She walked to Bobby's mirror—Bobby loved his mirrors—checked her makeup, grabbed her purse. She noticed his favorite cigarette lighter on the dresser, the one with the picture of that "Kilroy Was Here" guy on it, so popular during the war. She squeezed the lighter as if that could bring a memory from it, slipped it into her purse.

"Criminy," she said, holding back a tear.

She had flown in from San Francisco, but Bobby's old red-over-white sixty-one Corvette Roadster would take her where she had to go now, probably better than any new car. Bobby was a whiz with cars, always fixing them up and selling them.

She headed out the door, "La Tempesta" still spinning its magic.

She drove past familiar haunts from her childhood, down the Miracle Mile, past the fabulous streamline May Company building, the La Brea Tar Pits, where Bobby had taken her and Mindy on picnics, and the old El Rey Theatre, where they'd gone to the movies. Oh boy, how Bobby loved movies. Past Bullock's Wilshire, the art deco masterpiece, and by MacArthur Park, which Bobby insisted calling Westlake Park, even long after the name had been changed to honor the great World War II general. She jogged up and over, onto North Mission Road, looked for a place to park.

Heart tapping a hard four-four time in her chest, she walked toward the white-trimmed red brick building, beautiful despite its nature. It had been a hospital, once trying to save lives, now dealing with the remains. The green-and-white marble lobby seemed sober enough for its purpose. She did a double take at the Skeletons in the Closet gift store, a gift shop in the morgue that offered up all matter of items, from keychains to beach towels with body outlines on them, even body-shaped Post-it pads. Maybe she'd pick up a monogrammed body bag for some friends—enemies?—on the way out.

"May I help you?" a young man in suit and tie asked. He didn't look ghoulish, but who else would want to work here?

"I'm here to identify someone's remains." Diane thought that's how it should be put. She wished Mindy was here for moral support but she had refused to come. Some kind of ill-defined bad blood between her and Bobby. Something that neither could figure out how to resolve so they resolved to avoid each other, even though Mindy only lived an hour away from Bobby, up in Lancaster. Something that would never be resolved now.

The young man pointed her to the elevator in a small vestibule. The short trip seemed to take forever. A ride down, into the past.

She stepped out into a world that was more what she expected.

3

Sterile, tile, gurneys. People in white smocks. An attendant escorted her to the viewing room. A spikey-haired doctor joined them.

"I'm Doctor Takamura. I'm sorry you had to come down here."

"I guess it's something that has to be done."

"We don't usually have people come down to the morgue to identify remains anymore. That's just in the movies. But this was a special case."

Diane wasn't sure why Bobby was a special case. Maybe because he'd been a fairly well-known musician at one time, though that was long ago.

The doctor knocked on the glass. An attendant on the other side opened the blinds and pulled back the glaring white sheet. Diane walked closer to the window, almost pressing her nose against the glass. Bobby had almost made it. Today was the last day of the year; tomorrow would not only bring a new year but a new millennium, the twenty-first century. How Bobby would have loved to see it. He was always excited about things like birthdays and Christmas and New Year's. Everyone had to die sooner or later, but she wished he could have lived just a few more days. Just long enough to be alive in the new millennium.

"Yes, that's him. That's my father."

"Robert Saxon?" A look passed between the doctor and the assistant.

"Yes."

"There's something you should know," the doctor said.

Before Diane could respond, an ancient black man entered the room. His dark blue double-breasted suit with padded shoulders and long drape was stylish, if out of date. And she hadn't seen a Dick Tracy hat like that, well, since Warren Beatty's *Dick Tracy*. The fuchsia silk kerchief craning up from the pocket was just right. All topped off by an ebony cane with a gleaming pearl handle. "Help you?" Dr. Takamura said.

"Booker Taylor," the man said, sauntering in, very haughty. Lots of bling sparkled from his fingers. Booker "Boom-Boom"

Taylor. He was an old friend of Bobby's. She remembered him from her birthday parties when she was very young. He would toss her over his broad shoulders and play horsey. It started trickling back, Bobby and Booker and several of Bobby's other friends jamming at her parties. And she remembered a neighbor once remarking, why did Bobby have that *colored fella* over all the time?

"Are you sure you're in the right place?" the doctor said. Booker ignored him.

"Diane. Look at you." Booker's eyes lit up. "All grown up and quite the lady." He squeezed her hand. Turned to see Bobby through the glass. "Bobby, Bobby, Bobby." A long sigh escaped his lips. He went to the door that led to the little room.

Dr. Takamura stepped in front of him.

"No, it's okay," Diane said, smiling at Booker. He looked too sad to smile back. "He knew my father. They were in the music business together."

Booker opened the door and went inside, Diane trailing. He took Bobby's hand, tenderly massaged it.

"We weren't in the music business together. We owned it. We had this town of Los Angeles locked up tighter than a bass drum. And your pop, he really could have gone somewhere. And no one could tap the eighty-eights like he could."

"Eighty-eights?" the assistant said.

"The piano, hon. Tickle the ivories. Back in the day, Bobby Saxon was the man. And he knew one thing better than anyone, that we're all bluffing our way through life." Booker tripped on his words as another man entered the room. Dressed casual-cool.

"Who're you?" the doctor said.

"Irvin Hernandez, *L.A. Times.*"

"The Times—what does the Times want here?"

"This is Bobby Saxon, right?"

"Yes."

"I want his story."

"I didn't know anyone remembered my father. He hasn't

played music in years."

"You're his daughter? You must have some story to tell."

To Diane, Bobby was just dad. She didn't have much to tell. Her puzzlement must have been clear to everyone in the room.

Booker sat on a chair in the corner, leaning his chin on his cane. "*I* have a story to tell," he began. "It was the middle of the war when I met Bobby..."

CHAPTER ONE

Los Angeles—The Homefront, World War II

Bobby Saxon stood across Central Avenue from the Club Alabam, watching the crowds spilling into the street, lingering on the sidewalk. A near-lone white face in a sea of black. Dragging on his cigarette, trying to steady his nerves, he watched the people in their swanky duds entering and exiting the club, working up his nerve to go inside. Sure, he'd been in the Alabam before, but this time was different. He wasn't there just to see the bands blow and the canaries sing.

Everyone played the Alabam, or wanted to, including Bobby. Young, inexperienced—white—he knew he could knock 'em dead, if only Booker Taylor, one of the band leaders, would give him a chance.

Central Avenue was something to see. The heart of *colored* Los Angeles in the forties during the war. And at the heart of Central was the Club Alabam, and the Dunbar Hotel next door. Neon marquees lit up the night sky, beckoning passersby to enter their realms of music and mystery and see the likes of Duke Ellington, Cab Calloway, Bill "Bojangles" Robinson, and every other colored act you could imagine.

Cars, with their bright white headlights and trailing hot red taillights, crawled like lifeblood up and down the avenue. Cigarette smoke wafted in and out of the clubs, wrapping around streetlights, forming halos in the L.A. fog, creating an ethereal world—another world. And it was another world from most of L.A. and the L.A. Bobby grew up in. A world that Bobby would have sacrificed almost anything to be part of.

He darted into traffic, dodging oncoming Buicks and Fords and Pontiacs. He brushed past people dressed to the nines, ladies in furs and heels, gentlemen in tuxes and fashionable suits. Even zoot suits. They strolled and strutted up and down the street like peacocks showing their finest feathers, ducking in and out of the clubs and restaurants. They smoked cigarettes from beautifully crafted holders. He strolled to the front door, made his way inside. Smoke wafted up and through the palm tree decor as Ruby, the hostess, recognized Bobby and gave him a ringside seat. She knew he was hep, even though he didn't drink. The two-dollar tip didn't hurt his getting that good seat either. He ordered Bubble Up and grooved on the Booker "Boom-Boom" Taylor Orchestra—only in this case orchestra meant one hot jazz big band.

Bobby's foot tapped out the beat as he eyed the dance floor. Black couples. White couples. Coloreds and whites dancing together. One of the few places in L.A. you could do that and not walk away with your head in your hands. Whites from all over Los Angeles—even movie stars—came to hear the bands, cut a rug, and maybe get a little crazy. And though there might be some coloreds or whites who would look on disapprovingly, mostly no one cared.

Bobby watched set after set, tap-tap-tapping and smoking butt after butt of Viceroys. "Thank you, thank you, ladies and gentlemen," Booker's voice boomed from the stage mic. "We'll be back after a short break. Have a drink and enjoy!"

The jam-packed dance floor emptied as the jitterbugs scattered back to their tables or the bar. Bobby stood, ready to make his move. He scooted through the narrow lanes between the closely placed tables, through the crowd, dodging drunken dancers. He wanted to catch Booker wherever he might land between sets, maybe on stage, maybe in the hall leading to the dressing rooms. Before he could, Booker snapped his head in Bobby's direction, crooked his finger at him.

"Me?" Bobby mimed.

Booker nodded.

Bobby climbed onto the stage as the rest of the band departed. Just being on the Alabam's stage with Booker was enough to make his heart pound out prestissimo time, even if he wasn't playing with the band. At over six feet, Booker towered over Bobby. Up close Bobby could see the fine line of Booker's moustache, the longish, slicked-back, processed hair. He envied Booker's threads—the draped, broad-shouldered double-breasted suit, the pleated pants and fine, lilac silk scarf. But the most striking thing about him, besides his baritone voice, were those piercing eyes. Bobby felt those eyes burning a hole in his skin.

"You're up here every night, kid. Every night all alone. What's up?"

"I dig the music."

"You *dig* the music. Jungle bunny music?"

Jungle bunny rolled so easily off Booker's tongue. Bobby had heard it before and was surprised to hear Booker use such a negative word, even if he had said it sarcastically. "I didn't come down here to jive you."

Booker stared at Bobby through several puffs of his cigarette in a sleek, ebony holder. Bobby wanted to squirm or scram; held himself in check. Finally, Booker said, "Let's go to my office."

Bobby actually believed Booker had an office at the back of the club. Booker's *office* was the alley behind it, lit by a few bare bulbs swathed in fog, shadowy and creepy. Like something out of a Universal horror movie—*Dracula, Frankenstein*—that Bobby might have seen when he was a kid, not all that long ago. Several band members hung out there, talking, smoking, drinking. Bobby heard a grunt. Turned to see a couple screwing in a semi-dark doorway a few feet up.

He didn't know what he'd gotten himself into. What if Booker pulled a knife on him? He swallowed it down, though his father's warning about coming to this part of town with *these* people nagged at him. He was scared, but he couldn't show it. He was a man now.

Booker fished in his coat pocket, pulled something out. A hand-rolled cigarette, lit up. Offered a hit to Bobby. Bobby didn't go for it.

"Yeah, kid, reefer. The evil weed. You barely look old enough to drink. Are you old enough for this?" Booker said, inhaling. "You even old enough to be in here?"

"I'm old enough to pound the eighty-eights in a hot jazz band," Bobby said with all the bravado and self-confidence he could muster. He felt shaky fingers fumble a Viceroy from the pack. He'd been smoking since he was twelve—his hands had never shook before. "You don't look old enough to stand up to piss."

"I'm old enough."

"Hardly even looks like you run a razor over that pearly, baby-smooth skin." Booker slammed down a long drag, held it. Let the smoke out slowly. "What're you comin' down here for anyway? Why don't you try to get a gig with a white band?"

"I'm here. You wanna let me sit in?"

"Fresh cracker kid. Lemme see your hands."

Booker grabbed Bobby's hands. Ran his long dark fingers over them. Bobby hoped Booker wouldn't feel them shaking.

"Soft."

"Give me a shot, you'll see how soft."

"You know, Herb Jeffries is going to do a couple tunes next set—heard of him?"

"The Bronze Buckaroo. I love cowboy movies."

"You come down to Central to see colored cowboy movies?"

"By myself." Against his father's wishes, like so many other things he did.

"You got more balls than I thought, kid. All right, Herb's gonna sing 'Flamingo,' know it?"

Bobby nodded.

"He's also gonna sing 'The Yellow Rose of Texas.' If you can tell me what that song's really about, you can sit in."

Bobby shuffled his feet. He knew the answer, at least he thought he did. He wasn't sure if he should say it, if it was a trick question. "I know it's not about a flower."

"C'mon, kid, we don't got all day."

"The yellow rose in the song is a light-skinned colored woman, a *high yellow* woman. Do I pass?"

"All right, kid, we got no eighty-eight man tonight. You can sit in. If the audience throws shit—well you know." Booker took a last drag on his jive stick, pinched it out between his finger and thumb and put it back in his pocket. He headed inside, followed by Bobby and the band.

Bobby's eyes adjusted to the dusky Alabam light and stinging smoke. He started to push the piano into a position where it would be part of the band. No one offered to help. Booker nodded at a couple of horn players. They leisurely walked to the piano, pushed and heaved until it was in place. Bobby thanked them, limbered his fingers. Booker looked over to him, shot him a wink of encouragement. Before he could get fully situated on the bench, the band launched into "Take the A Train." The dance floor filled. The rhythm insinuated itself deep inside him. Every inch of him pulsed with it. He joined in with the band. Butterflies jumped in his stomach as he tried to play Duke Ellington's part half as good as the Duke. But his fingers stopped shaking. He hit the keys with joy and passion. Nobody left the floor. Nobody threw anything. Nobody paid much attention to the single white face among all the black faces in the band, the one person, besides Booker, not in the band uniform of white jacket, dark slacks, bow tie. Everyone applauded at the end of the number.

"And now ladies and gentlemen, as our usual vocalist, the sweet Loretta Martin, isn't with us tonight, we have a special guest. Mr. Herb Jeffries, the Bronze Buckaroo. The Sepia Singing Cowboy. The song stylist who, with Duke Ellington, made

'Flamingo' his own."

Jeffries sauntered on stage. A handsome man, over six feet tall, who truly did look bronzed. The crowd went wild.

"Thank you," Jeffries said in his rich, deep voice. Booker's hand swung on the downbeat and the band launched into "Flamingo." Bobby played along. He knew the song well. People crowded the stage to watch the singer. Others slow-danced, close and tight. The band was smooth. Jeffries spectacular with his beautiful baritone. And Bobby knew he was doing more than a serviceable job winging it. Booker glanced his way, gave him a quick grin. Bobby shot him a hasty salute. The crowd swelled and rose like a tidal wave, in a wild frenzy for the music. When the song ended, a hush fell over the room as Jeffries launched into "The Yellow Rose of Texas."

The song over, Jeffries took his bows and left the stage. Booker looked at Bobby. Bobby knew what that meant—his turn in the spotlight. Staring into a follow spot like a deer in headlights, he didn't know what to do. Then he whipped into Count Basie's "Jumpin' at the Woodside," banging away on the ivories. The crowd surged. Danced. Jitterbugs bopped to the music. Booker smiled, impressed. He looked to the band. They nodded while continuing to play—this kid could really blow.

Bobby dove deep into the music, swam with it. It was part of him, one with him. His thoughts were hardly conscious as he grooved to the beat. Fell in with the rhythm. This was the only place he wanted to be. Nothing else existed at this moment.

The number over, Booker motioned to Bobby to take a bow. Sheened with sweat, he stood and looked out at the crowd. The applause deafened him but made him happier than he'd ever been. The applause died and the band went back to its set. Bobby knew all the songs and played along just fine. When the set was over, drained and wiped out, Bobby went to the bar and ordered a Bubble Up.

"On the house," the bartender said. "Good set."

"Thanks."

"Lawrence." He put his hand out and Bobby shook it. The man squeezed hard. He wasn't much taller than Bobby but he had the handshake of a hard man. The slicing scar over his left eye confirmed it.

"Bobby Saxon."

Booker came up behind Bobby. "Welcome aboard."

Bobby tried to maintain his composure, his cool. He hoped it was working.

"You look spooked, man," Booker said, "and that ain't a word one should be using in this joint."

"Just taken aback."

"They like you, man."

"I got the gig?" Bobby was giddy. He only half-expected to get the spot, no matter how good he might be. Booker had never had a white player before. Bands weren't integrated, except for Lionel Hampton with Benny Goodman. This was almost a first.

"Yours, at least on a trial basis. We'll see how it works out for both of us. But when I said welcome aboard, I meant it. To-night's our last night at the Alabam for a few weeks."

Was the band going to travel? Bobby didn't want that. Booker must have seen the concern on Bobby's face.

"I know you're kinda young. Maybe don't wanna stray too far from home. And it ain't. Just onto the Apollo."

"The gambling ship?"

Bobby knew the Apollo was one of several gambling ships that operated off the shores of Los Angeles and Long Beach, just outside the legal limits. The law couldn't touch them. "The same. Man that boat's like a floating luxury hotel. Queen Mary ain't got nothin' on the Apollo. One day maybe we'll make it to the Apollo in Harlem."

"What about sleeping arrangements?"

"You shy, boy?"

Bobby didn't respond.

"You can sleep on the nice safe shore. Get your land legs back every night. There are sleeping arrangements on board, but most of my boys don't want to stay there either. Being colored and all, we don't get the best accommodations." Booker pulled out a Lucky Strike. "Take the last shuttle boat, water taxi, whatever you call it, home with the tourists every night. You bein' white and all they won't mind sharing their boat with you."

"Do you?"

"Do I what?"

"Mind sharing your boat with me, your band?"

Booker laughed. "I don't care 'bout color, boy. I care that my people can play. And you're not bad...for a white boy."

CHAPTER TWO

Bobby stood in front of the bathroom mirror, which also reflected the framed poster of Julien Eltinge from *The Fascinating Widow* on the opposite wall, trying on one fedora after another. If clothes make the man, Bobby wanted his clothes to make him. He loved hats and had a fedora for every occasion and every suit. Black, gray, tan and brown. Wide brimmed and wider brimmed. Wide band, narrow band. He pulled a snazzy gray-on-gray down over his eye. Picked up a multicolored, hand-painted tie with bold geometric patterns, tried it on. He tried on several ties. Booker was giving him the break he'd been waiting for. He didn't want to mess it up. Wanted to look sharp. And even though the band all wore the same suits, Bobby wanted to be seen around the ship or town in a classy outfit.

He picked up a pipe, also copped from his dad, when he thought smoking a pipe made you a man. "Too highbrow."

A cigarette. "Hmm, maybe."

Bobby eyed himself in the mirror. Baby faced. Could he pull it off? Brushing his index finger over his upper lip, he wished he could grow a mustache. He grabbed a pack of cigarettes off the sink.

He looked out the window to the low green hedge that divided his building from the one next door, longing for a view of anything other than a wall. He put the radio on. War news in between the songs. The Japs were dominant in the Pacific. Hitler was conquering Europe. American boys were already in the

African, Pacific and European theaters of war. Bobby wanted to escape news of the war, finally found some music and listened until it was time to leave.

A fine briny mist bit Bobby's skin as he waited in the throng of people on the Santa Monica Pier for the water taxi that would take him to the gambling ship Apollo. The little cartoon-like "Kilroy Was Here" drawing glared at him from the water taxi shack. Kilroy was everywhere these days. He had to shield his eyes from the fiery late afternoon sun, wished he had a pair of sunglasses. Only movie stars and musicians wore sunglasses. Maybe he'd get a pair of shades.

A group of colored men huddled off to the side. There was no rope or barrier separating them from the rest of the people, but there might as well have been.

"Bobby, over here!" Booker shouted above the din of the crowd and waves.

Bobby walked over to Booker and the band.

"We don't have to stand in line. There's a special water taxi for the band."

"We royalty," said another band member.

"Royalty my ass," a large, very dark band member muttered. It was one of those mutters that was meant to be heard. "We have to take the colored taxi. Slave ship."

"Bobby Saxon meet James Christmas. Don't let his name fool you. He's more of a Scrooge than a Christmas but a fine sax man and pretty damn good on the eighty-eights too."

Bobby camouflaged his concern. If Booker had another possible piano man, maybe he wouldn't need Bobby. He put his hand out to shake with James. James didn't offer his.

Bobby met James' eyes with his own. He wasn't going to let this man intimidate him. James held Bobby's stare for a moment, then looked away as if it were beneath him to waste his time on Bobby.

Booker turned to the band member standing next to James Christmas. "Bobby, meet Leroy Perkins, first trumpet—"

"—When Booker's not playing. Booker plays most any instrument. Still, welcome aboard the Booker Boom-Boom Taylor Orchestra and Yacht Club." Leroy put his angular hand out and Bobby shook it.

"I don't have a band uniform for you," Booker said to Bobby. "But then you're not a real member yet either."

Bobby tried not to show his disappointment.

"Most of the boys are bigger than you, so I don't have any outfits that would fit you right now. But you look fine. Sharp."

Bobby hoped so, he'd spent enough time trying on various outfits. "Is this the band's first trip to one of the gambling ships?"

"Naw, we play 'em once or twice a year. They like to move people in an' out so nobody goes stale. Not the bands, not the audience. It's like that."

"Hey, piano man," Leroy said, "where your axe? In your pocket—pretty small tinkle box."

Everyone laughed except James Christmas. Bobby joined in—he wanted the group to accept him.

"Yeah, man. How come we got to haul our axes with us?" said Cannonball, the tallest band member, with a piled high conk hairdo. He held up his trombone case. More laughter all around, except for James Christmas—again.

A water dog wearing a yacht captain's hat festooned with gold anchors and braid signaled the band to board their taxi.

"Three miles in this little boat, I hope no one gets sick," Leroy said. Everyone turned to Bobby, the rookie. He flashed a weak smile. He didn't know if he'd get seasick or not; he'd never been on the water before.

The boat moored alongside the Apollo after an uneventful trip. Once on deck, Bobby pulled Booker aside. "Booker, I really haven't had a chance to practice with the band."

"It's okay, Bobby. Just vamp. Improvise. You did swell at the Alabam."

James Christmas approached them. "Booker, I need to speak to you."

"You can speak in front of my man."

"It's about your *man*." He shot Bobby a look. "Fine by me. What're you doin' hirin' this ofay to gig with us?"

"He's good."

"This is a colored band, man."

"This is my band. You don't like it you can take the next taxi back to shore."

James dog-eyed Booker for a split-second, shook his head, and walked off under a full head of steam.

"Don't let him bother you," Booker said.

"Maybe none of them want to play with me."

"It's my call. See in the larger society, you're the man, the king. But in our world, well we got to look out for our own. But you're good and when they see you got the chops that's all they'll care about. Oh, and not being able to say shit 'bout white people." Booker clapped Bobby on the back. They headed to the band room, a large cabin below deck with dank, cold metal bulkheads, but large enough for the band to practice. The rest of the band was already there, noodling on their axes, reading the *California Eagle*—a newspaper for Negroes that Bobby liked too because it had great coverage of the band and music scenes. Bobby looked around. Since he had no piano to practice on, he started asking questions.

"Hey, Booker, do I need to join the union?" he said.

Everybody laughed.

"What's so funny?"

"Which union would that be?" Cannonball said.

"There's more than one?"

"There's separate unions for colored and white," Booker said.

"Guess we know which one he'll be joinin'," James said, without a hint of levity or irony.

The door opened. A light-skinned colored woman walked through. Bobby looked at her as long as he dared; she was beautiful. Long, straight black hair pulled back to reveal a near-perfect face with sharp features, like Lena Horne. Shimmering jet hair rippled on a diaphanous white gown sparkling with sequins.

"Yo, Loretta. Didn't know you'd be back so soon," Leroy said.

She smiled her million-dollar smile at the band, went and sat on one of the drum cases.

"Hollywood didn't work out for you? Those white boys—" Cannonball stopped short, noticing Bobby. He nervously jerked his trombone's slide back and forth.

"See what I mean, it's already different," James said.

Booker ignored him. "Loretta, meet Bobby Saxon. Our new hands on the eighty-eights."

Bobby looked over, walked to Loretta, shook hands.

"Pleased to meet you," she said. Bobby liked her contralto voice. "Just make sure he keeps his hands off Loretta," James muttered. Bobby heard, everyone did. No one said anything. Bobby was getting the feel for the band, for James in particular. He was a killjoy or maybe worse.

"Loretta's our little canary what flew the coup," Leroy said with a grin. "But now she's back to sing for her supper, at least for tonight."

"At least I'll be dining on steak and champagne, Leroy," Loretta said

Everyone laughed again, even James.

"Loretta, you and Bobby should get to know each other. Maybe work up some arrangements. Bobby, can you arrange?" Booker stared straight at Bobby. "I'm getting tired of doin' all the charts."

"I think I can."

"Think don't cut it."

"I can."

"Good." Booker turned to the band. "All right, let's get a little practice in before show time."

Bobby didn't know how the hell he'd manage that without a piano. Booker told him it was in the ballroom, but he'd have to limber up without it. Bobby's pulse drummed under his skin, nervous excitement racing through him. He'd have to play with the band cold. He hoped he was up to it.

Bobby peered over the sea of faces in the ballroom—white faces in expensive suits and chic dresses. The Apollo wasn't the biggest or fanciest or the most seaworthy ship in the world. But if she went down, half of Hollywood, the Los Angeles political establishment, and business movers and shakers in the Southland would disappear into Davy Jones' Locker. That didn't stop the people who ran her—gangsters everyone knew—from decking out the main ballroom as if it were Versailles. The ceiling was tall and sparkled with lights under a false ceiling with a gauzy, azure-painted sky. Below it, the dance floor in the center of the room, surrounded by gambling tables—craps, roulette, blackjack, and the like. And in rows behind the gambling tables, dining tables.

The band launched into its first set, running through several numbers, "Take the A Train," "Harlem Nocturne," "Sing, Sing, Sing," "Opus One," and "Strangeland"—a Booker original. Bobby jammed tight with them. No one in the all-white crowd seemed to notice a white piano player in the otherwise all-colored band. People danced. Gambled. Drank. Had a swell time.

Crash! The sound of glass breaking. Bobby looked down at the dance floor. A man's highball glass was shattered on the parquet floor. Two men yelling, raising fists. Bobby couldn't tell why. But the bulky white bouncers cooled them off before anything serious happened. Booker signaled the band to keep playing, while the bouncers handled the problem.

"And now ladies and gentlemen, please give a hand to our little canary, Loretta Martin," Booker said into the mic. The audience applauded as the band launched into "Brazil," a song

Jimmy Dorsey had made famous. Loretta sang the Helen O'Connell part; Booker did the Bob Eberly vocal. Loretta had a melodious voice.

Bobby played hard, not in the sense of pounding keys, but wanting to be there for her as an accompanist. Loretta did another number, then the band did some up-tempo tunes. At one point, Leroy leaned over to James, while glancing at Bobby, and said, "That cat does a mean walking bass." James shot him a dirty look.

"And now ladies and gentlemen, it's time for us to take a break. We'll be back in fifteen or twenty. Hang loose, have a drink, play some blackjack. Enjoy." Booker and the band left the stage to mild applause. It seemed the audience had other things on their minds. The break was as much to get people off the dance floor and at the gambling tables as it was for the band to take a rest.

He was about to step off the stage onto the main floor—deck? What do you call the floor on a ship?—when a movie-star handsome man in an elegant suit crossed in front of the stage, arm in arm with a woman of equal good looks. Bobby pretended to fiddle with one of his buttons, hoping David Chambers wouldn't look up and see him. He'd known David in high school, though David was a couple years older. They'd been friends, but Bobby didn't want to be judged. Luckily David seemed preoccupied with the woman on his arm.

Bobby followed the band down the passageway. Several of them headed for the restroom. Bobby got in line. Leroy turned to him, pointed to a sign on the door: *Colored Only.*

"The white bathroom is that way." He pointed again. Bobby didn't know what to do. He didn't mind using the colored restroom. He was part of the band. But he knew that in some places using the wrong bathroom could cause an explosion. He headed for the Whites Only toilet.

As he neared the restroom, Bobby could hear two men talking animatedly, one of them in a German accent, the other

American. Two tall white men stood by the lavatory door, one middle-aged, heavy-set, dressed expensively, like he'd stepped out of a Paramount white telephone movie. The other, thirty-fivish, lean. Pure blonde hair, like someone in one of those German propaganda films. James Christmas came out of the Whites Only head. All eyes turned to him as did the conversation.

"—*Der Fuehrer* was right in not shaking hands with the *schvartze* Jesse Owens at the 1936 Olympics," the blonde said in his mild German accent, turning his scowl on James.

"Say what?" James glared at the blonde man. The blonde glared back, neither one wanting to be the first to avert their eyes. Booker, standing near the end of the hall, turned to see what the commotion was about.

"Hans, pay no attention to him," the middle-aged man said. "He's just part of the band."

"You Americans are so much more tolerant than we Germans." The blonde turned to James. "Are there no colored toilets here?"

"You like my music. You come here to listen." James balled his hands into fists.

"I come here to gamble," the blonde man said.

"This ain't Jim Crow Georgia, you know," James spat.

"When we take over—"

"Yeah, Fritz, I know, today Deutschland, tomorrow the world," James shouted.

"My name is not Fritz."

Booker darted between James and the blonde man. James edged Booker aside, moving in on the blonde man until they were nose to nose. Booker and Bobby pushed back in between them. "Gentlemen, let's settle this like, well, gentlemen," Booker said. But it was too late. James' fist swung up, the German dodged it. Two beefy white bouncers jumped between them, pulling James off the blonde. They didn't lay a hand on the tall blonde German. James struggled; the two bouncers held him tight.

"I'll see you again," James sneered at the blonde man. The German chuckled as he and his friend walked off.

A stocky man in a tailored pinstriped suit walked up. Shorter than the bouncers, he looked tougher and meaner. "What goes on here?"

"It's all taken care of, Mr. Tierney," one of the bouncers said.

"This a band member?"

Booker nodded.

"Keep your people in line, Booker."

"Yes, sir." It was clear to anyone watching that Booker was seething, holding his temper in check.

"Let's go." Tierney led Booker, James, and Bobby to a large, well-appointed office, filled with blonde art deco furniture, not the cheap stuff. Signed celebrity photos adorned the bulkheads, Cary Grant, Carole Lombard, Jean Harlow, Clark Gable, Bogart, Joe Bascopolous, Errol Flynn, and more.

Bobby sized up the nattily dressed man behind the desk. Tony Leach—L.A.'s number two gangster, though nobody would ever say that to his face. In his mind, Bobby knew, Leach was number one.

"Booker, my friend, I can't—" Leach ran his fingers through his slicked-back black hair.

"I apologize, Mr. Leach. Sometimes things just get a little— especially with the war and all—"

"Well, it's your job to stop them from getting 'just a little.' Leastways if you want to keep working on the Apollo. I can't have you and your employees roughing up the guests."

"Booker was just trying to break it up," Bobby said.

"The honky Nazi bastard started it," James spat.

"Now you sound like my six-year-old nephew, my friend. You've met my other friend here. His name is Cabot Tierney, but we call him Carnie. You know those carnivals that travel through Southern towns, well Carnie here would break up fights with the good old boys, and believe me they grow them big down there. Carnie could one-hand them, up and out. And God bless anyone who tried fighting back."

"I'll take my lumps," James huffed.

"Listen, James. I like you. I like the Booker 'Boom-Boom' Taylor Orchestra, with a white piano player even." Leach gestured toward Bobby.

"Mr. Leach. The man James was arguing with is a German and he was insulting my people."

"If by that, Booker, you mean the American people—"

"The blonde guy's a Nazi," Bobby said.

"Mr. Dietrich is a guest. We make a lot of money on this tub. So far we're protected by the cops and sheriffs. But if there's trouble…We don't need no trouble."

"There won't be anymore trouble, Mr. Leach." Booker tried to maintain his dignity, though it was obvious he knew he wasn't top dog here.

"We understand each other then?" Leach looked straight at James and Booker.

"Yes sir," Booker said.

Bobby could tell Booker was tough. He was surprised to see him being so deferential. Maybe everybody's deferential to a real live gangster like Leach.

Leach nodded. "Good. Now I'm sure the folks want to hear another set."

Booker, Bobby, and James headed out to the passageway.

"Gangsters," Booker said.

"You lost your balls, man?" James said.

"Why make trouble? We need the gig."

"I could bust that ofay motherfucker's face for him."

"Which one?"

"All of 'em. But you, man, you done it." James pounded his fist into the wall.

"I don't own up to that one," Booker said.

"Everybody knows you did—killed that boy down in—"

"Well this ain't of that level," Booker whispered. "Now take it out on your horn, man."

The three of them walked toward the backstage area. James stopped.

"Let's go," Booker said. "Got a set to do."

"I need some air. I'll catch up with you." James hung back.

"You do that, James. And don't get yourself in anymore trouble."

Booker and Bobby headed backstage, where the band members wanted to know how it went. Booker told them, then called out to Bobby. "I been thinking. You need to come up with a signature song. Something that will make everyone sit up and take notice. Got anything?"

"Let me think on it, Booker. I'll see what I can come up with."

"You do that."

But right now Bobby wasn't thinking about a signature song. He was thinking about what James had said about Booker killing that boy.

The band took the stage, started wailing. People flowed onto the dance floor, a sea of jitterbuggers. It was amazing how crowded it was, but the gaming tables around the edges of the huge room were packed too.

Bobby went to a different place when he played. Cloud Nine. A place where no one else could go and no one could touch him. He didn't need booze, didn't need reefer; he had Cloud Nine or maybe he was over the rainbow in his own Land of Oz. Between numbers he'd briefly touch down on planet Earth. He looked out at the crowd, dressed in their finest, all the swells. One massive blur of humanity. Once in a while someone would look familiar—a movie star, the mayor, maybe even someone he'd known, like David Chambers—and he'd try to get a better look, hoping they wouldn't recognize him. The past was the past and that's where he wanted it to stay. He was glad when they'd be swallowed up by the throng before they recognized him. So why was he scanning the crowd for David? And there he was, dancing with that gorgeous woman.

Bobby noticed that James hadn't rejoined the band onstage. Probably off sulking. Booker gave the downbeat. The band launched into its next number and Bobby floated up to Cloud Nine again.

The band paused between numbers, just about ready to blow again when a tearing sound ripped through the ballroom. Everyone heard it, but no one was sure where it was coming from. Bobby looked around, didn't see anything. The band started to play just as the ripping sound got louder. People stopped dancing. What the hell was going on? A man by the stage looked up. A dancing couple looked up. Finally everyone was looking up as the gauzy azure *sky* of the false ceiling was shredding in two. People moved aside, clearing a space in the center of the dance floor.

A beam broke loose, swinging down.

People scattered.

Something fell out of the ceiling. A man. Hanging by his neck.

His deadweight dropped him two-thirds of the way from the beams to the dance floor below. He looked just like a hanged man in the movies, dangling by the neck from a rope that went somewhere up inside the false ceiling. Everyone stared. No one was quite sure what to do.

Bobby recognized the grotesquely distorted face as that of the German man James had threatened. Dietrich's lifeless body swayed above the crowd.

CHAPTER THREE

"Calm down. Everybody calm down," Booker said into the mic. His words echoed through the ballroom, careening off the walls. But they didn't do much good. People shouted, screamed, tried to run.

A woman fainted. She would have hit the floor except for the mass of people around her wedging her in.

James joined the band on stage. Booker threw him a glance as if to ask, *Did you do this?*

The bouncers blocked the doors, but otherwise didn't seem to know what to do with themselves or the guests. Seeing that no one was listening to him, Booker retreated to the folds of the band. The band members huddled.

"This's gonna be a shitload of trouble for us." Booker glowered at James. James looked from exit to exit. "Where you gonna run to, man?"

Bobby stayed at his piano, unsure what to do. He was still the new kid and didn't feel he had the right to give his two cents. James definitely had a chip on his shoulder, maybe with good reason.

Leach charged into the room followed by Carnie and some big, rough-looking men that made the regular bouncers look like schoolboys.

"My God, what the hell's going on here?" Leach looked up to see Dietrich dangling from the ceiling. The boat swayed and the body with it.

"Jesus fucking Christ," Carnie said. "It's a fucking zoo."

"Cut him down!"

"The cops ain't gonna like that," Carnie said, biting the head off a stogie, putting it in his pocket.

"Like I give a cow's fart what the cops'll like. Timber."

"Yeah, boss." Timber, called that for obvious reasons, pulled a knife from his pocket. Walked off.

"This ain't gonna be good for business," Carnie said.

"You're telling me." Leach took the stage. Spoke into the mic. "Ssh. Ssh, ladies and gentlemen. It appears we have a tragic accident here—"

A loud nervous laugh pierced the crowd.

"As I was saying, let's calm down. Unfortunately accidents do happen. It looks like a member of the crew was up in the scaffolding and—" He wiped his brow. "Let's all head out on deck."

Nobody headed topside. Morbid curiosity held them tight. Carnie leaned over, whispered to Leach.

"Drinks on the house," Leach said. "On deck."

A cheer went up in the ballroom. Some people slowly started heading out, while others stayed behind to gawk.

"That always gets 'em." Carnie smirked.

Bobby stayed at the piano, trying to be invisible. At least he hoped he was. He didn't want Leach to think he was eavesdropping, even if he was.

"These swells, you can buy 'em off cheap."

"Let's hope we can do the same with the cops, boss."

"They can be bought too. They're just a little more expensive."

A creaking sound cleaved the ballroom from high above— Timber gingerly making his way across slim, threadlike catwalks until he finally reached the rope holding the dangling body. He tried pulling the body up. Holding onto the trellis with one hand, he couldn't raise the body with the other. He looked down to see Leach slice a finger across his neck. Timber slit the rope Dietrich was hanging by. Several bouncers ran to the center of the floor and caught the body. A wail escaped the lingering crowd.

"No more fainting, please," Leach muttered. "I guess this means another round of drinks."

They watched the bouncers lower the body to the deck.

"Stop the water taxis."

"Already done, boss."

"Get me out of here," a woman screamed.

Leach paced the stage near Bobby's piano, bouncers surrounding him. "We're gonna have to call the cops in on this one. Ain't no way to hide it with a thousand people on board. They been wanting to shut me down forever. Now they're really gonna have a reason." He lit a cigarette with a gold lighter. He pushed Carnie into a corner, spoke under his breath. "This is the end, Carnie. The *farshtunkenah* end. Go radio the Coast Guard or sheriffs or whoever the hell we gotta be calling. And stow the men's weapons before the cops get here."

"What about the band?"

"Put 'em in their room."

"You think that hot-headed Negro did it?"

"Don't know, but I know we didn't. Did we?"

"Not on my orders, boss."

"Good. Put a man on the door. Let's keep this neat and clean. Wrap it up in a bow for the cops and hopefully we'll be right back in business."

Carnie made his way past the bouncers.

The band room was like a steam bath of smoke, everyone chain smoking one cigarette after another. Loretta and Cannonball sat in a corner playing gin. Booker walked up to James. Though larger than Booker, James' eyes showed fear where Booker's showed none.

"I need to know, James, you do this?"

"No way."

"You weren't with us last set."

"I was in a lifeboat, smoking reefer. Had to get away after all that BS."

"Don't give me no shuck 'n' jive, boy. He couldda been put there—hidden up there—any time."

"I swear, Booker, I didn't do it."

"Well if you did, I'm gonna knock the black off-a you." Booker's face was a sea of calm. Everyone relaxed. Then Booker, tapping into a reservoir of rage, hard-charged into James, shoving him against the wall, his hands wrapped around James' throat.

"Don't lie to me."

"I'm tellin' you the truth."

"They'll be wanting to pin this on a colored man."

Bobby watched Booker and James. He knew what it was like to be the outsider. And here he was an outsider in a group of outsiders. How hard must that be, to get up every day and know you didn't quite fit.

"I didn't do it."

"Yeah, but is that gonna matter to the cops? You got in a fight with the dead man. An' you're as colored as they come. I'd say you got two strikes on you already. An' with the umpires being part-a their team, I'd say a third strike is on the way."

A loud knock pounded the door. The bouncer opened the door and stuck his head in. "Boss says everyone to the ballroom."

Everyone took long drags on their cigarettes before heading out single file. Now there were sheriff's deputies and coast-guardsmen at every door. Throngs of customers sat or stood in their evening wear, smoking, talking, all looking uncomfortable, the party atmosphere drained away. Deputies had people cornered here and there, questioning them, while Dietrich's body lay in the center of the room, covered only by a thin sheet.

A uniformed deputy stepped up to Booker's mic. "Quiet, quiet. I'm Deputy Wes Hardin of the L.A. Sheriffs and this is Lieutenant Toby Norman of the Coast Guard. We'll be leading the investigation of what happened here." He conferred privately with Lieutenant Norman before continuing. "James Christmas, step forward," Hardin said into the crackling mic.

Booker turned to Bobby, "Strike three."

He looked around for James. No sign of him. The cops up on the stage were looking too. Hardin and Lieutenant Norman huddled together. Signaled for a couple of their men. The huddle broke. Deputies and coastguardsmen talked to Leach and Carnie. To the bouncers.

Hardin, Norman, Leach, and Carnie headed for Booker and Bobby.

"Where is he?" Hardin said.

"I don't know."

"Booker, my friend, if you do, you'd better tell these gentlemen." Leach, Hardin, the deputies, and the coastguardsmen walked off.

"You think he did it?" Bobby said.

"I told him not to be arm wrestling with that dude. He's always got to be goin' against the grain. Just like he did with you. Can't leave nothin' alone." Booker pulled a marijuana cigarette from his pocket, thought better of it, shoved it behind a sofa cushion. Pulled out a Lucky, lit up.

Even though it appeared that they saw James as their prime suspect, deputies continued to question everyone in the ballroom. A dark-haired man with finely tuned blue eyes walked up to Bobby. He filled out his cheap double-breasted detective's suit the way Charles Atlas might after a few years of sitting at a desk. Bobby didn't like the looks of him, a meanness around the eyes.

"You a member of the band?"

"Yes."

The plainclothes deputy looked at the other band members. "What are you, the black sheep of the family?"

"Wouldn't that be white sheep?"

The man cracked the slightest grin. "I'm Sergeant Nicolai with the sheriffs. So what's a white sheep doing with all these black sheep?"

31

"Do these questions have anything to do with—" Bobby pointed to the dead man crumpled on the floor.

"Let's go outside, or topside or deckside or whatever the hell they call it." Sergeant Nicolai led the way. They stood at the railing, watching the flickering lights of Santa Monica in the distance. Bobby sucked in a deep breath. He felt like he'd landed in the middle of a Bogart movie.

"So where were you during the band break when *Herr* Dietrich was last seen alive?"

"You say 'Herr' with some distaste, Sergeant."

"I gotta job to do, but I got no truck with the dead man. We're already fighting the krauts—again! So where were you?"

"Having a smoke, hanging around."

"In any particular room or whatever they call it on one-a these tubs?"

"I don't know, I think I got a drink at the bar. Bubble Up, if you want to know." Even with only Bubble Up in him, the chunk of the waves was getting to Bobby.

"I thought all you band guys were hardcore alkies."

"Well, you know, a white sheep in a black herd."

"All right, let's cut the jive. You were at the bar the whole time?"

"Before the fight, I think I might have hit the head." Bobby didn't want to get involved, didn't want to be the one to point the finger at James. He already had a strike against him being the only white in the band; he didn't want to be kicked out because he squealed on James.

"Hit your head?"

"The head. What they call the bathroom on a boat."

"Serves me right for having been in the army instead of the navy." Nicolai scratched at the rail. "The head's where the fight was. Did you see it?"

"From a distance." Bobby wondered if his see-no-evil-hear-no-evil act seemed obvious.

"That's funny. I thought you were a lot closer."

"And then we went back onstage for another set."

"Was Mr. Christmas there for that set?"

"I don't know, Sergeant, I was just digging on the music." Bobby watched the shoreline bob up and down, hoping he would keep his dinner down.

"Okay, what do you know about James Christmas?"

"Sax man. Pretty good."

"I hear you and him had a tiff."

"Tiff, such a delicate word, Sergeant."

"All right, a fight." Nicolai lit up.

"It was nothing. Just the usual hazing when someone new joins any group." Bobby knew this was a line of BS. He had gotten his dream job; he wasn't about to jeopardize it. "I heard it was more than that. Something about not wanting a white boy in the Booker band."

"You're good, Sergeant. Yeah that too."

"And something about Mr. Christmas not wanting to use the colored *head*."

"Criminy, Sergeant. Can you blame him?"

"So what are you doing in a black band, slumming? I hear you're pretty good."

"I dig their style, the way they play." Bobby's eyes darted back and forth. He had to look the sergeant in the eye but he couldn't tell him the truth. And he knew he wouldn't fit in with the white big bands. He would always be the outsider with them. But he wanted to play, so he gave it his shot down on Central. "Besides, I couldn't get in with Goodman or Dorsey. And Booker's local. It's a good training ground."

Bobby heard a commotion. He looked up to see a hand-cuffed James being led toward the ladder and the waiting Coast Guard boat below. The other passengers and guests were boarding water taxis. They pushed and shoved to get to the front of the line. None of this women and children first stuff.

"Looks like we got our man." Sergeant Nicolai started to head off.

"Found him in a lifeboat, Sarge," one of the deputies escorting James shouted.

"Doesn't it seem just a little too easy, Sergeant?" Bobby said.

"It's not my call. It's Deputy Hardin's."

Bobby glanced at James' face. He'd never seen such a defeated look on a man, not even on his father. As the deputies led James past Bobby, he could see the cuts and bruises on James' face, the tears in his clothes.

"Well, I guess that's it for now. Write your personal info down here in case we need to get in touch with you." Nicolai handed Bobby a notebook. Bobby scribbled in it. Nicolai headed off, calling behind him, "Have fun slumming."

Bobby wanted to push him overboard, but why aggravate things for himself?

CHAPTER FOUR

Bobby's head swirled with thoughts of James and the dead guy, Dietrich. Had James done it? Bobby didn't know him very well but James seemed like a hot head. The way he overreacted to everything and seemed angry all the time, Bobby wouldn't put it past him, especially since the dead German had made comments about colored people.

His wristwatch read five to twelve, almost the witching hour, but not very late by musicians' standards, when he pulled up in front of his apartment in his 1935 Oldsmobile Six convertible. Several years old, it had been in an accident, so Bobby got it cheap. It was still one snazzy car and he loved the running boards, rag top, rumble seat, and magenta color. Not the original color, but a hot jazz color if ever there was.

Bobby grabbed his stuff, didn't bother locking the car, headed up the walk. His building was like a thousand others in Hollywood, a million in L.A. White stucco and Spanish style, but it had seen better days. He opened the wood-and-glass-paneled front door, walked down the carpeted but threadbare hall to his tiny apartment in the back. He'd thought about going to a Gene Autry Western at the all-night theater to unwind, decided against it. A smoke and his couch would help him unwind just fine.

He threw off his hat and coat, yanked off his tie and shoes, and flopped on the sofa. It was too much trouble pulling down the Murphy bed. He pulled out the ever-present pack of Viceroys, lit up, drew hard, turned on the radio—war news, what else? It was as good as anything to drift off to sleep to.

Intense morning sun streamed through the venetian blinds, casting long shadows, while dust mites jitterbugged on the light. Bobby, asleep in his clothes on the couch, turned. A loud knock on the front door seeped into his semi-consciousness. Who the hell was it, the cops?

He got up, adjusted his shirt carefully, making sure everything was in place. He ran his hand over his chin and cheek, then headed to the door, saw Booker through the peephole. Booker was in the same suit he'd worn last night; looked like he'd slept in it.

"Booker," he said, opening the door.

Booker stumbled in. "You got any coffee?"

"Sure." Bobby walked to the kitchen on the far side of the room, followed by Booker. He started the percolator while Booker made himself comfortable at the banquette. "How 'bout some breakfast?"

"I didn't sleep at all, Bobby. You?"

"Nothing keeps me from sleeping."

"You're lucky."

"In some ways." Bobby thought this was a slip, but Booker didn't pick up on it. Bobby started frying up some eggs and bacon. Making toast. They would use up most of his rations for the week, but Booker was a guest.

"I got a funny look from one-a your neighbors coming here."

"Probably Mrs. Hazelton, the landlady."

"I don't think she likes colored folk in her neighborhood."

"She looks at everyone like that. I've been living here a year and she still looks at me funny."

"I don't know if you're telling me the truth or not, but it makes me feel better anyways. Bobby, this is a nice place."

"This dump? It's all right, but I'm aiming to move to better digs."

"You ain't no rich white boy just slumming, playin' on Central Avenue with the *darkies* to stick it to your folks?"

"Nope."

"You go to school?"

"I graduated high school. I like to read. But I've never been to college."

"That's good. I don't want no eggheads in my band. They tend to intellectualize everything." Booker sipped the coffee Bobby gave him. He looked the room over. "So, where's your piano?"

"If there was a piano in here there'd be no room for me. I go to my old piano teacher's house in Edendale to practice."

"Edendale? The land of kooks and crazies."

"Maybe that's why I fit in."

Booker laughed. "So who do you like? Musically."

"Benny Goodman. Dorsey. Ellington. Armstrong."

"All the usual suspects." Booker threw a hard glance at Bobby. "So whatd'd ya think about them hauling James off?"

Booker's abrupt change of subject threw Bobby for a moment as he put out the plates of food and topped off Booker's coffee. He set a bottle of ketchup on the table. Both of them dug in. Anyone looking at this scene from outside would have seen two pals chowing down.

"Do you think he did it?"

"I don't know, man," Booker said. "What I do know is that the cops don't care. They got a suspect. A colored suspect. They're happy. I know you and James aren't exactly tight, but maybe you can do some checking around."

"What do you mean?"

"You know, ask some questions. See what you can find out."

"Criminy, Booker, I'm no detective."

"I know that. But you got something I don't, something no one else in the band has."

"What's that?"

"A passport."

"Passport?"

Booker pinched Bobby's pink cheek. "White skin. You can go places we can't. Ask questions we can't and get away with it. Maybe even get some answers."

"You want me to play Sam Spade? Like in that movie *The Maltese Falcon?*"

"Sure, why not? But you ain't no 'spade' far as I can see." Booker looked Bobby up and down, grinned.

"I'm no Humphrey Bogart either."

"Hell no, you're ten times better looking."

"I'm not sure how much that says about me," Bobby said. "But I do have a fedora. What else is there?"

"A gun."

"Well, that I don't have."

"And hopefully you won't need one."

Bobby hoped not. He had never fired a gun, though he'd seen Gene Autry and Roy Rogers and Bogart all do it in the movies a million times. What was he getting himself into?

"What about the gig, I'll have to be there every night to play."

"There is no gig. The Apollo's shut down, at least temporarily. And you're on probation with the band. You solve this, you got the gig."

"I thought I'd get the gig 'cause I can play."

"That too. 'Sides, what else you got to do now that we're on hiatus since they shut the Apollo down?" Booker shrugged. "If you get James off, I'll give you a permanent spot with the band."

"What if he's guilty?"

"If he is, if you prove him innocent or guilty without a doubt either way, you got the gig."

"So where do I start?"

"You seemed to be talking to that plainclothes deputy a long time. Maybe start with him. See what they have on James. I'm

gonna try and get him a lawyer. White lawyer. Jewish lawyer."
Booker took a drag on his cig.

"I want a spot, but I want it 'cause I'm a good musician."

"You are a good musician. Now go and be a good detective."

Bobby had no idea where to begin, but something inside him liked the idea of playing detective, at least for a little while, even if he wouldn't admit it to Booker. It might make him more of a man.

Bobby parked across the street from the Los Angeles County Hall of Justice, an imposing building and right now it was imposing itself on Bobby. The top five floors of the 1926 beaux arts structure housed the main jail for the county and that's where Bobby was headed. He stood in its shadow, trying without success to light a cigarette in the wind. He stopped, looked at the columns of highly polished gray granite, tossed his match. Headed inside.

Ionic columns, marble walls, a gilded ceiling, and a vaulted foyer, looking like a Grecian palace and running the length of the building, belied the jail that lay on the top floors. All that majesty changed when Bobby got off the elevator on the fifth floor. The unwelcoming yellowed linoleum and hard-tiled walls made Bobby's footsteps carom off the ceiling. The visitor's area, with its filtered yellow light and stained dull green walls, didn't improve his mood. And if this is what the county presented to the public, he couldn't imagine what the jail's cells were like. He longed for a drag on a cigarette.

A uniformed deputy sat him at a long wooden table. The scarred surface bore the marks of almost every prisoner who'd sat there. A large, pissed-off-looking man shuffled in, accompanied by a larger, more pissed-off deputy.

"Yer the last person I expected to see here," James said, looking even angrier upon seeing Bobby.

"Booker asked me to come."

"'Course you wouldn't come on your own."

Why the hell would I the way you went after me? "Do you hate everyone or just whites?"

"Mostly whites. But I pretty much hate everyone equally."

"I think you hate yourself more than anyone else."

Instead of shutting James up, he came back with, "Don't go being no Freud on me. Why don't you go home to your silver spoon and perfect family?"

Bobby stifled a laugh. "Booker asked me to help you."

"An' what can you do for me, white boy? You who's wet behind the ears and don't even look like you started shaving yet."

"I see that you don't need my help. Enjoy the food, I hear it's *yummy* in here." Bobby got up to leave, turned his back on James.

"Bobby?" James stood. The deputy shoved him down on the chair—hard. "Wait."

They stared at each other across the table. The deputy stood rock solid behind James. The look in his eyes said he hoped the big man would make a move. James disappointed him. In a very small voice that admitted defeat, he said, "Got a smoke?"

Was that James' way of asking Bobby to stay, maybe even to help? Bobby shook out a Viceroy, started to pass it across the table. The deputy took it, rolled it around in his fingers, probably to make sure a Bowie knife wasn't hidden inside, and handed what was left of the crumpled cigarette to James. He put it in his mouth and Bobby lit it for him.

"Maybe I do have a small chip on my shoulder."

Bobby sat down again. "I'll say. Only about as small as the Rock of Gibraltar."

"Well, could be bigger. Could be as big as Everest." James cracked the slightest smile, held up his arm. A long, angry slash. Fresh. He pulled up his shirt. More bruises. The deputy slapped his billy club on James' shoulder. The shirt went down.

"What happened?"

James leaned in, talked softly, "They beat me. Of course,

they kept away from my face. But they had a hell of a good time doin' it. And my chip keeps growing. So what'd Booker send you here for? Got a hack saw up your sleeve?"

"He thought I might be able to help."

"You got friends or maybe your daddy's on the *po-lice* force?"

"No. But why don't you tell me where you were when Dietrich was killed."

"That his name? No one ever told me." He sighed. "'Course no one knows exactly when he was killed. But they had to have enough time to haul the body up to the rafters. I think I was probably back in the lifeboat, smoking reefer. Wasn't feeling too good that night. Seasick, you know. And mad as hell after my confrontation with this Dietrich."

"Uh," Bobby didn't know how to proceed. He was no private eye. "Was anyone with you?"

"I know I'm just a lowly *spade*, but I don't have to have someone holding my hand every minute."

"I'm trying to help. It would be good if we had someone to alibi you." Bobby was getting into the rhythm of being a detective.

"Got no alibis. All I got is my sax and I don't even have that here."

"And we miss it in the band." Bobby stared beyond James, at the grimy walls. "James, did you do it?"

"Hell no!"

Bobby figured people in jail lied. He didn't know if James was lying or not. But for now he'd take him at his word. "I'll do what I can."

He pulled out his pack of Viceroys, tossed it on the table. The deputy grabbed it. Stuck his fingers inside, pulled two cigs, tossed them to James. Stuck the pack in his pocket.

Out on the street in front of the jail, Bobby sucked in a deep breath of fresh air, opened a new pack of smokes. Lit up and took one long drag. He looked across the road to the rundown

Bijou Theatre, playing a re-release of *The Maltese Falcon*. Bobby darted across the street. Short of a correspondence course on private detecting, he figured this would be about as much of a class in the subject as he could hope for.

Bobby emerged from the theater a couple hours later to a dark Los Angeles, lit by streetlamps haloing in the low-hanging fog that had rolled in.

He got in the Olds, cut over to Beverly Boulevard, drove west. *I should be playing music, not hunting for a killer. I didn't take a correspondence course in Detecting 101. Criminy, I'm even more of a fish out of water than Booker knows.*

Where the hell do I go now? I guess it would help to know who the, uh, dead guy is, was. I have to look at this logically, Bobby thought on the drive home. *The answer's probably right in front of my face.*

He flopped on his sofa, listening to Artie Shaw's sweet clarinet on the radio in between war news. Bobby flipped through the pages of his high school yearbook. He had tried calling Deputy Nicolai. He had gone home for the day. The desk sergeant wanted to take a message. Bobby didn't leave one.

The Andrews Sisters' "Boogie Woogie Bugle Boy" followed Shaw. Bobby's eyes grew moist. All those boys overseas. The service flags in almost every window, gold star flags in too many of them. Sometimes he wished he could join the boys in Europe or the Pacific. He didn't want to think about that now. He wanted to look at the pictures in the yearbook. Johnny Larkman, senior class president. Very handsome. Is that why he was prez? Jane Feldman, most likely to succeed. What else could she be with her glasses and librarian hair? David Chambers. Handsome, smart. The reason Bobby had pulled out the dusty old yearbook in the first place. David in drama club with Bobby. They had appeared in *Cyrano de Bergerac* together. In the lead roles. Georgiana Greene, voted prettiest and homecoming queen.

Bobby had had a major crush on her. Who didn't? Mary Cooper. Bobby'd sent her a love note in fifth grade and gotten in trouble for it. Mary never said another word to him. They all went through school together, elementary, junior high, high school. And now they were all out on their own, facing their demons. Facing the world. He kept turning pages and reliving memories. Band. Drama club. Lunches in the quad.

It was fun seeing David Chambers the other night, even if Bobby had been too shy to go up to him. He must be doing pretty good to have money to spend on the Apollo.

Bobby fell asleep on the sofa again.

The Malibu sheriff's outpost, or station, wasn't much to look at. At least parking was easy. Bobby got out of the Olds Six, inhaled fresh ocean air. Walked inside. After some palavering with the desk sergeant he was allowed back to the detective room. It looked a lot like detective rooms in the movies did. A bunch of wood desks with blotters, file cabinets, and telephones. Men in shirt sleeves and shoulder holsters, some with fedoras on their heads, some with their hats on their desks or hanging from a rack.

Bobby and Sergeant Nicolai sat at a desk in the corner, by the water cooler. Bobby explained he'd come to find out what he could about the Dietrich case.

"Why're you so interested?"

"James is a member of the band. I'm a member of the band."

"Doesn't sound right. Gotta be something more."

"We have no gig. The Apollo is shut down. We need to hold the band together," Bobby vamped.

"With a murderer?"

"What if he isn't?"

Nicolai thought a moment. "I'd like to help you but I can't divulge information on an ongoing investigation."

"Is it ongoing, Sergeant? And that sounds like a very nice,

very formal 'don't bother me, kid.'"

"I don't buy your spiel. That *boy* a friend of yours?"

"I'd hardly say that. But he is a bandmate and we need our first sax."

"So why doesn't your leader, Mr. Booker Boom-Boom, come down here himself?"

Bobby's eyes wandered the room. Nicolai followed. He knew the answer.

"All right, I know why he doesn't come down. Still—"

"Can't you give me something?"

"His name's Hans. Hans Dietrich. I believe he worked in the import-export field. That's all I know."

Bobby looked down, then up and straight into Nicolai's eyes. "I got that much from the papers."

"You're a persistent little cuss, aren't you?"

"I got Booker to give me a spot in the band."

"And now you think I'll just give you information in an ongoing—"

"Tell me something I don't know and I'll get out of your hair."

"Something tells me you'll never be out of my hair." Nicolai drew a deep breath. "He and his partner, Harlan Thomas, an American, worked as Dietrich Enterprises, on Third Street. Dietrich's a German citizen, moved here a couple years ago. Forty-five. Unmarried. Blonde over blue. No arrests."

"That should get me started. Thanks, Sergeant." Bobby stood, tipping his hat to Nicolai.

Bobby lit up a Viceroy, stepped out into the raging sun and wind and fresh, stinging ocean scent.

"So who are you," Bobby sucked in the cigarette, exhaled, "Mr. Hans Dietrich?"

CHAPTER FIVE

Bobby hit a phone booth in a Richfield service station on Wilshire in Santa Monica. He ripped through pages in the phone book looking for import-export companies, finding Dietrich Enterprises' address on Third Street. Judging by the number, he assumed it was near La Brea, not all that close to where he was now, but close to where he grew up. He yanked out the phone book page, fled the booth like Superman, only instead of flying he *flew* to his car.

Dietrich Enterprises took up a small suite of offices on the second floor of a three-story beaux arts building.

"Can I help you?" the receptionist said, setting her bottle of RC Cola down on the desk, missing the blotter by a good six inches. The stain from the bottle would match the others already there.

"Is Mr. Thomas in?"

"You another cop?"

"Another cop?"

"Yeah, you guys have been all over this place this morning."

"You don't seem too broken up about Dietrich's passing." Bobby thought that sounded like something Bogart might have said in *The Maltese Falcon*.

"I'm broken up. He was a good boss, as bosses go. But I have a job to do." She fluffed her hair, adjusted the pencils in their holder, rolled her chair closer to the desk. Her makeup—a little too much of it—was perfect, unspoiled by tears. She stood to adjust her dress, a slinky number that seemed better suited to Ciro's or the Trocadero than the office, especially this soon after the boss died.

"I'm not a cop."

"Then you are?"

"Bob—Robert Saxon. Not a newspaperman either. So you don't need to be scared of me."

"Scared of *you*?" she scoffed. "And what is your company?"

Bobby knew he didn't exactly project that tough Bogart veneer. He fumbled in his pocket, as if looking for a business card. "Looks like I left my company at home."

"I don't have time for jokes, sir."

"Uh, no company."

"Then maybe I can help you?"

"I'm a musician. And I wanted to talk to Mr. Thomas about importing musical instruments from Europe." Bobby talked on the fly, not even sure they were making instruments in Europe with the war on. He had no idea what would come out next but found that he enjoyed the game. "They make superior pieces there and I thought I could make a little money on the side."

"Well, I'm sorry, but Mr. Thomas is on vacation at the moment."

"Is there someone else who can help me?"

"Only Mr. Thomas, but he's out, as I said."

"Does anyone else work here?"

The receptionist's face went to stone.

"I'm sorry. I'm just so excited about my idea. Listen, I'm starving and it's almost lunch time. Maybe you'd like to get a bite?"

"I don't know you, sir."

"That's how you'll get to know me better." Bobby smiled his most winning smile.

"I am rather hungry."

Bobby drove them to Nickodell, across from the Paramount and RKO studios in Hollywood. There were closer places, but

Bobby thought they might see some movie stars and that might impress her. She seemed the type, especially so when she sashayed in as if auditioning for a part in a movie about a New Orleans cat house. That said, she did have a fine figure and a pretty enough face. They sat opposite each other in a red leather booth, scanned the menu and scanned the restaurant for stars.

"Y'know, you never asked me my name."

"I saw it on the plaque on your desk, Lois Templeton, right?"

"Right. And you are—"

"Bobby."

"That's right, I remember now. Robert Saxon."

A waiter in a penguin suit took their drink orders. Bubble Up for Bobby, a Tom Collins for Lois.

"I love this place, when I can come," she said. "There's so many movie stars all the time, being right across the street from both Paramount and RKO."

"Do you come here often?"

"Naw. It's out of my league. I usually eat at the counter at Woolworth's or JJ Newberry's. Have you ever been here?"

"I come here sometimes. It's a music biz hangout." Bobby didn't know if that was true; he'd never been to Nickodell before.

"That's so exciting. Romantic." She caught onto what she'd said. "I didn't mean it that way, I mean, I have a boyfriend and all—"

"Don't worry about it. I know what you meant."

The waiter brought their drinks, took their food order. Lois sipped her Collins.

"Look, there's Veronica Lake. Now if only Alan Ladd were here, that would be something."

"It sure would." Bobby looked over to Veronica Lake. Indeed, he wouldn't mind getting to know her.

"So what kind of musician are you?"

"I play piano—mostly—in a band."

"Big band? I love hot jazz. What's your band? Maybe I've

heard of it."

He was hesitant to say. Even if she'd never heard of Booker's band before today, the cops or the papers probably told her that the man suspected of killing her boss was in the same band as Bobby. He had no choice. "The Booker 'Boom-Boom' Taylor Orchestra."

"You're in that band?"

"Yes." He waited a second. She said nothing. Maybe she didn't know. "Have you ever seen us play?"

"Well, no," she said with a halt. "I...don't go down to dark-town on Central Avenue. You know—"

"I understand."

"But how come you're in that band? I thought they were all Negroes."

"There's an exception to every rule—I'm the exception." Bobby's fingers tightened on his glass—and what an exception he was. Times like this he wished he had a real drink. This wasn't the conversation he wanted to be having. At the same time he felt he had to *woo* Lois.

"You look awfully young to be in a band. Is that why you're not in the service?"

Bobby's fingers squeezed the glass harder, as if he were wringing a neck. "Old enough to vote."

"Old enough to vote is old enough to join the army."

"I have a deferment."

"Lots of girls won't date guys with a deferment, but if it's legit, hey, everybody has something."

Bobby shifted his feet under the table. "So, tell me a little about your business."

"There's not much to tell. We used to import stuff from Germany and export stuff over to them. But now we just do business with other allied countries in Europe, when we can. That's where Mr. Dietrich is from, Germany. Business hasn't been so good since the war started."

"Have you been working there long?"

"A couple years, give or take. I'm taking acting classes at night. But I have to pay my bills and help my mom with the mortgage, you know, until I get my break."

He didn't think any casting agents would be corralling her anytime soon, unless she had some hidden talent that he couldn't see over lunch.

"I know how that goes."

"You're in the biz. Well, the music biz and that's close enough. Maybe you know someone who could help me? An agent or a producer." She put her hand in Bobby's. Left it there. "Soft hands. I guess playing an instrument isn't exactly like manual labor."

"I guess not." He left his hand around hers. "So what do you import and export?"

"Cuckoo clocks, regular clocks. Watches. Some business machines, typewriters and the like. And toys, though that's dried up since the war started. In fact, the whole business is drying up since the war started. They told me I might not have my job much longer. I'm trying to get a gig at the Hollywood Canteen but they want people with names—that is, I have a name, but they want stars." Lois leaned her face close to Bobby's. He smelled the gin from the Collins on her breath.

"Personally, I've often wondered if Mr. Dietrich was a Nazi," she said, "you know, being German and all."

"Not all Germans are Nazis."

"That's not how my father sees it. He fought the Germans in the first war."

"There weren't any Nazis in the first war."

"Well, all Germans are Nazis as far as my father is concerned."

"What about Mr. Dietrich, you really think he was a Nazi?"

"I don't know," she said coyly.

They were talking about a dead man, about Nazis and she was flirting. Bobby didn't know if he would ever fully understand women.

"Did he ever attend any Bund meetings?"

"Not that I know of, but he didn't talk much about his personal life. Besides, the Bunds are kinda kaput now, aren't they? If he did, it would have been before my time with the firm."

The waiter brought their food. Bobby wasn't interested in his. He was getting into playing the role of detective. He was good at role-playing, drama club had helped with that. So had life. He wanted to talk about Dietrich. Lois wanted to flirt. Every time she did, he brought the subject back 'round to his investigation.

"Were you and Mr. Dietrich, uh, romantically involved?"

"What kind of girl do you think I am?" Lois blurted. Her lips formed a pout. Whether she was really hurt or insulted or just acting, Bobby didn't know. "I told you, I have a boyfriend. Besides, why should I tell you anything when you're in the band with the guy who killed Mr. Dietrich?"

Heads turned.

"It didn't seem to bother you five minutes ago," he said. "So maybe you're fishing, trying to see what I know."

Lois stormed out. He sat there, unsure what to do.

"Criminy," Bobby said. He knew everyone, guests, waiters, busboys, were looking at him. He had two choices. Leave or eat.

He started in on his food. A handsome couple sat at the booth across from him. Up and coming stars, no doubt. They were both too beautiful to be anything else. Bobby stared as long as was permissible. Without finishing his meal, he threw some money on the table, got up, and left.

He ducked into the lobby phone booth, paged through the book. Tore a page out and walked into the glaring sunlight.

CHAPTER SIX

Bobby looked at the ripped-out phone book page as he drove down Wilshire, past the Ambassador Hotel, with its famous Cocoanut Grove nightclub. He'd never been, but one day he hoped to play there. Past Lafayette Park, until he came to the Bryson Apartments. Bobby'd heard a rumor that Fred MacMurray was an owner. He parked, got out of his Olds, holding the torn page. He gazed up at the ten-story classical revival building, with its carved lions sitting atop huge pillars guarding the entrance, wishing he could live in as nice a place someday.

"I'm sorry, sir. But if you're not a relative I can't let you into Mr. Dietrich's apartment," the snooty desk clerk said.

What would Humphrey Bogart say? "I'm a friend of the family. They want—"

"Unless your driver's license says Dietrich, I'm afraid I can't believe you."

"Are you calling me a liar?"

"In a word—" Before the clerk could finish he was distracted by someone heading for the elevators. "Sergeant."

Nicolai tipped his hat, pressed the elevator button.

"Sergeant," Bobby said, echoing the clerk. Nicolai must have recognized him because he started walking over.

"This guy giving you trouble?"

"As a matter of fact, yes, well, no, Sergeant."

"He's a real pain in the ass."

Bobby grunted, spoke in deep bass tones, as if he were another cop the sergeant was kidding. "Thanks, Sarge."

"Why didn't you say you were a cop?" the clerk said.

"I—"

"He's on probation. And you can see why."

Nicolai started for the elevator. Bobby stood by the reception counter watching the elevator dial head for the bottom floor.

"You coming or you gonna stand there chewing the fat all day?"

Bobby lurched toward the elevator, jumping in just as the doors were closing.

They stood in the elegant little box heading for the sky. After a few seconds of stilted silence, Bobby said, "Thanks, Sergeant."

"I figure if you can't beat 'em, join 'em and I know I ain't gonna beat you so I guess I'll let you join me on a limited basis. A very limited basis. But you turn up anything, you let me know. Get it?"

"I get it." Bobby was sorry for thinking the sergeant had mean eyes. He didn't know what to say next. He thought about asking Nicolai if he was out of his jurisdiction, this being LAPD territory, not sheriffs'. "Y'know, I've heard that Fred MacMurray owns this building."

"I've heard that too."

"I wonder if it's true."

The elevator doors opened on a grand eighth-floor hallway of luxurious Egyptian deco-patterned carpet and cut-glass chandeliers. Expensive-looking wainscoting marched down the hall. Bobby followed Nicolai to Dietrich's door and in.

Dietrich had good taste. Everywhere Bobby looked he saw expensive European furniture. Sofas, tables, lamps. A gorgeous burled wood martini bar, still open, glasses, colorful bottles of gin and vermouth, and mirrors sparkling in the filtered sunlight.

"Be careful what you touch."

"Aye-aye, sir."

"I ain't in the navy. You'd never find me in the navy. Army all the way. And you look too young to have ever been in the service, though why you ain't in it now, I don't know."

"Flat feet."

"Sure, that's what they all say."

Bobby knew the sergeant was kidding him along. Felt they were building a bond, some sort of male friendship. Still, he felt guilty about not being in the service with so many others overseas fighting Hitler or the Japs.

"Let's get to work," Nicolai said, pulling a pack of Chiclets from his pocket. He took a couple, offered the pack to Bobby, who declined.

"Do we know what we're looking for, Sergeant?"

"Only God knows and He's not talking to me lately. I've been through this joint two times already and I still don't know what I'm looking for."

Nicolai sat down on a plush burgundy settee. Weary.

"All right if I smoke?"

"Why not?" Nicolai pulled out his own pack of Winstons, put a cigarette between his lips and lit up, still chewing on the Chiclets. "Okay, the guy's German. He's on the gambling ship Apollo. He's bumped off, why? He's stowed away up in the ceiling—why?"

"To hide him?"

"Sure, that's the first thought. Or is it to send a message? Does the killer know the ceiling's not all that sturdy and that the body will swing free with the swaying of the ship and he'll come flying down—swinging to and fro? Is there a message in that?"

"I'm impressed, Sergeant. I just thought he was trying to hide the body."

"He? Who's even to say the killer's a he? Though the odds are for it. 'Sides you need some strength to lift it up there. And don't be too impressed, kid. I been doing this a long time. When I was green I learned from the older guys too."

"How did he die?"

"Knocked on the head with the usual blunt instrument. And

if that wasn't good enough for the killer, he knifed him in the gut for good measure."

"Did you find the knife?"

"No. I'm sure it's deep-sixed."

Bobby took a drag on his butt. "You don't think James Christmas did it, do you?" When Nicolai didn't respond, "Sergeant?"

Nicolai continued to ignore Bobby's question.

"If you did you wouldn't be here."

"He might have done it," Nicolai said. "Leastways, everybody loves him for it."

"Everyone but you?"

"I just like covering all the bases." Nicolai stumped out his cigarette in one of Dietrich's imported ashtrays, kept chomping on the Chiclets.

"Why you being so nice to me, Sarge?"

"You're suspicious of everything, ain't you?"

Bobby nodded. "I had lunch with Dietrich's secretary."

"You are working this case, kid."

"I'm trying."

"What'd she have to say for herself?"

"Not much. Didn't want to talk about Dietrich. Mostly wanted to flirt. Oh, and get a free lunch. When she saw I was all business, she got pouty."

"You learn anything from her?"

"Not really."

"She give you this address?"

"Nope. Phone book." Bobby pulled out the crumpled page.

"She say anything about Thomas, the partner?"

"Said he was on vacation."

"He sure picked a convenient time to be on vacation. Sounds like you got about as much from Miss Templeton as I did. Feel free to have lunch with her again. Dinner even. If you get some good dope, I might even pay for the meal." Nicolai stood. "Let's get to work."

They started rifling drawers, looking under the sofa cushions. Bobby walked into Dietrich's bedroom, the same good taste as the living room. Matching blonde art deco bed, nightstands, dresser. He looked through everything he saw. Wondered what he might not be seeing. Came back to the living room, walked to the balcony. The south and east views were magnificent. He could see people boating in Westlake Park, a couple blocks east. What a wonderful life that must be, picnicking in the park with your family and friends.

Nicolai was in Dietrich's second bedroom, set up as a study, with a blonde desk that matched the bedroom set, while Bobby scrounged around the kitchen. He looked in the cabinets and the Frigidaire, though he wasn't sure why he looked there. He looked in the wastebasket under the sink, which had clearly already been gone through. He was about to put it back when he noticed a sliver of paper behind a can of cleaning powder. He gently took the paper from the crevice between the wall and floor so as not to rip it. Scribbled on it were the letters *IBM* and a time, *4pm*.

"What's that, kid?" Nicolai said appearing behind him. He took the paper from Bobby, read aloud, "I-B-M."

"What is that?"

"I don't know, maybe the initials of a friend of his or something."

"Or something in Germany, like the Gestapo. Something like that?"

"I think you're on the wrong track there, kid. I ain't never heard of no German initials like IBM, *SS*, but not IBM."

"Do you want it?"

"Naw."

Nicolai gave the paper back to Bobby.

"Let's call it a day. I been through this apartment twice already. This is my third strike."

"Did you ever find an address book or something?"

"Our friend Hans' little black book? Yeah, I found it."

"Can I have a look at it?"

"It wouldn't be right."

"It wouldn't really hurt either, would it, Sarge?"

"Stop calling me Sarge like you're a member of the department."

Nicolai pulled Dietrich's black book from his pocket, gave it to Bobby. Bobby flipped pages. Nothing stood out. There was no entry for IBM or anything with those or similar initials under *I* or any other letter.

"Find anything?"

"Nope. Just a buncha names." Bobby memorized Harlan Thomas' address. It was easy, sort of like remembering the notes in a song. He'd pay a visit to the man's house soon.

"You know, kid, maybe we're both on the wrong track, maybe it is your colored friend."

"He's not my friend. Just a bandmate."

"Sure kid. That guy doesn't seem like he'd have any friends."

"If he wasn't such a mean reed man, he might not."

"You did say reed and not reefer, right kid?"

Bobby nodded. They headed down in the elevator. The clerk waved obsequiously. Neither Nicolai nor Bobby acknowledged him, though Bobby did notice how ostentatious the lobby was this time. Huge, sparkly crystal chandeliers that made those in the upper hall seem puny, marble stairs, rich, in both meanings of the word, mahogany furniture. Outside, Nicolai got into his unmarked police car. Bobby delayed at the phone booth. He looked up IBM, tore a page from the book, and headed to his car. He made a U-turn in the middle of Wilshire, drove by Westlake Park, slowing to a crawl. He looked longingly at the people drifting along in their rented boats. Families picnicking. Lovers lying on blankets, watching each other's eyes. He pressed the pedal, the car gained speed. Bobby headed for downtown.

* * *

From the outside the Bradbury Building looked like any other office building, brown brick and sandstone in an Italian-Renaissance-meets-L.A. style. Inside, it was like being transported to a great European palace or maybe a train station of the industrial age. Bobby had heard of this building, though never had occasion to visit. He was awed by its breathtaking beauty. A glass skylight let shards of light fall on glazed brick and wrought iron grillwork. Marble flooring. Bobby stopped for a moment to catch his breath before heading to the open-caged elevators. He told the operator his floor, rode to the top, walked to room 501. The writing on the pebbled-glass door said *International Business Machines—IBM*. The directory had listed several names under the company, but George Stinson seemed to be the head man. Bobby also remembered seeing that name in Dietrich's phone book.

"Can I help you?" the switchboard operator-receptionist said. *Another wall to go through.*

Bobby looked at the fine wood paneling. The original old master oil paintings.

"Is that an original Rembrandt?" Bobby could hardly catch his breath.

"Yes. And you are—"

"I'm looking for George Stinson."

"Do you have an appointment?"

"No, but I'd like to discuss some business with him."

"Maybe if you tell me your business I can direct you to the right person. Mr. Stinson doesn't—"

"Well, you give me your phone number at home and I'll tell you my business."

"Fresh."

"Can I just wait for him?"

"It wouldn't do you any good."

"Then I'll make an appointment."

She looked in her book. "Let's see, he has an opening three weeks from today."

"I'll take it. Robert Saxon. What time?"

The secretary's eyes widened. She had clearly thought that three weeks would be enough to scare Bobby off. She made a show of writing his name in the book. "Thank you, Miss Cooke," Bobby said, noting her full name on the wooden desk plaque: Gwen Cooke. It might come in handy. He smiled and gently opened the door.

Riding the elevator to the lobby, he again marveled at the building's exquisite beauty. He bought cigarettes at the lobby magazine stand. Lit up.

"Thanks, pop."

"Sure kid."

"Why does everyone always call me kid?"

"Why does everyone call me pop? I guess we got something in common." The old man winked at Bobby. "Maybe it's 'cause it don't look like you're old enough to shave yet, kid."

"I shave all right. Listen pop, can you do me a favor?"

"Depends."

"There's a fin in it for you."

"Still depends. Lotta slick guys like you give money for bad ends."

"I just want you to point someone out to me."

"That could be a bad end. Who is it?"

"George Stinson."

"Oh, you mean George Stingy."

"Stingy?"

"He don't give me nothing at Christmas. Barely says hello. But he 'spects me to bring him up cigarettes, candy, whatever. An' I gotta leave the booth unattended. He don't think nothing of it. I'll be glad to point him out to you. Might be a while though. He don't usually leave till after five."

"What else have I got to do?"

"Let's see the fin."

Bobby gave Pop a five-dollar bill, sat down on a ledge by the newsstand. Pop brought him a *Life* magazine.

"This'll help pass the time. Just don't bend it up soes I can't sell it."

Bobby nodded, flipped through the magazine. Time passed slowly until people finally started trickling out of their offices. He looked at his watch, five after five. Some stopped to buy things from Pop. Bobby looked up, expectant. Pop shook his head.

At six-seventeen p.m. a distinguished looking man with graying temples, perfect nose, steel gray eyes, and a dark blue suit came down the stairs, walking fast. He looked familiar, though Bobby couldn't quite place him. Pop edged over to Bobby, nudged him. Bobby slipped the *Life* back to Pop.

"Good as new."

"Almost."

Bobby discreetly followed Stinson. Should he go up and talk to him right now or follow him and see where he goes? He decided to follow on the better-than-even chance that Stinson wouldn't talk to him. This way he'd be able to see where he lived. Maybe know his routine. Find him again outside his office, if he had to.

Bobby barely had time to get to his car to follow Stinson's Packard. They drove west to the Wilshire Brown Derby, famous for the movie stars it served as well as its bowler hat shape. Another place Bobby had never been. Stinson went inside. Bobby circled the block, parked nearby so he could see the front of the building. He tried not to doze.

What am I gonna do if we don't get another gig?

I need to practice. I need an apartment where I can fit a piano.

I don't want to do the same damn thing every day. Go to the office at nine. Leave at five. Do whatever they do inside those airless places.

He lit a cigarette. It helped pass the time.

Why am I doing this? For James, that rotten bastard? No, for Booker. And maybe, just maybe, to prove something. To who? Booker? Myself? My dad?

Several smokes later, Stinson came out with a group of well-dressed people. Bobby's foot tapped the floorboards as they spent several minutes waiting for their cars and saying goodbye. He thought he recognized one of the people who came out with Stinson. David Chambers? Were they together or was it just coincidence? He squinted to get a better look. He thought it was Chambers, but at this distance it could really be anyone.

Something popped. He knew Stinson looked familiar as soon as he'd seen him in the Bradbury Building. Now he knew from where. He was the man that Dietrich had been talking to on the Apollo. Chambers had been on the Apollo. Was there a connection—was the man he was looking at now even Chambers? Or did he just want to see connections, even when there weren't any?

The valet brought Stinson's car; he drove off. Bobby followed him to an impressive Spanish colonial revival house in Los Feliz, not far from the Greek Theatre in Griffith Park. Stinson parked in the driveway, went in.

Should I go in or just give him some rope? At least I know where he lives now. Bobby looked at his watch. Drove off. He thought it had more to do with being scared than the time. What would he do if he went to the door?

Luckily it was Bobby's ration day, so he gassed up on the way home. While the attendant was cleaning the windows, Bobby checked the phone booth. Turned to the Ts. No Harlan Thomas. No Thomases at all. Some jerk had ripped the page out. *Damn!* Bobby huffed over to the attendant, paid, and sped off. Only then did he realize he had memorized Thomas' address from Dietrich's black book. He brought it to the fore of his mind and kept repeating it over and over like a musical bar so he wouldn't forget it.

Lights twinkled in most of the houses on Thomas' block in the Hollywood Hills. Not his. It didn't appear that he was home. Bobby wanted to walk the outside of the house. But he never got out of his car. He'd check again tomorrow. Drove home, feeling like a coward for not confronting Stinson or even going up to Thomas' door.

Bobby parked near his apartment. Walked up to see two white cops hassling Booker on the front lawn walkway. They had him between them like a baseball player in a pickle. They weren't leaning on him physically, but just being between the two large white cops in a white neighborhood must have been intimidating. Though maybe not for Booker.

Shit!

CHAPTER SEVEN

"What's going on here?"

"Bobby, Bobby, kindly explain to these gentlemen who I am and why I'm here."

"Who're you?" the older cop said.

"I live here."

"That's who I was coming to see," Booker said.

"He's a friend of mine."

"He works for you?" The cop scrutinized Bobby.

"He's a friend."

"This man was reported prowling around this building," the younger, taller cop said, glancing toward Mrs. Hazelton. Bobby's landlady stood a few yards away on the grass. The young cop pulled Bobby aside, while his squatter, wider partner grasped Booker by the arm.

"What're you doing with colored friends?"

"What difference does that make?"

"People see a colored boy in this neighborhood—"

"He's not a boy."

"Show me some ID," the younger cop said, his left hand scratching at his holstered baton.

Bobby proffered his driver's license photostat. The cop looked at it for what seemed longer than necessary. Bobby's heart raced; the photostat was a fake that his friend Marion— his former piano teacher—had helped him get. He hoped the cop wouldn't figure it out.

"All right, but get him off the street."

Bobby walked up to Booker. "Let's go."

The cops watched Bobby escort Booker up the walk. Mrs. Hazelton gave them the evil eye, then she turned it on the cops for not hauling Booker in. Bobby returned the look.

Bobby closed his apartment door on Mrs. Hazelton. "You seem awfully calm, Booker."

"Sometimes you just gotta swallow it down, 'specially with the cops. It's not worth it. Know what I mean? I got a pretty good life for a colored man in Los Angeles. Jeez, can't go anywhere and everywhere. But I make a good living. People come to see Booker blow. Got a nice house down in Central. What am I complaining about—just 'cause I'll get my head knocked off by some trigger-happy cop 'cause I made a wrong turn into a white neighborhood or went to visit one-a my band?"

Bobby didn't know what to do. He wished he had something to drink. "I'd offer you a drink but I don't have any alcohol."

"What kinda musician are you? Don't drink, don't smoke—"

"—I smoke up a storm," Bobby said, shuffling a cigarette from his Ronson Mastercase lighter. He put it in his mouth. Offered one to Booker.

"I mean reefer, boy."

"I know." Bobby shook out another Viceroy. Booker took it. Bobby lit it for him.

"How do you afford this place?"

"I told you, I've been working forever. I love to tinker, been working as a mechanic's assistant since I was a kid."

"Or maybe you have a rich white daddy. What troubles have you seen? You're a pretty white boy. All doors are open to you. You got a future. And right now you're playing in a colored band, taking a job from a colored boy, probably on some whim. Then some day you get tired of it and move on. Meanwhile the colored boy whose job you took is in jail since he doesn't have a job with the band."

"You hired me."

"I thought it would add some color to the band." Booker howled with laughter.

"Have you been drinking?"

"Not me. Just stewing."

"Well hold on then, I'll get you some beer to cry in." Bobby went to the fridge. "No beer."

"Let's go out and get a bite," Booker said as he grabbed his hat.

They headed for Marny's Café on Melrose by RKO and Paramount Studios in Booker's car.

"If you were in my position, you'd get down on yourself sometimes too." Booker rolled down the driver's window. Why did he want to let that smoggy air inside the car?

Bobby knew about getting down on himself.

"I'm sorry, Bobby, man. Sometimes I just gotta blow off steam, know what I mean? I mean, Jesus, James is in the slam and we got no gig."

"I know what you mean."

"Bullshit you do! And now the war's on. I'm sure they'll want black men for cannon fodder." Booker drove the speed limit exactly. Probably didn't want another run in with the cops. But Bobby could see him gripping the steering wheel as if he wanted to choke it to death. "What's the news on James?"

"You ever heard of a company called IBM?"

"They make musical instruments?"

"Nix."

"Then I ain't heard of them."

"Neither had I."

"So what's that got to do with James rotting in jail? You don't know what it's like for a colored man in jail. White time ain't the same as black time."

Bobby scanned Booker's silver 1941 Chrysler Thunderbolt Roadster from front to rear. It looked like something out of

Flash Gordon. It also looked like something the cops would want to pull over, especially with a colored man driving. "Maybe my being in the band isn't such a good idea."

"Am I making you uncomfortable—think how uncomfortable James is. You wanna be in a colored band, white boy, you gotta pay your dues." Booker dragged on his cigarette. "I'm just a little p.o.'d right now. Now what's any of this IBM jazz got to do with James?"

Before Bobby could answer, Booker pulled into a parking place near Marny's. Bobby felt uncomfortable with Booker. People stared at them. He felt less threatened when he went down to the colored part of town.

He held the café's door open for Booker. The place wasn't very crowded, but whoever was there turned and looked. The heat off their eyes felt like bayonets ready to strike. Booker didn't seem bothered. In fact, he seemed to enjoy it.

The guy behind the counter came out to greet them. "Help you?"

"Two."

The counterman eyed them suspiciously. Seated them near the back door. Booker took the seat against the wall. "Coffee," Booker said and the counterman walked off. "I always sit with my back to the wall."

Most of the patrons went back to their meals. Not all. "Hey," the burly guy at the next booth shouted. "Do you have to seat them next to us?"

Bobby could see Booker's shoulders hunch up. The tendons in his jaw tightened. His eyes turn to slits.

"Booker..."

"I can't eat. And let them pay the bill."

"Let it go," Bobby said.

"Guess I'm still pissed about those cops hassling me." Booker jerked out of the booth, turned to stand over the two men in the booth behind theirs. He grabbed the man's collar, yanked him up. The man was at least two inches taller than Booker, but

Booker's rage made up for the difference in their heights. "You wanna take this out back?"

"Let a nigger in and everything goes downhill from there."

Bobby grabbed Booker's sleeve as the counterman ran over.

"Why don't you all go outside?" he said.

Booker grabbed a ten from his pocket, threw it down on the table. "Here, I'll pay your bill. My mama said never to waste good food. 'Course on you even air is wasted."

"Get out. All of you." The counterman ushered all four of them out onto the sidewalk. Booker stared the man down. His friend grabbed him by the arm. Bobby took Booker. They headed off in different directions as if to neutral corners.

"Remember what you said about the cops, sometimes you just gotta swallow it down."

"This guy ain't no cop."

"No, but the counterman was ready to call them and you know who they'd slam."

"Yeah, I know who they'd slam.

"Sometimes you just gotta let it go."

"And sometimes you just gotta bust heads," Booker said. "I guess I just didn't swallow hard enough."

They reached Booker's car. "That was a swell cuppa coffee," he said.

"Yeah, sweet." Bobby stared out the window, his mind drifted back to the case. "I'm not sure yet."

"Not sure 'bout what."

"IBM, before we hit the diner you asked what IBM has to do with James. They make business machines. The initials stand for International Business Machines. Right now it's the only lead I have. I've talked to Dietrich's secretary and been to his apartment. Zip."

Bobby slid down in the front seat of the car, trying to relax.

"This guy Hans Dietrich work for them?" Booker asked.

"I'm not really sure, I don't think so. He had an import-export business."

"So you got nothing."

"I got IBM," Bobby snapped. Booker didn't flinch.

"Well, I guess that's better than nothing."

"Booker, you got anything lined up? I'm gonna need some scratch to pay the rent on my Gone-With-the-Wind-White-Bread-Southern-Plantation-Mansion here and my fingers are getting rusty."

"Yessir, massah, I be workin' on it. I really be. Might have somethin' lined up, yessuh."

"Stop with the Stepin Fetchit routine."

"Yessuh, massah."

Bobby reached for the door handle. "All right, Booker, let me out here. I quit the band. I quit playing detective. I quit."

Booker pulled up to the curb outside of Bobby's place. "Calm down, boy. I'm tryin' to line up a gig, Bobby. It ain't easy. Besides the Apollo'll be back up and running as soon as those gangsters pay the cops off."

Bobby figured Booker was making amends. He swept his fingers across an imaginary piano keyboard. "I need a place to practice. No piano."

"I'll see what I can do about that too. You keep working on James. Worse comes to worst, I'll front you some money. Since you'll be working as a detective, you should get paid as one."

"I don't want your money for that, Booker. Just a gig and a place to practice."

Booker reached into his breast pocket, shoved a C-note into Bobby's hand. "Take it. You're a private eye now."

Bobby jammed the money down into his pocket.

"I'll let you know. You just stay on with James," Booker said. Bobby got out, closed the car door. Booker tipped his hat, drove off. Bobby watched the silver bullet recede down the road.

He walked to his apartment and into the center of the living room. Looked around, stopping long enough to glance in the mirror. Booker's words echoed in his head, *What troubles have you seen?*

Bobby walked into his bathroom.

He took off his fedora, hung it on the hook behind the bathroom door. It was such a part of him, he hadn't realized he still had it on. He looked in the mirror. For a man he spent a lot of time looking in the mirror. Tired, puffy red eyes. He ran his fingers over his face the way a man does when he's checking his beard to see if he needs to clean up that five o'clock shadow.

More of Booker's words echoed. *You're a pretty white boy. All doors open to you. You got a future.*

Bobby slipped his jacket off, put it on a hanger, hung it on the hook below the hat. He very deliberately untied his tie, slid it off. He ran his right hand over the silk. Then he ran his left hand over the right. His hand was almost as smooth as the silk. He delicately set the tie on the tub edge.

Bobby fingered the buttons on his shirt, hard, sleek. He unbuttoned, hung the wrinkled shirt under the jacket on the same hanger, smoothed it out. He stared at himself in the mirror. Ran his hand over his face again. He began tugging at his undershirt. Hesitated. *What troubles have you seen? You're a pretty white boy. All doors open to you. You got a future.* Echoing. Swirling in his head.

Bobby finally removed his undershirt. A wrap-around bandage scored his chest. He removed the bandage and stared not at the chest of a man, but that of a small-breasted woman. Because Bobby was a woman through and through, born Roberta Saxon. And instead of Bobby, with a *y*, staring back at him was Roberta—Bobbie, with an *ie*. He, she, stared at her reflection. The close-cropped hair, smooth skin, chin too small for a man. His eyes settled on his chest, the small round breasts—and he was no longer Bobby, but Roberta.

"Oh yeah, all doors are open to me."

Bobby had been born Roberta and still was, at least underneath the double-breasted pinstripe suits and Dick Tracy hats. But in order to pursue her dream of being a musician in a hot jazz band, she had to pretend to be a man. She had grown up under the HOLLYWOODLAND sign. Hollywood, where people came to make dreams come true. Where dreams did come true, as long as you weren't Peg Entwistle, who had jumped from the sign's *H* in the thirties when her dream shattered like broken glass. Roberta, Bobbie, didn't want to be a canary, a singer, though she had a good voice. She wanted to be one of the players, something unheard of for a woman. But no band, white or colored, would have a woman except as a singer. Bobbie didn't mind singing on occasion, but she wanted to wail on the eighty-eights, so she did what she had to do. She became a man for all intents and purposes. She didn't like living a lie, it wreaked havoc on her love life—which was another story altogether—but it did everything for the love of her life, music. It was a tradeoff she had to make and one that was well worth it. Still, that's why the idea of going on the road scared her to death. She couldn't afford to share a room with one of her bandmates and have her true self revealed.

With the help of Marion, her piano teacher, she had obtained a fake driver's license under the name Robert Saxon and started a new life as a man. As far as she knew the ruse worked. Nobody suspected. Or if they did, no one said anything. And that was fine with her.

Staring in the mirror, she watched herself, wondering what it might be like to live as a woman once more. She was confused. What was she really, a man or a woman? She didn't think her crossdressing, a word she'd picked up somewhere, only related to wanting to play in a band. She'd given it lots of thought and didn't have any good answers. As a child, there was no one to talk to, to bounce ideas off. She knew she wasn't like the other girls, never having really outgrown the tomboy stage. She always preferred jeans to dresses. And while putting on makeup and fussing with her hair could be fun, mostly all that girly stuff was just tedious. She was pretty in an offbeat way and had dated boys in high school, though somewhat reluctantly. It always felt awkward, except with David Chambers. He always made her feel comfortable in her own skin. But her father despised seeing her dress up like a boy and then a man. Her mother was weak. Her brothers were in their own worlds of baseball and movies. People in high school made fun of anyone who was different, so for the most part she kept her boy-side to herself. But it gnawed at her.

She could go to one of those fancy-schmancy psychiatrists. No money, not for that.

Oh yeah, all doors are open to me. Little rich white boy. Girl.

"Am I a man or a woman? I don't even know who to date, men or women. If I'm Bobby do I date women? And Bobbie dates men? Or do I just want women? And what does that make me?" The thought sent a shiver through her entire body.

Before Bobbie had gotten the art of male dressing and grooming down, she-he had taken a few beatings along the way. They didn't really bother her, him. They made him stronger. More determined. And he could have moved to New York or somewhere where he wasn't known, because in Los Angeles he occasionally ran into people he did know, though if he saw someone he thought he knew, he might cross the street to avoid bumping into them. That didn't always work. Some people recognized him, most didn't. Still, he chose to stay in L.A. and follow his dream here.

Did Booker know the truth? If he did he'd given no sign. What about Nicolai? Or James—is that why he was so hostile? He was hostile to everyone, but even so.

Bobbie's piano teacher—Marion—had noticed something off with her right away. She'd been coming to Bobbie's house to give her lessons. One day, not long before Bobbie graduated high school, she invited Bobbie to her home in Edendale. Bobbie rode the red cars there. Marion was very bohemian and her little

Spanish house bore that out with its original Salvador Dali painting and Richmond Barthé statuettes. Marion didn't beat around the bush. She told Bobbie she knew something was up with her. Admitted her own attraction to women. She called herself a lesbian, the first time Bobbie'd heard that term. Marion helped Bobbie explore her desires to dress like—to be a man. But she never came on to Bobbie. Once Bobbie moved out of her parents' house the summer after high school, she—he—worked as a piano tuner and a mechanic. She'd always been good with her hands. And Marion helped her to accept herself. She invited Bobby to parties, but Bobby and Bobbie were always too scared to go. She hadn't been to Marion's in a while, maybe she should go back and practice.

Bobby—Bobbie—didn't know if he was a man or woman, though obviously born a woman. Or if he, she, was interested in men or women. Indeed, he had some things to work out. But right now the biggest was keeping his dream alive—finding the real killer and staying in the band.

Bobby ran his hand across his forehead. "Jeez, I could use some reefer now."

Roberta walked out of her bathroom.

CHAPTER EIGHT

Bobbie sat on the sofa in her male skivvies, coffee in one hand. With the other she flipped pages in her high school yearbook. Her eyes traveled up the page. There he was. Tall, light, and handsome. Striking eyes. Great actor. A great Cyrano to her Roxanne. She had almost thought she was in love with him. Almost. Or did she just want to be like him? And right now she was playing the part of *Bobbie*, at other times she played *Bobby*. She'd always felt like she was acting out a part for most of her life. Pretending to be a *girl*. Pretending to be a *boy*. Pretending to be a detective. Some day she just wanted to stop pretending.

David Chambers' smile beamed off the page at her. She scrutinized his face. Was that the face she had seen with Stinson outside the Brown Derby? She cursed *Bobby* again for not having had binoculars. For not being a better detective. Bogey would have had everything he needed. Bobby had no idea what was needed, at least not ahead of time.

A crimson knife edge of sun blinded Bobby as he drove west on Sunset. The trip to the Malibu sheriff's station seemed to get longer each time. Bobby dressed in his usual *uniform*, double-breasted suit, shirt, tie, fedora. Breasts tightly tucked. No makeup, God forbid. Though sometimes he wondered about dabbing a little mascara on his cheeks and upper lip to give the illusion of a five o'clock shadow.

Bobby's heart danced. He hadn't been this nervous in some time. He had been passing as a man for a good while now. So why was he scared to go into the sheriff's station and ask for Sergeant Nicolai, especially since he'd been there once before? Nothing had changed, nothing except thinking about David Chambers, someone who could blow his cover. Was he now worried that everyone would blow his cover? That he no longer passed as a man? He didn't know. All he did know was that his palms were sweating, hands shaking. He decided to watch the parking lot to see when Nicolai pulled in. He would approach him outside and there'd be less people to scrutinize him.

Nicolai seemed like a nice enough guy. Didn't go to town on Bobby for not being in the service, yet he'd said he was army all the way. Didn't know if the sergeant was married. Didn't really know much about him at all. Did that matter, as long as Nicolai didn't bother Bobby, didn't see through him? The real question was, did Nicolai really believe James had done it? It didn't seem so. Why else would he be at Dietrich's apartment? There he was, pulling into the lot. Bobby got out of his car.

"Sergeant."

"I was wondering when I'd see you again. Solve the case yet?"

"No. Have you?"

Nicolai rested his foot on his bumper, tied his shoe. "Ain't the killer in jail?"

"I thought you didn't think James did it?"

"Why?"

"'Cause I found you going through Dietrich's apartment. 'Cause you seemed to want to help me find the real killer."

"Yeah, well the brass thinks we got the real killer."

"What do you think?"

"I think what the brass tells me to think."

"C'mon, Sergeant. Surely you have an opinion of your own."

"I got lots of opinions." His voice trailed off as two deputies walked past them into the station. "But nobody wants to hear 'em."

"I know how you feel." Bobby looked at Nicolai's ring finger.

No ring. But he knew that some men didn't wear a ring on the job. Why was he looking? Ever since last night his mind was a jumble of thoughts about his life, his sexuality.

"You wanna come in?"

Bobby's heart jumped. "Uh, you really don't want them seeing me with you, do you?"

"Guess not. No more than necessary."

What did that mean?

"What can I do for you today?"

"Well, now I feel a little funny asking."

"Hey, you drove all the way down here. Might as well get a lick in, so to speak."

"I'm trying to find Harlan Thomas—"

"The partner?"

Bobby nodded.

"Have you talked to their secretary again?" Nicolai thought a moment, "Lois."

"Naw, she doesn't wanna talk."

"Yeah, but not too hard on the eyes."

Bobby worked up his best wry smile. "I went to Thomas' office and his house. He's nowhere."

"Did you ever stop to consider that maybe he is around and isn't really on vacation, but he hasn't been around when you've been to his office or house? Maybe, just maybe, he don't wanna talk to you."

"Does he want to talk to you, Sergeant?"

"No, he doesn't seem to. He's never been around when I've tried either." Nicolai rubbed his chin, as if debating whether to give out to Bobby. Finally, he said, "I hear he's got a cabin somewheres but nobody seems to know where."

"Can you track it down?"

"Not yet and this case has become low-pri for me."

"Is the cabin even in this state?"

Nicolai shrugged. "Maybe Lois can tell you over a nice T-bone and beer."

"There's more to this than James just beating on the guy 'cause they got in an argument."

"I think so too," Nicolai said, not bothering to whisper. "But my hands are tied."

"Hey, Sarge—"

"Good luck, kid," Nicolai saluted, disappeared inside the station.

Bobby knocked on the door of Dietrich Enterprises. No response. Knocked louder. Nothing. Maybe the business was closed, Lois let go. The narrow hall pressed in on Bobby, one small window at each end letting in a squat rectangle of dusky light. He wiped his damp forehead with his pocket square.

He wished he could get inside, look around. Maybe he could, but not now. Not when people were coming and going in the building. When he—she—was young, playing with his brothers, they had picked locks on some buildings, gotten inside them, looked around. They might have stolen a turkey leg or a cookie, but nothing else, no real property. It was fun, until they got caught and their father turned their butts a glowing red. Maybe being a detective wasn't such a stretch. Though if he messed up here the consequences would be a lot worse.

Bobby hit the phone booth on the corner, looked up Lois Templeton. She lived on Detroit. He snatched the page from the book.

The duplex on Detroit and First streets was within walking distance of Dietrich Enterprises. Made sense for Lois to work somewhere close to home. Bobby wondered if she walked the few blocks in her heels every day or changed shoes once she got to work. Three blocks in high heels, ouch! Bobby preferred his solid oxfords. The duplex was a side-by-side. Well-tended. Green with grass and plants. Fuchsia bougainvillea and brightly colored flowers. Bobby wished he could live in a place like this instead of the dump he lived in.

He straightened his tie, placed the fedora on his head just so, headed to the door.

"Yes?" The woman swept a strand of gray hair off her face, while holding the door open only a few inches behind a chain.

"Hello, I'm a friend of Lois. Is she home?"

The woman's mouth turned down. She scanned Bobby from head to toe. "Who did you say you were?"

"I had lunch with Lois a couple of days ago."

"You're a friend?"

"Yes, ma'am."

"I'm her mother. She lives here, but I haven't seen her in a couple of days." Worry spilled from her voice.

Bobby ached for a cigarette. Didn't want to light up in front of Mrs. Templeton. He wasn't sure why.

"Is it like her not to come home like this?"

"No. She comes home every night," she said, defending her daughter. "Or at least she would phone."

"Have you called the police?"

"Not yet. I didn't think it was that bad."

"I'm not saying it is."

"Do you have any idea where she might be?"

Mrs. Templeton bit her lip.

"It's all right, Mrs. Templeton. I'm not here to judge her."

"She goes around with this crazy man, Sam Wilde. The name couldn't be more appropriate."

"Do you know where he lives?"

She shook her head.

"Works?"

"No. Besides, that good-for-nothing wouldn't know a job if it hit him over the head. But I know she would go with him to a pool hall down on Pico. Near Western I think. Are you going to help find her?"

"I'm gonna try."

Bobby didn't want to give Mrs. Templeton false hope. And he wasn't sure how much time he needed to spend on this aspect of the case. Hell, for all he knew Lois was shacking up some-where with this Wilde guy.

Bobby wanted to call Sergeant Nicolai. He didn't want to talk in front of Mrs. Templeton so he stopped at the first gas station he came across. The phone booth quickly filled with cig-arette smoke. Nicolai wasn't in. Bobby cruised down Wilshire in the direction of Western. He slowed near the Bryson Apartments, scanning for Nicolai's car. Didn't see it and hit the pedal. Turned south on Western. After a few blocks he started looking for pool halls. Seemed to be a popular place for them. Where the hell to start? He parked. Called Nicolai again.

"Where are you?"

"Pico and Western."

"What'chu doing there?"

"Lois Templeton is missing. Her mother said she sometimes hangs out with a guy at a pool hall down here."

"Good luck. There must be ten within a three-block radius."

"I just figured that out. Hey Sarge—"

"Don't call me Sarge, unless you want to join the department."

"Deputy Nicolai—"

"Better."

"Maybe you can check into it."

"That's LAPD territory. They don't like us stepping on their toes."

"But you checked out the Bryson and that's LAPD."

"Part of an ongoing investigation—Dietrich—and I had LAPD permission."

"Well, Lois is part of that same ongoing investigation. Can you call someone at LAPD?"

"Listen, kid, my hands are tied. Your call would do just about as much good."

Bobby doubted that. He looked down the street. Three pool halls just in what he could see from the booth.

Bobby hit the first pool parlor: "Sam Wilde? Name doesn't ring a bell. What does he look like?" the manager said.

Bobby had no answer for that. He'd forgotten to ask Mrs. Templeton. He described Lois instead.

"Can't say she sounds familiar."

The next pool hall was a bust and the one after that. Bobby turned the corner onto Pico. Walked into Brownie's Pool Emporium, a red brick building that sliced diagonally across the corner of Pico and Western at a forty-five-degree angle and stank of cigar smoke. It seemed more like a snake pit than an emporium, with unfinished brick walls and low-hanging lights. Worse than the others. He wanted to cough. Seeing the tough hombres—he'd learned that expression from the B Westerns he liked so much— he thought better of it. Tough hombres or not, he struck paydirt.

"Sure, Sam, he come in here 'round ten when he comes," the straw boss said.

"Will he be in tonight?"

"I'm not his social secretary, you know." The little man sucked on his big cigar. Blew smoke out. Bobby stifled a cough. Looked at his watch. Ten p.m. was several hours off. He drove to the Belasco Theater on Hill Street. Caught a Gene Autry-Roy Rogers double feature. Still had some time. Had a plate of spaghetti and a Coke at Delmonico on South Hill. Bobby felt funny eating alone in such an elegant, white tablecloth establishment. He stared at the murals on the walls until his food arrived, avoiding eye contact with the other customers.

Bobby didn't understand Nicolai. One minute he wanted to help, the next...Didn't understand himself either. Was he doing this to help James or just to get a slot in the band? Maybe a little of both. He thought about Gene Autry's Cowboy Code, had the whole thing memorized, all ten points:

1. The Cowboy must never shoot first, hit a smaller man, or take unfair advantage.
2. He must never go back on his word, or a trust confided in him.
3. He must always tell the truth.

4. He must be gentle with children, the elderly, and animals.
5. He must not advocate or possess racially or religiously intolerant ideas.
6. He must help people in distress.
7. He must be a good worker.
8. He must keep himself clean in thought, speech, action, and personal habits.
9. He must respect women, parents, and his nation's laws.
10. The Cowboy is a patriot.

Bobby had no one in his own life to model himself after. So he looked up to the cowboys on the silver screen. He could do a hell of a lot worse.

He had to use the restroom and though he'd been dressing and living as a man for some time, this still caused a tremble of the heart. Clearly he would never use a urinal and nobody paid attention to a man in a stall. But there was always that little flutter of nerves.

The walk back to the theater from the restaurant felt good, a chance to work off a little of that spaghetti. He picked up his car, drove back to Brownie's pool hall. Several men in work clothes hung around by the front door. The air outside was brisk, clean, until he came into clouds of pungent cigar smoke once he was inside the pool hall again. No empty tables at this hour. Bobby felt out of his element here. Tough crowd. Which wasn't to say that the Club Alabam or other places Bobby went didn't have toughs around. But here there was no pretense of civilization. If these guys knew what Bobby was under the suit and fedora he wouldn't make it out of here in one piece. Girlie jokes and Jew jokes filled the air as much as cigar smoke and Glenn Miller's "American Patrol," which spilled from the jukebox.

The little man with the big cigar nodded at Bobby, used the cigar as a pointer to send him to a man at table number nine.

"—that Jew bastard Roosevelt," an unshaved man said.

"Roosevelt's no Jew," said the man that the cigar-smoking manager had pointed to. Bobby watched Sam Wilde bank the eight ball to win his game.

"He might as well be." His opponent stomped off.

"Play?" Wilde said, scratching at his belly and side.

Bobby didn't want to play. Didn't know if he could. It'd been years since he'd held a pool cue. His father had tried to interest him in the game in an effort to get closer. It didn't take. Now he figured if he played Wilde, maybe he could bring the conversation around to Lois.

"I'm not very good."

"Well, you look like you do all right. You can afford to lose a few bucks. Two bits a ball."

Bobby nodded, chalked up a cue. They lagged for break. Bobby won. Or lost—he wasn't sure if it was better to go first or not. No balls were sunk on the break. Wilde squinted. He had small, dark eyes under a soiled and battered brown fedora that looked like it had been run over by a steamroller. He sunk three in a row. Bobby figured it would be a good time to bring Lois up.

"You're a friend of Lois Templeton—"

It sounded dumb as soon as Bobby said it. Squinty eyes turned on Bobby. Now he knew where the expression *shooting daggers* came from. He wore his amateur detective status like a badge. Wilde missed his ball. Stood erect.

"Let's go to my *office*." He shoved two gun-barrel-hard fingers into Bobby's back. Thrust him toward the men's room. "Get out," Wilde bellowed to the one man at the urinal. The man zipped up and scrambled out. Wilde spun Bobby around, glared at him nose to nose.

"Who the fuck are you and what do you want?"

CHAPTER NINE

If it came to a fight, Bobby didn't have the strength of a man. The broad shoulders of Wilde. And he certainly didn't have the fire in the eyes of the man staring him down.

"Talk, before I—"

"—I was just making small talk," Bobby cut in before Wilde could finish.

"Bullshit!"

The door started to open. Jimmy Durante's *Ink-A Dink-Doo streamed in from the pool hall.* Wilde slammed it shut on whoever was trying to enter. He shoved Bobby up against the sink. *Better than the urinal.* The sink's lip bit into his lower back.

Bobby decided to play it straight. "Lois is missing."

"You think I did it?"

"I didn't say that." Bobby wondered about Wilde's response. Instead of asking about Lois, he was worried about being accused. Sign of a guilty conscience?

"Why else you here in your fancy duds? A swell like you wouldn't be hanging at a joint like this."

"I'm a friend of her family."

"So her bitch of a mother sent you after me? 'Cause I don't fit into their circle. She's a goddamned secretary and I'm not good enough for her?"

"That's none of my concern."

"Damn right!" Wilde shouted. "I'm not her only boyfriend."

"You're the only one her mother told me about."

Rage flooded Wilde's eyes. His arm came up, ready to slug Bobby. He held it there. Bobby's heart stopped. He didn't want to show fear. He silently talked himself into breathing normally.

"You think I done something to her?"

"I never said that."

"You didn't have to, you little runt. You don't even have the balls to tell me straight out. You play pool soes you can work it in like it's just friendly talk."

You're right about the balls.

The cocked arm shot straight for Bobby's nose. Bobby reacted faster than he ever had, ducking out of the way. The large fist hit the mirror behind the sink, shattering it—no bullseye here. And Bobby learned a lesson: speed is almost as good as strength in a fight. But he knew that wouldn't work every time.

Bobby dived for the door, while Wilde was still nursing his bruised and bloody hand. Wilde started after him, thought better of it.

"You tell that bitch-mother I didn't do nuthin' to her precious daughter. And don't come 'round here again."

"Why? What're you gonna do, smash another mirror?" Bobby grinned and walked out slowly. But he knew he was tempting fate and would be even more if he came back.

Ink-A Dink-Doo, A dink-a dee, A dink-a doo, Simp-ly means In-A dink-A dee A dink-a doo.

Bobby bolted out of the pool hall, sucking down fresh air. He might have put on a show of bravado for Wilde, but now his whole body was shaking. He needed a drink and there was a bar next to the pool hall. But he didn't drink, and even if he did, he wanted to get the hell away from there. He hit his car. Before heading home, he drove up Western into Griffith Park with the top down, driving the winding roads up to the Observatory. The feel of the open road would help him unwind from the encounter with Wilde. He passed garrisoned soldiers on his way up the hill. The Observatory was still open during the day, not at night in case enemy planes could use it as a beacon.

Wilde stayed on his mind. That was a man's man—or just a crazy man? Bobby was still trying to find his way in the world of men. He needed role models. Sam Wilde wouldn't be one. Still, there was something magnetic about him and Bobby could see how Lois would be attracted to him. He wondered if women were attracted to him. Or he to them? He knew he wasn't really attracted to men, though he had dated some before he started living as Bobby full time. Lately his social life had been nil. Would it always be that way?

Bobby squinted in the morning sun as he drove east on Sunset, toward Echo Park, past Ciro's and Club Rendezvous. He didn't have a particular destination in mind. He needed to think. Normally he'd head west to the beach. Why was he heading in the opposite direction this time?

Most boys had their father to look up to. Most girls their mother. Bobby had neither. He had always looked to movie stars, not their real lives that he read about in the fan magazines, but their on-screen personas. Bogart. Autry. The other cowboy heroes, from Hopalong Cassidy to Hoot Gibson and John Wayne. Gable and Errol Flynn. They always did the right thing and somehow always knew what the right thing to do was. Bobby wished he knew what the right thing was. He wished he knew others like himself, but there was no one. He just lived his life as if he were a man. He had spent enough time in his father's house to see how a man lives, maybe not the best man, but a man.

Sometimes he wondered what made him like this. Why he couldn't just be the she *he* was born and live a normal life? He'd tried. It went nowhere. And now here he was, wondering what direction to go in, with no one to lead him.

Bobby needed someone to talk to. He headed for Edendale, near Echo Park and downtown L.A. Drove down Allesandro, past the enormous Angelus Temple of Aimee Semple McPherson. The huge domed structure almost reached out and grabbed him. He'd never been there, though he'd driven by several times; he knew it had space for over five thousand parishioners. Bobby didn't think he'd ever be one, not if they knew the truth about him. But who knew, maybe Sister Aimee was open-minded.

Bobby pulled up to a small yellow stucco Spanish job, buried in a nest of willow trees, shrubs, overgrown rose bushes, and meandering raspberry-colored bougainvillea. He climbed the steep cement stairs from the street to the house. Knocked. Marion Jones answered the door. As always, she dressed to impress, in a silk shirt and Marlene Dietrich men's tuxedo pants. It had been a while since Bobby had seen his piano teacher. But Marion was the same old Marion.

"Bobby, what a nice surprise. Have you come to practice?"

"Not today, Marion. I just thought maybe we could chat."

"Sure. Come in."

Marion led the way, bare feet padding on the scuffed hardwood floor. They made their way past the living room, with its shiny black-lacquered grand piano, down the hall into the kitchen. Bright sun filtered through the foliage outside, dancing on the kitchen surfaces, making brightly painted sunflower yellow walls even more yellow.

"Coffee? Coke?"

"I'll just have a Coke."

Marion opened the ice box. Grabbed a couple six-ounce bottles of Coca-Cola. "Glass? Ice?"

"Bottle's fine." Bobby took a bottle from Marion, nudged it into the opener on the side of the counter. Popped the top. "Cold."

"The pause that refreshes," Marion said, with only the slightest hint of sarcasm.

"Is that a new painting I saw in the entry hall?"

"Oh, I've had it some time. It's been a while since you've been here. It's nothing, a gift from Salvador and Gala." She motioned for Bobby to join her at the breakfast table.

"Do you have any students today?"

"Not until four, in fact I was about to head out for a bit. So what brings you out to this hotbed of commies and homos?"

"Edendale isn't all like that." Bobby knew that the neighborhood had a reputation as an avant-garde, bohemian community, that the first movie studios had been built here, Tom Mix's Mixville, Selig and Mack Sennett's studios. Bison and Fox. The Keystone Cops pulled many an antic on its streets. Bobby envied Marion. Her house. Her self-assurance. The fact that she knew what she was and was comfortable with herself.

"Not all." Marion smiled slyly.

"I just need someone to talk to."

"About *Bobby*?"

Bobby shook his head.

"Roberta?"

"No. I got a gig playing with a band down at the Alabam."

"Congratulations, that's what you always wanted."

"But it's all sort of blown up in my face."

"They made you as a woman?"

"No. I don't think so anyway. We were playing on that gambling ship, the Apollo."

"You were there when that man died?"

"He was killed. And the police, the sheriffs arrested one of the band members."

"Because he did it or because he's a Negro in the band? I read about it in the paper."

"I don't think he did it."

"Because he's a Negro. Figures." Marion lit a cigarette. Bobby did the same. "So no more gig?"

"More than that even, I'm playing detective."

"What do you mean?"

"Booker, the band leader, asked me to see what I could find out since he doesn't think James—the guy the cops have arrested—is guilty. And because I'm white—"

"—Booker thinks you can go places he can't."

Bobby nodded. "And I've been doing the best I can but I'm way out of my league. I went to see a rerun of *The Maltese Falcon*—I don't know how else to learn to be a detective except from Bogart, William Powell, and the movies."

Marion laughed. "I'm sorry. That's not the place I would think to go."

"Where would you go?"

"I don't know, but not to the movies." Marion laughed. "Have you learned anything?"

"I know the dead man's name, that he's German and ran an import-export company."

"Trading with Germany? That's odd. I thought all trade with Germany was halted when the war began."

"According to his secretary they were trading with other countries in Europe but not Germany anymore. Business isn't so good since the war."

"What else do you know?"

"I found a piece of paper in his apartment. All it says is *IBM 4pm*."

"What does that stand for?"

"International Business Machines."

"Is there a connection?"

"I don't know. Maybe. I'm still trying to work it out in my head."

"Maybe I can ask around."

"You do know a lot of people." Bobby didn't really think Marion would follow through. She rarely did, though her intentions were good.

"Anything else?"

"That's about it. I talked to his secretary, the dead man's, went out to lunch with her—"

"—A date? As Bobby or Roberta?"

"It wasn't a date-date. I just wanted to get some information." Bobby slouched deeper in his chair.

"And did you get it?"

"Not much. And now she's disappeared."

"The secretary?"

"She's gone. I can't find her. I tracked down a boyfriend her mother told me about. This is one scary man."

"How come he's not off fighting the war?"

"I didn't have time to ask as his B-17 Flying Fortress-sized fist swung toward me." Bobby ducked—a reflex.

"The army probably doesn't even want him."

"He has a bad temper—"

"—No doubt." Marion moved to the window. Dappled by the sunlight coming in, she looked like one of her impressionist paintings.

"I don't think he did it. It's too much of a coincidence. Dietrich is killed. Lois goes missing. And her boyfriend just happens to be a lout."

Marion's blue eyes bore down on Bobby. "So what are you really doing here, my friend?"

"I need a sounding board." Bobby eyed the photos on the wall opposite him. FDR. Autographed photos of Eleanor Roosevelt and Earl Browder, the American Communist Party presidential candidate.

"What about this Booker?" Marion said. "He knows more about it than I do."

"So does Sergeant Nicolai."

"Who?"

Bobby filled Marion in on Nicolai. Sipped his Coke.

"Sounds like he's not so bad...for a cop. Trying to help. Do you think he knows about Roberta?"

"He hasn't said anything to indicate it."

"You say that about everyone."

"Don't you think I pass?"

"You pass very well, unless someone is attuned to—"

"I think most people aren't attuned and they aren't looking for it and they wouldn't see it even if hit them like a brick."

"You're right. Most people don't see what they don't want

to see." Marion stubbed her cigarette in an ashtray with a picture of Hitler's face on the bottom. She seemed to relish jamming the burning embers into his eyes. "I'm sorry I can't be of more help on your, uh, case. But I will see if anyone knows about this International Business Machines."

Bobby knew that Marion was waiting for more. That she thought he'd come to talk about his life. His *confusion*. He didn't say anything, dragged on his cigarette.

"I can fix you up with a nice man. Or a nice girl. Or something in between. Whatever you want, darling."

"I don't know what I want, Marion. That's the problem." Bobby stubbed out his cigarette in Hitler's face. "And there's one more problem. I ran into a boy I used to know—"

"Boy?"

"Well, he's a man now. David Chambers. I used to have the biggest crush on him. I sometimes wonder if it was more that I wanted to be him than be with him. But right now I'm concerned he might know something about this IBM business, be involved."

Marion thought a moment. "There's no rule that says you can't go both ways. Use what you've got, be Roberta for a day. See what he knows, tease it out of him."

CHAPTER TEN

Bobby tore into his apartment, scrambling for the closet, digging through clothes and shoes and boxes of this and that until he finally found what he was looking for. Bobby pulled out an old dress and a pair of medium high heeled women's pumps. He, she hated these things. But *she* was glad now that she hadn't discarded all her girly clothes. If Marion was right, Bobby might get more information out of David as Roberta. The dress was pretty enough—even sexy—in a simple, plain way. Bobby laid it on the ironing board, smoothed it out with a hot iron.

"It'll have to do."

She began undressing. Shirt first. Then the bands holding her breasts down. She hunted through the apartment until she found an old bra. She put the bra over her breasts and slipped the dress over her head, shimmied it down. She walked to the bathroom mirror.

"Yechh!" Seeing herself in a dress for the first time since high school brought back her feelings of disquiet. The awkwardness she had always felt as a girl returned. She shooed those thoughts away, looked in the mirror again. "Good enough."

Bobbie removed the dress and bra, ran the water in the tub, finished undressing. She slid into the tub, the warm water feeling damn good on her aching muscles. She'd been doing a lot of leg work in the last few days. She didn't realize how exhausted she was. She rested her head on the back of the tub, closed her eyes and she was in another world. A world that wasn't as confusing. Wasn't as angry. Wasn't at war. She soaped her legs, picked up a razor and shaved them, something she hadn't done in ages. Her legs felt smooth and girlish. And she didn't have bad gams if she said so herself.

Bobby slept half the night in the tub, eventually waking just enough to dry off and hit the couch. Pulling down the Murphy bed would have been too much trouble.

Morning sun tricked Bobbie awake. She rubbed the sleep out of her eyes, sprinted to the bathroom for a quick shower. Instead of putting on a suit and tie she slipped into the bra and dress and those pumps, becoming fully Roberta for the first time in as long as he—she—could remember. She appraised herself in the mirror.

"Not bad. The dress could be a little more stylish, hon, but you don't make a half bad dame," she said from the corner of her mouth, trying to sound like Bogey. Her short hair was a problem. She combed it forward, then back. Well, maybe not such a problem. Veronica Lake had cut her hair for the war effort. People would understand.

But maybe she should get a wig to be safe. And she knew just where to go.

Finding a parking space on Highland Avenue was easy; walking to the front door, even on mid-high heels, wasn't. Bobbie stopped at the entrance, looking at the marble surround and gold doors of the Max Factor Building. The lines of the building were flowing beauty, like a Botticelli nude or Marlene Dietrich in a Hurrell photo. Like almost everything in Los Angeles, it was a hybrid, in this case of classical architecture and art deco. The jewelry box display windows floating up the sidewalk were filled with more than makeup and the things that made women beautiful—they were filled with dreams. Hollywood dreams. Looking at them made Bobbie wince.

She crossed the threshold, knowing that, like Dorothy entering Oz, she was in another land. The cream-and-salmon streamline moderne interior enveloped her and she almost wanted to become a full-time woman.

"May I help you?" the receptionist said in the snootiest tone.

"Is Mary Cooper here?"

"Do you have an appointment?"

"I'm an old friend, Bobbie Saxon."

"I'll see if she has a moment."

Mary Cooper appeared in the lobby as mysteriously as Glinda, the Good Witch, appeared to Dorothy in *The Wizard of Oz*. She looked every bit the glamorous Max Factor girl that Bobbie always remembered. Tall, buxom. Pretty in that all-American way.

"Bobbie?" Mary could barely conceal the bewilderment behind her smile. After all, they hadn't spoken since Bobbie's love note to her in fifth grade, even though they'd gone through grade school, junior high, and high school together.

Mary led her back to a consultation room.

"I guess you're surprised to see me."

"That's an understatement. We haven't spoken since when?"

"Fifth grade." Bobbie may not have spoken with Mary, but she'd heard where she worked through the grapevine.

"That's right. The...love note you sent me."

"I was just a kid."

"I guess it scared me."

"Well, I've come to retrieve it."

"Oh, I don't know what happened to it."

"Just kidding."

Mary sat on the edge of a makeup table. "So what do we do now, talk about old times? High school. Boys we liked."

"Actually I was looking through the yearbook. Brings back lots of memories." Bobbie didn't want it to seem like she had just come here for business. Thought a little small talk would help. Mary's polite but impassive face said she wasn't interested.

"High school's the past. I prefer to look to the future, you know like the 1939 World's Fair slogan: 'Dawn of a New Day; the World of Tomorrow,' that's how I like to live," Mary said.

"This is the twentieth century. Did you ever believe man would fly? I mean I guess since we were kids there've been planes. But c'mon. Our parents, our grandparents certainly, were going around in horses and carriages. We get to move forward on the 20th Century Limited."

Boy, she talks a lot, just like a girl.

"So what're you up to these days?" Mary asked.

That was the question Bobbie had hoped to avoid. What could she tell Mary? That she played piano in a band—as a man. That she lived ninety-nine percent of her life as a man, maybe more. That she wore men's clothes and shoes and ties and hats and that's why her hair was so short. Or should she tell Mary that she's a detective, like Humphrey Bogart in the movies. She wondered if Mary knew Bogey. "I'm still finding my way, I guess," is what she came up with.

"So what brings you here? Not just to hash over old times?"

"I, I want a makeover."

Mary looked Bobbie up and down. "No offense, but you could use one."

"Don't I know."

"Makeup?"

"Makeup. Hair. The works. And don't worry, I can pay."

"We're not cheap."

"I'm not looking for a discount or to take advantage of knowing you, or sort of knowing you. I just figured maybe someone I knew could help guide me through the process."

Mary circled around Bobbie. "Well, there's a lot to work with. You have great skin. Pretty, expressive eyes. Nice coloring. And a good figure. But that hair. It's so short. Who're you trying to be, Marlene Dietrich?"

"Not exactly."

"She's a dyke you know."

The scorn in Mary's voice surprised Bobbie. She tried not to let it show. Right now she needed Mary's help. Marion was a *dyke*; it didn't bother Bobbie.

"I've heard that. But you hear that about everyone in Hollywood, male and female. It can't all be true."

"More times than you'd think. All right, so I'm clear for," Mary looked at her watch, "the next ninety minutes at least." She ran her fingers through Bobbie's closely cropped hair. "More like Louise Brooks than Veronica Lake. But we'll manage something, maybe with a little styling it can work."

"Maybe I can get a wig?"

Mary eyed Bobbie's hair as if she was X-raying it. "If you want, but let's see what we can do with what you've got. Besides, you can always grow it out."

Bobbie enjoyed the full treatment, facial, eyebrow waxing, shampoo and a clear-coat manicure of her short nails. She wondered if Booker and the others would notice. She hoped she wouldn't be too feminine to pass as Bobby now. And while she didn't consider going back to living as a woman, there was something satisfying about being pampered. Several people worked on her, each having their own specialty. All were under Mary's guidance. If Mary held a grudge from fifth grade Bobbie didn't notice. Mary turned Bobbie around in the swivel chair so she could face the mirror.

"Voilà!" she said. "A new you."

"It really is," Bobbie said, enthusiastically, putting on an act for Mary. "Even the hair, I'm amazed at what you've done."

"You have nice thick hair; you should grow it out."

"I might. I just might." Bobbie knew she wouldn't.

"Now, I hope you're not going to stick with those rags. You have to get some nice clothes."

"I was thinking of going to Bullock's Wilshire."

"Good choice."

Mary didn't charge for her services, only those of the others.

"I'm happy to pay the full fare," Bobbie said.

"Consider it a gift from one Fairfax High gal to another."

"Thanks, Mary." Bobbie clutched a bag of creams and makeup. They would come in handy and, expensive as they were, they were cheaper than having to come back here for another makeover.

"Don't mention it. I guess, despite what I said before, high school is forever. To Lord Fairfax."

They clinked imaginary glasses, said their goodbyes. Just before leaving, Bobbie asked, "By the way, whatever became of David Chambers?"

"I thought you'd know. You and him seemed very friendly in drama club."

"We were, but we lost touch."

"Last I heard he was practicing law. Not sure if he's on his own or with a firm. Good luck finding him, high school forever and all of that."

Bullock's Wilshire proudly towered over Wilshire Boulevard, five stories of main building, a tower that rose to ten. All art deco garnishes and streamline moderne, copper and that tall tower with the searchlight that couldn't be turned on during the war. Huge display windows that could easily be seen from the street and a parking lot in the rear. That's where Bobbie went. A valet's mouth puckered at the Olds, then gave her the same treatment in her frumpy dress. But he also gave her face and body the twice over. She knew she looked dishy.

The store's interior reeked magnificence, with humongous murals and columns that rose as if to heaven. Bobbie thought she saw Errol Flynn at the jewelry counter. She was in too much of a hurry to look closer. She went straight to the dress department. More snooty looks. She was getting used to them. She wanted to shout, *I have money!* And she did; most of her savings was in her purse. She knew it would be an expensive day. If she got a real gig with Booker out of it, it would be worth every penny.

She sank down into a plush chair as models strolled by in various outfits. She waited for the more casual selections. She wanted something sexy, but not too formal, and she found it in a slinky wrap dress. The saleslady brought it to her in her size. She went to the dressing room. It fit like a glove in most areas. And where it didn't they said their seamstress would alter it. Bobbie didn't want to wait. It looked fine and she would make do.

When she paid, the saleslady seemed surprised. Good for her. Don't judge a book by its cover.

She retrieved her car, giving the same valet more of a tip than he deserved, drove off, feeling like a million bucks. Which was about what she'd spent today. Now she hoped for a return on her investment.

She had thought about going straight to David's office, but didn't feel quite confident enough, so she had come home, sneaking in past the landlady's closed apartment door.

She sashayed back and forth across the living room, practicing on her new Bullock's high heels. That was getting old. She stopped and looked at herself in the mirror. "Wow, if I were a guy I could go for a dish like you." She hoped she wasn't the only one who felt that way.

She grabbed the yellow pages, found David's office address.

CHAPTER ELEVEN

Bobby parked on Beverly. She opened the car door, one alluring foot reached for asphalt, then the other. She stood on wobbly high-heeled feet, a surge of butterflies swarming her stomach. *Am I doing the right thing?*

She wanted a cigarette in the worst way; forced herself not to. It wasn't too late to back out now. All she had to do was slip back in the car, close the door, and drive off. Instead, she closed the door behind her and headed to the building. She had parked several doors up and it took her that long to get her land legs on those unfamiliar heels. She was glad she didn't have to walk in them every day. A fluttery breeze tossed her dress up. Her hand shot down to smooth it. Is this what women have to put up with every day?

"I'd like to see David Chambers," Bobbie said, before the receptionist could open her mouth.

"Do you have an app—"

"—No appointment. Please tell him it's Bob—Roberta Saxon."

The receptionist could have used the intercom. Instead, she disappeared behind an expensive-looking carved wood door, returning a moment later with surprise on her face. "He'll see you."

She ushered Bobbie into David's office. In contrast to the building's exterior, the office was decorated in the height of art deco chic.

David rose when Bobbie entered, came around the desk and greeted her with a big hug. The receptionist retreated, closing the door behind her.

"Bobbie, you look great! So, so feminine." David drank her in.

"So do you, David, well great, not feminine." And he did. When she thought she'd seen him on the Apollo, she saw movie-star good looks and up close he was the real deal. And she didn't mean Bogart. More Tyrone Power, but taller. With a million-watt smile that could make Edison even richer. He filled out his double-breasted suit the way Bobbie could only do in her dreams.

"You finally outgrew your tomboy phase. I don't think I've seen you since, well—"

Bobbie remembered the last time she and David had seen each other. That disastrous date when they'd gone to see *The Adventures of Robin Hood* with Errol Flynn—in Technicolor—at the Pico Drive-In and he'd tried to make out with her. It's not that she wasn't attracted to him then—or now. Simply that she was scared, scared of him. Scared of herself and her desires. But if she could ever be attracted to a man in a romantic way, it would be David Chambers. Not only because of his good looks. Also because of his charm and intelligence. She felt herself getting mushy. Now wasn't the time. She had a job to do.

"Well, let's just say I haven't seen you since we both graduated Fairfax High."

"Lord Fairfax, he's our man," Bobbie said.

"It's really good to see you, Bobbie. Have a seat. What are you up to these days? Still have dreams of playing in a big band?"

They sat in a visitor's seating area across from David's desk. Bobbie sank into a warm leather sofa that must have cost more than her rent for a year. David sat in a leather chair opposite.

"It doesn't hurt to dream," she said.

"No, I guess not."

"It looks like you've done well for yourself. But if I recall you were voted 'Most Likely to Succeed.'"

"I've done all right—can't complain." He tapped his fist three times on the deco end table. "How are your folks?"

"I don't see them much."

"I know what you mean. Got to live our own lives, huh."

"I gig with a band sometimes. Booker Taylor's."

"Yeah, I've heard of them. Colored outfit, aren't they?"

Telling David about Booker was taking a chance. A chance she gauged worth taking. He didn't seem to react—or overreact.

She didn't think David, in his hundred-dollar suits, would venture down to Central Avenue when he could afford Ciro's or the Grove. But he might remember The Booker "Boom Boom" Taylor Orchestra from the Apollo. She thought she'd seen David on the boat. Was it him or did she just want it to be him, to give her an excuse to come here? And what was she doing here? Was she on the case or on a pre-date? She still didn't know who she was—what she was.

"It's not a regular gig. But it might turn into one."

"Great!"

They shot the breeze for about ten minutes—did you hear what happened to so-and-so? Johnny Miller got a Purple Heart in Africa, Mary Cooper's working at Max Factor. The usual.

"If you run into Mary Cooper again, tell her hello for me." David took a deep breath through his nose. "Nice perfume."

"I'm wearing too much, aren't I?" Bobbie's self-consciousness escaped her just as her perfume had.

"It's fine." He toyed with the ring on his left hand.

"You have a ring. Married?"

"It's a fraternity ring, not a wedding band. I don't know why I wear it on that finger." He showed her the ring. A carving of a skull and cross bones with 322 centered below it. *What the hell did that mean?* "It's from Yale, gives me something to do with my hands since I gave up smoking."

"Jeez, that's great. I wish I could."

"My doctor said I had TB, which is why I quit. Also why I'm not in the service. One-B, available, but fit only for limited military service. I'm better now, not contagious and pretty much cured. Let's just hope they don't change my classification to One A and that I don't get drafted in the meantime."

"Something tells me you've got that taken care of. You look pretty healthy to me," she said in the most flirtatious voice she could muster.

David twirled his ring. Bobbie tried not to stare at him, taken as she was.

"I always thought of you as the one who got away, Roberta," he finally said.

Her face turned crimson. She hoped the makeup held the color at bay as far as David could see. "You, too, David."

"You think about me sometimes?"

"Often."

David smiled that movie-star smile that Bobbie remembered so well and that made so many of the girls at Fairfax fall for him. "Well, that eases some of the disappointment. Though I always thought you might, maybe, go the other way."

"Other way?"

"You know what I mean. On the, uh, bohemian side."

"Everyone thought I was weird, huh?"

"Not everyone. Where is Renata? She usually pops in with some coffee or something." He stood, paced. He went to a burled cabinet, pulled out a green bottle. "I can offer you absinthe. The real stuff. Illegal now, but I have my little stash."

Bobbie declined.

"So what does bring you here out of the clear blue?"

She wasn't sure anymore. When she'd seen David on the boat it struck a chord with her. When she'd seen him—or thought she had—at the Brown Derby with Stinson it struck a different kind of chord. But here he was, sweet as ever. Why should she suspect him? Maybe he did know Stinson. Did some legal work for him. That didn't amount to a hill of beans, as Bogey said in *Casablanca*.

"I guess I had two reasons. One was to see you, of course."

"I'm flattered. And the other?"

"I thought maybe you could help me out."

"Sure, anything."

"I wanted to see if you knew anything about a company called International Business Machines."

"IBM. Sure. What do you want to know?" His expression didn't change.

"Anything you can tell me."

"Are you thinking of going to work for them?"

Bobbie wasn't sure how to respond. Should she lie just to get the info or should she shoot straight with her old friend?

"No." Now she wished she had a cup of coffee, anything she could fidget with without being obvious. "A friend of mine is and neither of us is really familiar with them. But you always had an interest in business, so I thought of you." She hated lying to her old pal.

"Trying to help a friend. You always were the inquisitive type and a little bohemian too."

"Still inquisitive." Bobbie smiled. "And still on the bohemian edge."

"You couldn't be any other way."

You have no idea.

"IBM, hmm. They make typewriters, tabulating machines, and other business machines, employee timecard machines, scales, even meat slicers, I think. But I don't really know much about them other than that. Does that help?"

Bobbie wondered if David would spill that he knew Stinson. She hoped so. She had a good feeling about him—hell, she was being seduced by him, whether he was meaning to or not. Some crushes never go away, no matter who or what you are.

"I think so. She's just not sure if it's a good place to work."

"I've done a little legal work for them. Nothing serious. They have big time lawyers for that. Mostly they're an East Coast outfit, but they have a branch office here. They seem pretty on the up and up to me. As far as I know they're a good, solid, and patriotic company. Everything, everyone helps the war effort. And since we're not fully out of the Depression tunnel, I'd think she'd just be happy for a job."

"You're right, David. I'll tell her that. She needs to get off the dime." Bobbie needed to get off the dime too. She wanted to find out what IBM did and now she had. She couldn't come right out and tell David she was playing detective. A wave a nausea swept over her. She felt shallow and crummy for suspecting David of anything. He admitted doing work for IBM. A bad guy wouldn't have admitted as much. And working for them didn't mean he was involved with anything underhanded. For that matter it didn't mean IBM was either.

Bobbie thought about Dietrich—pictured his body hanging from the rafters. Why would someone want him to die that way? She might never know unless Houdini had found a way to communicate from the grave and could act as go-between.

"It's nice to help friends, Bobbie. But don't get in over your head."

Was that just small or talk or a warning? How the hell could Bobbie know? The one thing she did know was that she was already in over her head. And right now she couldn't wait to go home, strip off these clothes, and put on slacks and a comfortable pair of oxfords.

Renata finally did return.

"Would you like something to drink?" David said.

"No, thanks. I really better be going. I have an appointment." She didn't, but she was too nervous to stay and too unsure how a girl would really act.

Renata left, leaving the door open this time.

"I'd like to see you again," David said.

"Me too."

Bobbie made a U-turn on Beverly, glad that no cops were there to see it. Her joy was premature. Flashing red lights glared in her rearview mirror. She pulled to the curb. The LAPD officer strode toward her.

"Hello, Officer."

The cop leaned in the window. She could feel his moist breath on her cheek, and on it maybe the slightest odor of alcohol. "Afternoon, ma'am. See your license?"

"Is it for the U-turn?"

"'Fraid so."

"Any way I can talk you out of it?"

He looked around, including down her dress, at her cleavage. She wished she had more to show. She noticed the name tag pinned on his chest.

"Aw, never mind. Just don't do it again."

"Thank you, Officer Daley." She smiled the most seductive smile she could manage. He saluted, walked back to his motorcycle. *There* are *some advantages to being a woman.*

She waved goodbye as she pulled out, heading east on Beverly. At Poinsettia she turned left, cruised by a Spanish colonial house, slowing as she neared it. She peered out the window at the house, then hit the gas and was out of there.

CHAPTER TWELVE

She drove out of her way to go by Thomas' house in the Hollywood Hills, using up precious rationed gas. She thought if the neighbors saw a man going to the door they might be suspicious, but a woman, maybe not. Besides, even though she couldn't wait to get back into Bobby's clothes, there was something fun about playing dress-up.

She headed up the cracking front walk, up two steps into a Spanish-tiled portico. The massive wooden door was like something out of a castle in an Errol Flynn movie. She banged the huge iron knocker on the highly varnished door. No answer.

She tried to peer in the windows of what appeared to be the living room. The tightly drawn drapes didn't allow any view of the inside. She peeked in every window along the driveway. Every one was covered with closed blinds, shades, or curtains she couldn't see through. The blood rushed through her, making her hot all over like when she had her period—another damned girly thing she could live without.

She thought about going down to the Bradbury building to see if Stinson was there and if Bobbie, as opposed to Bobby, could talk to him. She started off in that direction.

"I can't do this," she said out loud. "If Stinson or that receptionist make me I'll never be able to find who really killed Dietrich. I'll never get the job with Booker."

As a compromise, she stopped at a gas station, put a nickel in the pay phone and called the IBM office. She tried to sound sexy when asking for Stinson. Not in. When would he be back? The receptionist didn't know.

"Is he ever in—he does work there, doesn't he?"

"Give me your number and I'll have him call you back."

Bobbie hung up. Drove home.

Tomorrow she would be back on the case. Tonight she wanted to get out. Do something fun. She could have gone to the Alabam or one of the other clubs on Central Avenue, but she didn't want to run into Booker. She wanted a night off from the case, James, Booker. She scrubbed the makeup off her face, not caring that she rubbed raw her delicate female skin. Rinsed the spray out of her hair, washed it and slicked it back—dressed as Bobby in slacks and double-breasted jacket, and headed for the Casino Gardens ballroom on the Ocean Park pier. In the early days of the war, the pier, the coast, had to black out at night. Those restrictions had been eased now and everybody was back in business, which was also why the Apollo could operate again, at least before Dietrich was murdered.

All the big bands played the Casino Gardens, including the King of Swing, Benny Goodman. Bobby didn't know who was there tonight. It didn't really matter.

He got lucky, Harry James was playing. He'd become well-known as a trumpeter with Goodman. Now he had his own band and Betty Grable—the G.I.'s favorite pinup girl—to boot. Bobby waited in line to get in, then headed straight for the bar. He ordered a blackberry brandy on ice. The bartender looked at him like he was nuts. He settled for his usual Bubble Up. The band opened with "Sing Sing Sing," made famous by Benny Goodman when Harry was in the band. That got people moving and in the mood but fast. Bobby edged toward the dance floor. How he wished he could be dancing.

A young woman in a rayon dress came up to him. Asked him to dance. He looked from side to side, unsure why. Oh, what the hell. He took her hand, led her to the center of the floor. They cut the rug with a jumpin' West Coast swing. People stepped aside to watch. Bobby led, the young woman followed. They did an outside turn. A slide. He wished he could do an over-the-head, but knew he didn't have the confidence.

"Thank you," the young woman said when the song was over. Bobby hoped maybe she'd spend some time with him. Instead, a sailor came up to her and off she walked with him.

Bobby felt naked and alone on the dance floor as the next tune started. He retreated to the edge. Three soldiers came up to him. It felt like they were surrounding him. He avoided looking them in the eye. They crowded him more. He stepped farther back. They moved with him. He saw their faces, even though he was trying not to. He wanted to get the hell out of there, but he also didn't want to look like he was running. He couldn't go to the men's room, they could follow him in. And he definitely couldn't go to the ladies' room. He decided to leave, though he'd only been there half an hour.

"I know you, don't I?" one of the soldiers said.

Bobby slid into the crowd, headed for the exit. Outside on the pier, he sucked in a deep slug of briny air. Lit a cigarette and walked past arcades and food joints. He walked to the edge of the pier and stared out across the Pacific. It was dark and foggy, but in his mind he saw what was happening far across those waters. Marines slogging through the mud of Guadalcanal, fighting everything from Jap soldiers and snipers to malaria mosquitoes. He wished them well. Wished he could be with them.

He heard footsteps pad up behind him on the damp timber of the pier. He knew who it was. Turned around.

The three soldiers formed a half moon. Bobby could either surge through their gauntlet or jump over the railing into the roiling sea. He half thought that would be the better way.

The three's eyes were beady, cold steel, like the muzzles of their M1 Garand rifles, which Bobby was glad they didn't have with them. He didn't know what they might have, switchblades, brass knuckles?

A cold breeze blew in off the ocean, pitting Bobby's face with stinging bullets of salt. He felt the uneven, rotting planks of the pier beneath his feet.

"How come you're not in the service?" the soldier with acne scars asked. The three soldiers inched closer.

"Yeah. You're the right age," said the one with corporal stripes.

"There's three branches, army, navy, and marines. It's kind of like a multiple-choice test in school," the third soldier said. He was the only one Bobby didn't recognize. His piercing blue eyes bored into Bobby.

"Yeah, pick one."

They took another half step toward him.

Bobby had nowhere to go.

"I know you. This is Bob*ie*, with an I-E. B-O-B-B-I-E," acne said. His name was Howard Gibbon. Point guard on Fairfax High's basketball team. If it wasn't for his height and the fact he scored, he would have been more of an outcast at Fairfax than Bobbie. "Or should I say Roberta?" He laughed snidely, almost snorting.

The corporal, Phil Bartel, turned to the soldier Bobby didn't know. "We went to school with Bobbie here. Didn't we, Bobb-ie?"

Bobby held his ground. He wouldn't back up farther to the railing.

"I thought we were here to smash a draft dodger," blue eyes said.

"You might like to date this draft dodger," Gibbon said.

"Huh," said the soldier, slow to catch on. "I'm no faggot."

"Neither is Bobbie here. In fact, he's really a she. Not a bad looking one either. But for some reason she likes to dress as a man."

"Sick, ain't it? Damn dyke." Gibbon's long arm rushed for Bobby's head. Bobby ducked. But now all three soldiers were on him—her. Pummeling.

"Leave her face alone," Bartel said.

Gibbon started to rip Bobby's pants off.

"I don't want no part of this." Blue eyes backed off.

"We done enough." Bartel backed off too. Gibbon unleashed one more good slug. Bobby's gut caved as blue eyes yanked Gibbon off him. The three soldiers backed off, fading into the fog. Bobby slumped against the clammy pier railing. His gut wrenched and he felt his dinner coming up, pushed it down. He gasped for breath but didn't think he was seriously hurt.

So this is what it's like to be a man. Gotta learn to fight.

He lay there for several minutes, until his breath approached normal, finally pulled himself up the railing, leaned against it. A white chalk drawing of Kilroy, drawn on the pier planks, mocked him.

Was this really because he was different? Or was it because he'd—she'd—turned Gibbon down for dates, including the prom, when he'd repeatedly asked her? Or did it matter? Ultimately it was for no good reason. But he knew these boys would be off fighting the Japanese or Germans soon. They were scared. Bobby was different. They took out their fears on him. He didn't even wish them ill. He could have hoped that they would take a bullet or worse, end up in a prisoner of war camp. He didn't. He just hoped he never saw them again.

Bobby pushed off the railing, brushed himself off. Strips of ragged cloth hung from his once-beautiful suit, beyond fixing. He looked through the fog as best he could to see if the soldiers were ahead of him. He knew they wouldn't be—they wouldn't want to hang around for the police. Of course, the police might side with them. It probably wasn't a chance they wanted to take.

Bobby walked to the land end of the pier, past soldiers and sailors necking with girls, headed to his car and drove home.

* * *

He looked at himself in the mirror. This suit was definitely a goner. He'd give it to war relief, maybe they could fix it up. His left chin and cheek were turning slightly purple. "Leave her face alone," one of the soldiers had said. Bobby knew it couldn't have been that bastard Gibbon. Must've been Bartel or blue eyes. But someone's elbow or fist had whacked him in the face but good. Damn that jackass Gibbon. The bruise wasn't big or bad and could be covered with makeup if Bobbie needed to meet with Chambers again.

He disrobed, examining his body. There were several black-and-blue marks. He didn't think any were serious, dabbed iodine on one small cut.

"Damn, that stings."

Bobby picked up an old cigar box on the table next to the sofa. Inside sat his treasured baseball cards, Babe Ruth, Lou Gehrig. And his favorite, Hammerin' Hank Greenberg. Bobby felt a special kinship with Greenberg. One of the first Jewish ballplayers, he'd endured taunts and jeers and worse. "Throw him a pork chop! He can't hit that," the St. Louis Cardinals shouted at him during the 1934 World Series. Bobby wasn't Jewish, but he had his own cross to bear—so to speak—and so he related to Greenberg. He loved baseball and, along with Lou Gehrig, Hank was his hero. Sometimes Greenberg fought back, once charging into the White Sox clubhouse to challenge their manager. Bobby hadn't fought back on the pier. But he didn't run either. He had held his ground and wouldn't let the three soldier boys push him back any farther. Since he was raised a girl he didn't really know how to fight. But if that's what it took to be a man, he would learn.

"Fuck them!" Bobby said out loud and slid onto the couch to sleep.

Sounds from the garbage truck woke Bobby in the morning. His chin felt a little raw, his gut sore, but overall he didn't feel too much the worse for wear. He hoped those boys would do more damage to the Japs and Germans than they did to him. He felt good—he'd taken what they dished out and was the better man for it.

He rubbed the sleep from his eyes, went into the bathroom. The bruise on his chin was a mark of toughness.

He needed to get back on the job, find out more about Dietrich. Leach might know something. Bobby had to track him down.

Fog shrouded the Santa Monica pier, just like it should in all good mysteries, Bobby thought. He walked up the pier toward the water taxi station. It looked like all the taxis were moored.

"Water taxis running?" he asked a local fisherman.

"Not since that fellow was killed on the Apollo."

Bobby scanned the horizon. The gambling ship still rested at anchor off the coast. "Anyone on board the Apollo now?"

"I think there's some folks there."

"Take me there."

"Sorry, I don't want no trouble."

Bobby produced a roll of bills quicker than Houdini could get out of a locked trunk. He peeled off a twenty from the savings he'd taken out of the bank to buy his girly clothes. When he got no response, he peeled off another. Being a private dick didn't come on the cheap.

"That boat and them that run it is bad news. Sorry."

"Well, is there someone who will?"

The fisherman pointed to a man eating a sandwich on a nearby launch.

"Thanks." Bobby walked over to the man on the launch. "Can you take me to the Apollo?"

"Ten bucks."

"Steep."

"You want me to wait for you, it's another fin."

"Okay, but I give you the last fin after you bring me back to shore."

The launch captain nodded. Happy for the cut rate from what he offered the fisherman, Bobby climbed into the boat and they rode choppy gray seas to the Apollo.

Bobby had stopped for a hamburger at a greasy spoon on his way to the pier. He thought the rolling swells would bring that burger up for sure. He managed to keep it down.

"Who's that?" someone shouted from the Apollo's deck.

"Bobby Saxon, I play piano in the band," Bobby shouted back.

"Band? This boat's closed down."

"Can I come aboard or whatever one says?"

"Request permission to come aboard," the launch captain corrected him.

"Request permission to come aboard?"

"What do you want?" the deckhand yelled over the crashing waves. But he lowered the accommodation ladder anyway.

"Don't forget, you're waiting for me," Bobby said to the launch captain, as he climbed to the deck.

"What'd you do, forget your piano?" the deckhand said.

"I want to talk to Mr. Leach."

"If I'da known that I wouldn't-a let you onboard. I thought maybe you forgot something, came to pick it up. That's what I get for being a nice guy." Up close the deckhand looked more like a thug than a sailor.

Carnie, in a pinstriped suit with a diamond tie clip and a cigar, walked over. "What gives?"

"This pipsqueak wants to see the boss."

"What for?" Carnie said, sucking on his cigar.

Carnie and the thug stood on either side of Bobby, making him feel short. *What the hell did I get myself into?*

"Look, I played in the band the night that German fellow was killed. I just want to talk to Mr. Leach about—"

"—About what?"

About anything, about the Brooklyn Dodgers and the Giants, the Yankees, Hank Greenberg being off to war. About Gable and Lombard. FDR. About anything, as long as I don't have to talk to you.

"I'd rather just speak to him."

"Well, he's not here today. And even if he was, you couldn't talk to him." Carnie tossed the cigar overboard; it hit the water with a hiss. Bobby started toward the launch. "Hey, kid, you might check the Sunset Tower. But I wouldn't interrupt his *social time.*"

The boat ride back to shore was more choppy than the ride out had been. The launch heaved and pitched on its way back to shore. *I went there for this, a saltwater bath and no info. How badly do I want this gig with Booker?*

CHAPTER THIRTEEN

The zigzag moderne Sunset Tower Hotel, with its rounded corner windows, statues, and friezes, sprouted tall and stately from Sunset Boulevard, reaching for the sky, like an elegant art deco palm.

The lobby at the Bryson had been ritzy. The Sunset Tower's lobby made the Bryson look like Skid Row.

Someone bumped into Bobby.

"Excuse me," the man said in a familiar voice.

Bobby was too flustered to respond to Clark Gable, as the King of Hollywood walked past. Bobby went to the front desk.

"May I help you?" the clerk asked.

"I'd like to see Tony Leach." The words stumbled out. Bobby hoped his nervousness didn't show. He'd heard that Leach lived here. Bugsy Siegel too, as well as several movie stars off and on. Infamous gossip columnist Hedda Hopper had said so. "Can you just call up and tell him Bobby Saxon, from the ship's band, is here."

"You play in a band on his ship? I'm afraid he's too busy for—"

Bobby wanted to strangle this jerk, but as discretion is the better part of valor, he bit his tongue and kept his hands in his pockets.

"Fine, do you have a bar?"

"It's for residents and their guests."

"It's for the public and I'm John Q. Public." That felt good, sticking it to another snooty gatekeeper, just like Bogey would. He looked around, waiting to be stopped by some thug in a

Sunset Tower uniform. No one came. He still couldn't get over seeing Clark Gable as he made his way to the bar. Movie stars and dignitaries filled the cocktail lounge—Katherine Hepburn, Howard Hughes, and others—and probably a lot of behind-the-scenes people that Bobby didn't recognize. Maybe even some gangsters. Bobby drank Bubble Up at the bar. Finally, Leach entered, waving to everyone, a king to his vassals.

"The usual, Mr. Leach?" another waitress said, pulling out a chair for Leach at the table with the best view. Leach nodded. Bobby tried not to stare. Everyone said that Bugsy Siegel was the first good-looking gangster. Leach made Siegel look like a piker, though Bobby wouldn't say that to Siegel's face. In fact, Leach was Cary Grant handsome and just as well dressed.

Bobby walked straight up to him. The waitress looked like she wanted to shoo him away. The bartender came out from behind the bar.

"Excuse me, Mr. Leach," Bobby said.

"Do I know you?"

"Bobby Saxon." Bobby put his hand out for Leach to shake. Leach was too busy or too important to be bothered.

"You that kid that came out to the boat?" He shifted in his seat. His coat flapped open slightly. Bobby saw a nice, shiny semi-automatic in a holster. *What the hell am I getting into?*

The bartender grabbed Bobby's coat lapels, ready to toss him out on the street. Leach waved him off.

"Yes."

"You got some nerve, kid. People don't usually have the chutzpah to come at me directly. Especially after my goons politely turn them away. Alright, you got one minute to make your case."

Bobby started to pull a chair out. Leach shook his head— Bobby remained standing. He remembered the pistol under Leach's jacket and he knew that, unlike in a Cagney movie, it wasn't filled with blanks.

"I'm looking into the murder of Hans Dietrich—"

"—What are you, a shamus now too, besides an alligator?"

"Shamus?"

"You a dick, detective? I thought you were in the band."

"I am. But as you know one of our members has been, uh, fingered for the murder." Bobby was pleased with himself for using a hard-boiled word like *fingered*. "I, Booker, we don't think he did it."

Leach's eyes bored a hole into Bobby the way the pistol in his shoulder holster could bore a hole into his gut. Bobby hoped Leach didn't think he was accusing him. But he was a gangster. What else could he think?

"Are you implying I had anything to do with—" He pounded his glass on the table, the amber liquid spraying like Old Faithful.

"Not at all, Mr. Leach. I just wondered if you knew Mr. Dietrich and might be able to point me in the right direction." Bobby chose his words carefully. Measured his breaths so his nervousness wouldn't show on his voice. He was trying hard to be a man.

The waitress brought a replacement drink for Leach faster than a short-order cook whipping up a burger. Leach sipped. "Young man, it is my understanding that the...*fingered* man is a hot head who got into a fight with the deceased just a few minutes before he decided to wreck my boat and my income stream with it."

"James is a hot head. Not a murderer."

"I suppose they don't have to be one and the same. Go on."

"I want to see the real criminal put behind bars. You hired Booker's band and people will say it's your fault for hiring him, but I know it was someone else, someone who didn't respect your business."

Leach signaled Bobby to sit down. Bobby sagged into his seat, relieved that if nothing else he made a smaller target. He felt more comfortable being on the same level with Leach, though his foot beat a tattoo under the table. "What're you drinking, kid?"

"Uh, scotch on the rocks."

"Your best single malt for my friend here. Same for me." Leach tapped his glass. The waitress walked off. Bobby didn't really want the scotch but he remembered too many B Westerns where some mean hombre got offended if the hero wouldn't drink with him and then all hell broke loose. "I hardly knew the man, kid—what's your name again?"

"Bobby, Bobby Saxon. Anything you might know would be helpful. Any of his friends. I'm sort of at a dead end."

"What's a pretty white boy like you doing playing in a band of *schvartzes*?"

"I—I'm too young. The white bands want people with more experience."

"I'd think the colored bands would have the best musicians."

"Well, Booker had an opening and I guess I was in the right place at the right time. Besides, I like the way they blow."

"They do make a good sound, I'll give them that." Leach lit his cigar. Didn't offer Bobby one, for which Bobby was grateful. "Hans Dietrich. He was a high roller. Liked to bet against the odds. Take chances. Good customer. Always paid his bets. He was in the import-export business, but I bet you knew that."

"Do you know what he imported or exported?" Bobby knew the answer, wanted to see what Leach would say.

Leach's eyebrow jumped imperceptibly, but Bobby saw the *tell*. Leach knew more than he would let on; Bobby would be glad for any morsel of info at this point.

"I think a little of everything, *chachkas* from Germany, Europe. I think his business might have been suffering since the war. Not able to get stuff out of Europe to sell here or to get our stuff there. He might have been expanding into other areas."

Bobby shot him a *like what* look. There went that eyebrow again.

"He wanted me to go into business with him."

"What kind of business?"

"We never really got that far in our discussions. He was just trying to court me. Tease me. That's all. But I wasn't sure about doing business with a kraut."

"Do you know any of his other associates? Even what kind of people he hung around with?"

"You mean gangsters like me?"

"I, I didn't mean that."

"I'm just pulling your leg, kid. Bobby."

The waitress brought their drinks. Leach raised his glass.

"*L'chaim*, kid. To life."

They clinked glasses. Bobby could hardly get the harsh brown liquid down. Tried to conceal his distaste. Leach took a huge swig. "I like a good single malt."

As if Bobby had any idea what that meant.

"What kind of man was he?"

"Decent enough in his own way."

"Did he have any enemies? Was he a Nazi?"

"I didn't know him that well, kid. He was a customer. Good customer. We'd comp him drinks, food, even girls."

"What about family, friends?"

Leach thought a moment. His face softened. He looked like he wanted to help or was he trying to think of a dodge? "He used to go with this girl, Margaret...Lane. The answer to your next question is 'no.'"

"What's my next question?"

"Do I know how to reach her?"

Bobby nodded, impressed. Maybe if he'd been doing this a little longer, he wouldn't have been so impressed with Leach or in bumping into Clark Gable.

"Maybe I should do a mind-reading act on the boat—if we ever reopen." Leach smiled. Not a happy smile.

"I thought that was about to happen. Booker said—"

"News to me."

News to Bobby too. He'd gotten the impression from Booker that the reopening was imminent.

"Don't believe everything Booker tells you, kid. And don't turn your back on him."

Bobby's head was spinning. Now Leach was throwing Booker into the mix. He waited a minute, then decided on an end run. "Do you know Harlan Thomas?"

"Dietrich's partner? Met him once. We all had dinner at the Brown Derby, I think it was. Funny eating in a hat, you know."

Bobby didn't know. It was a popular place. Movie stars. Big wigs. Gangsters. Stinson. David Chambers?

"But I didn't really know Thomas." Leach took another swig. "Like I said, Dietrich was trying to get some money out of me so he wanted me to meet his partner."

Maybe Dietrich had tried too hard. Maybe Leach didn't want to be tapped—maybe he tapped back with the butt of a pistol and a noose? Or a switchblade?

"Wish I could help you more, kid."

"You've been a big help, Mr. Leach, in more ways than one. I appreciate it."

"Booker's band is coming back—as soon as we reopen. Come see me then, maybe I'll have thought of something."

"Thank you, Mr. Leach."

"And don't be so scared. I ain't gonna bite—or shoot."

"It shows that much?"

"Like a *fagala* at a burlesque show. But you got balls, kid. Consider me your friend."

Bobby wasn't sure if that was a good thing or not. He guessed it was better to have Leach on his side than against him.

Leach dismissed Bobby, with a nod and a wink. Bobby couldn't believe he'd just spent twenty minutes with a gangster—a real live gangster. He went to the lobby, head swirling, crashing into a dashing man. Movie star? No. Bugsy Siegel, who didn't get the name Bugsy for no good reason. Bobby apologized and jammed out of there, barely noticing Leach waving Bugsy and his men off. Maybe saving Bobby's life.

He hit a phone alcove in the Sunset Tower lobby, collapsing onto the seat, knees rattling. He wiped his damp brow with his handkerchief, set his hat on his head, and started to leave.

Thought better of it and closed the door to the little booth.

He had been able to hold himself together talking to Leach. Now he was a mass of jellied nerves. *Why is it you're always more scared after the fact than while the trauma is happening?*

He spread out the phone book, turned to the L's in the white pages. There were no Margaret Lanes, but three M. Lanes. He figured those were women, as women often used their initials—it was a dead giveaway. He tore out the page.

He drove down Sunset, turning into Dolores' Drive-In. A car hop took his order. He slumped down, resting his head on the seat-back. Artie Shaw's "Frenesi" finished; the war news came on. Rumors about what was going on in the concentration camps. Setbacks on the Italian front, camouflaged to make them look like victories.

The hop brought Bobby's cheeseburger, Suzy Q fries, and chocolate malt. Luckily the music had returned. Bobby ate to Glenn Miller instead of General Patton.

Bobby parked across the street from a large Mediterranean house in Hancock Park, old money, unlike the nouveau riche of Beverly Hills. A well-attired woman, no doubt dressed by Bullock's Wilshire, came out of the house to look at something. Bobby stepped out of his car, gingerly approached her. She didn't look wary. In fact, she smiled.

"Mrs. Lane?"

"Who wants to know? If you're selling something I've already got plenty of everything."

"Not selling."

"Good. I thought you might be the Fuller Brush man. Though he's always very nice."

"I'm looking for Margaret Lane."

"That's me."

The woman had to be at least sixty-five, if not older. Her blue-gray hair and matronly dress and figure said this wasn't

Dietrich's girlfriend. Still, Bobby had to make sure.

"Are you a friend of Hans Dietrich?"

"Now that doesn't sound like someone anyone should be friends with these days."

"I'm sorry," Bobby said. "I don't think you're the Margaret Lane I'm looking for."

"That's too bad. We might have had some fun."

"We might at that. Sorry to have bothered you."

"No bother. I wish a nice young man would come calling on me again." She smiled. Bobby smiled back, tipped his hat. Drove off.

He drove to the next address on his list, 357 Edinburgh Street, back near Poinsettia, close to David Chambers' office. A single-story duplex. He looked at the torn phone book page. Headed to the door of 357-A. Bobby passed a *For Rent* sign, with a special warning stapled to it that read *No dogs. No Jews!*

He knocked. A middle-aged woman answered.

"Hi, I'm looking for Margaret Lane."

"No one here by that name, nor in 357-B. You interested in renting a lovely duplex?"

"I'm afraid I couldn't afford it."

"Too bad. My man's off at the war. Would be nice to have a man around. Though why aren't you in the service?"

"Four-F," Bobby said.

"You look healthy enough to me. Goldbricker."

Bobby looked at the torn phone book page. "Isn't this 357 South Edinburgh?"

"*South*—Kikeville you mean. This is *north*, North Edinburgh." She slammed the door in Bobby's face. He walked past the *No dogs. No Jews!* sign again, thinking about the rails to concentration camps that Roosevelt wouldn't bomb, got into the Olds, made a U-turn, rolling south.

CHAPTER FOURTEEN

Bobby parked in front of 357 South Edinburgh, another side-by-side duplex, very similar to 357 North. One big difference, no *No dogs. No Jews!* sign. He walked through a courtyard overflowing with birds of paradise. Before he could knock, an older man with thinning white hair and sallow skin opened the front door, while shrugging into a suit coat. He already had the tie, slacks and overly shined shoes on. Was he going somewhere or was this how he always dressed?

"Hello, I'm sorry to bother you. I'm looking for Margaret Lane."

"That's my daughter. Is something wrong? Has she been hurt?"

"No. I'm a friend of a friend."

"Uh huh," Mr. Lane said.

"Do you know where I can find her?"

The old man scratched his chin. "Why should I tell you? I don't know you—"

"I'm a friend of Hans Dietrich's. I'm trying to find his killer, not to hurt your daughter."

"How do I know this for a fact?"

"Look, I already know where she lives since I'm here, right? And if I was a bad guy, why would I be asking you all nicely here, I'd just wait for her to come home?"

"I guess if you know where she lives—she works over at the May Company on Wilshire."

"She there now?"

"Ladies gloves and hats."

"Thank you."

Bobby lammed out of there, shooting down Fairfax. He drove past the glittering gold streamline moderne cylinder that anchored the May Company building to Fairfax and Wilshire. He parked in the lot at the back and entered the equally impressive marqueed rear entrance. This was, after all, L.A., and just like Bullock's Wilshire the May Company knew they were catering to the carriage trade, who now arrived in horseless carriages.

Bobby charged through perfume and lingerie, first-floor staples. Even if he hadn't been on a mission he wouldn't have paid much attention. Ladies' Gloves and Hats was presided over by a woman staving off middle age, wearing a hat that would have made Hedda Hopper proud. She looked like she would have made a good drill sergeant. He didn't think that would be Margaret Lane; he hoped not.

"Can I help you? Something for your wife maybe?" said a svelte, strikingly attractive young woman with jet black, shoulder-length, permed hair—no hat. But why was she dressed in mourning black?

Was she mourning Hans Dietrich?

Bobby blushed. "Margaret Lane?"

The young woman startled. Frightened.

"What do you want?"

Bobby didn't know how to play it, sensitive or tough. He chose the latter, putting an edge in his voice. "Why are you so upset?"

"I, I'm not upset. It's just that people don't usually come in here and ask for me by name, at least not my full name. My customers just ask for Margaret. I—" The words blasted out in a torrent.

"All I did is ask a simple question."

"I'm at work. It's not right to be seen talking to a man when it's not about business." She looked over her shoulder to the D.I. in the Hedda Hopper hat.

"How do you know it's not about business? I haven't said

anything one way or the other."

Margaret took a deep breath.

He picked up a hat, caressing it lovingly. "Well then, let me look at some hats."

"Okay. I can show you this lovely Lilly Daché, with a genuine ostrich feather."

"It's quite lovely—" Bobby caught himself being too feminine. "It's very nice."

The *sergeant* went back to doing her inventory, while Bobby and Margaret went through the motions of looking at hats.

"Now what do you really want?" Margaret said, under her breath.

"I understand you were a friend of Hans Dietrich's."

Margaret's face dropped. She quickly lost the official salesgirl's smile.

"What are you, some kind of detective?"

"I'm a shamus." Bobby did the worst possible imitation of Bogart.

Margaret smiled. The first genuine smile Bobby had gotten from her. She glanced quickly over her shoulder; the sarge was busy with another customer.

"She your boss?"

Margaret nodded.

"Maybe I can talk to you on your break?"

"I just got off break. What is it you want?"

"Hans Dietrich."

"I knew him, okay."

"Well?"

"What business is that of yours?"

The sarge walked over. "How are we doing, Margaret? Is this gentleman finding what he needs?"

"I'm doing fine," Bobby cut in before Margaret could respond.

"Perhaps I can be of service."

"No thanks, I'm perfectly happy with—" Bobby looked at Margaret's name tag, playing the part of the good customer,

"—Margaret."

"All right then."

"Thank you, Mrs. Ford," Margaret said as the sarge huffed off. "She doesn't like me."

"I don't see why not."

Margaret hesitated, "Because I'm Jewish. So if that makes a difference to you—"

"—Slow down. I'm not even here to buy a hat, remember? And if I was that wouldn't make a difference to me." Bobby shrugged. "It's funny that a Jewish girl would be friends with a German man with what's going on over in Germany, the concentration camps and all. Was Hans Dietrich Jewish?"

"No. And I already talked to a Sergeant Nicolai of the sheriff's department. I don't see why I should talk to you. But we can talk on my next break 'cause I have the feeling you aren't going to leave me alone."

"Unfortunately, Miss Lane, you win the prize. I'll wander around, but don't you wander off. I just came from your house, and I'm a pretty good shamus. It'll be hard to lose me," Bobby said with as much false bravado as he could muster.

"Like chewing gum on my shoe."

Was that where the expression gumshoe *came from?*

"Something like that." Bobby tipped his hat, traipsed up the aisle, quickly looking at this and that, but the thises and thats on this floor were all for women and those things didn't interest him. He didn't want to leave the floor as he wanted to keep an eye on Margaret to make sure she didn't try to ditch him. He picked up a girdle. *What the hell is this?* Women's underthings were as foreign to him as lederhosen.

Margaret removed her name badge as she and Bobby entered the May Company tearoom. Crisp white linen draped over every table. It wasn't crowded at this time of day, but there were still some women here and there in their white gloves and *lovely* hats, even with wartime shortages of various materials. Bobby preferred his fedora.

"Why'd you remove your name tag?"

"They don't like employees to use the employee cafeteria."

"Well, at this moment you're not an employee, you're my guest."

Bobby's thoughts flew from concentration camps, Dietrich and Margaret to the lingerie he'd just been looking at. He remembered a time when his mother had forced undergarments like that on him—her. Thank God that was a long time ago, at least it seemed that way.

"What're you thinking?" Margaret said.

"I probably shouldn't say." For a moment, lost in his thoughts, he'd almost forgotten about Margaret.

"If you want me to answer questions you're going to have to answer some of mine and this one's pretty simple."

"Quid pro quo."

Margaret furled her brow. It was cute. What if he was feeling the beginnings of a crush? This was business. Keep business and pleasure separate. Besides, if the feeling he felt was pleasure, it scared the hell out of him.

"It means tit for tat," he said.

"So what are you thinking?"

"That Lane doesn't sound like a Jewish name."

"That wasn't my name originally. It was Levy. Seems that a lot of Lanes used to be Levys."

"Why change? This is America, not Nazi Germany."

"You saw Mrs. Ford. I'm sure a handsome young man like you wouldn't know about prejudice, but take my word—"

Bobby knew prejudice, but he wasn't going to say that here. He had to keep half of his life secret. He could barely go home in case he might run into his father, who'd kicked him out for not being Roberta. "But surely there aren't...Well, I did go to North Edinburgh before your house and there was a sign—"

"—'No dogs, no Jews.' I know. And we don't even get top

billing."

They both laughed, dissolving some of the tension. A waitress brought menus and water. They already knew what they wanted and ordered.

"And, of course, there are, or were, Bund meetings. They stir up a lot of trouble and hate. She sipped her water. "I'm sorry to be rambling so. What can I help you with? Why are you so interested in Hans Dietrich?"

"A friend of mine is accused of the murder; I want to clear his name." Bobby's fingers tensed calling James a friend. "How well did you know him?"

"Well enough, we were friends."

"I heard you were going together."

"Where did you hear that?"

"There's some things I can't tell you. But I'll be as open with you as I can."

"We dated on occasion. He liked to take me places."

"Was it serious?"

"Marriage, you mean?" She strained to keep a tear from falling from her eye. "I don't know, it really didn't get that far."

"Wasn't he a lot older than you?"

"We were friends. Friends."

Bobby let it drop. For now. "He was German. German-Jewish?"

"No."

"But he dated a Jew?"

"Like you said, this is America, not Nazi Germany."

Bobby thought about Margaret. Her last name, Lane. Maybe Dietrich didn't know she was Jewish. He wondered if that played into Dietrich's death somehow.

"Were you there that night, on the Apollo?"

"What are you implying?" Margaret snapped.

"I'm not implying anything. I just want to know if you saw anything."

"I wasn't there. If I was, maybe then it wouldn't have happened."

"Do you have any idea who might have wanted him dead?"

"No, I wish I did." But the twitch at the corners of her mouth said something else.

"He was in the import-export business?"

The waitress brought their snacks, smiled, and quickly departed.

"Yes, and business wasn't so good lately—the war."

"Maybe a creditor?"

"He didn't do business with the kind of people who have you killed for not paying a bill. They take you to court or collections."

"Then who?"

"I wish I knew. The Germans wanted him back."

"Wanted him back?" Bobby said.

"They wanted him to return home to join the *Wehrmacht*, the army. He didn't want to go."

"You'd think they wouldn't go after someone just for that. Not in this country."

"Maybe not, but that's all I know."

Bobby knew it clearly wasn't all she knew.

"I hear he was friends with Tony Leach."

"The gangster?"

"Don't sound so surprised."

"Okay, they were friends. I don't think they were good friends."

"I heard they were going into business together."

"Hans didn't discuss his business with me, why don't you ask Mr. Leach?" Her chin jutted out.

"Can you tell me some of his friends and associates?"

"So you can harass them?"

"So I can find out who killed your boyfriend."

Margaret looked down at her plate. It was clear she didn't want to talk about it anymore.

CHAPTER FIFTEEN

Bobby crashed on the sofa like a Stuka dive bomber that had been shot from the sky and spiraled straight to earth. He knew now why cops were called flatfoots. His feet ached, from wearing those heels. He'd been dogging it and maybe even making a little progress on the case, though he wasn't quite sure about that. "Opus One" by Tommy Dorsey tickled out of the radio. Bobby grabbed a *Life* magazine from the end table, flipped pages. He came to a big ad: Ronald Reagan, the movie star, touting Chesterfields. Bobby liked his Viceroys—which he reached for—but thought he might give Chesterfields a shot.

He put the magazine down, pulled a crinkled piece of paper from his pocket—a list of some of Dietrich's friends and associates that Margaret had given him before they parted.

"Now what? Start all over?"

He glared at the list. The jangling telephone woke him from his reverie. Bobby looked at the phone, willing it to stop ringing. Whoever was calling let it ring at least fifteen times. Bobby made no move to answer it. He looked at the list. The only names he recognized were Stinson's, from IBM and, of course, Lois, Dietrich's secretary, and his partner, Harlan Thomas.

Stinson's name had jumped out at Bobby when Margaret first handed him the list. She'd said that he and Dietrich had done business together, though she didn't know the nature or the extent. Bobby didn't know whether to believe her.

Thomas and Lois made sense. And obviously Dietrich had

that scrap of paper with Stinson's company, IBM, on it, so it made sense that Margaret might know him too. *But he won't talk to me—why?* Bobby had thought that maybe Margaret would mention David Chambers. She hadn't. Even so, he looked the list up and down again, making sure Chambers wasn't there. He was glad of Chambers' absence. He'd—she'd—always liked David and it was good to renew his acquaintance with, hopefully, no strings attached.

Bobby put the list back in his pocket, drifted off to "We'll Meet Again" on the radio. He woke to a sinking late afternoon sun. Still dressed in the suit he'd worn that morning, he grabbed his smokes and headed for the Alabam to get in some practice before the evening crowds arrived. He could have gone to Marion's but that would have meant confronting things he didn't want to confront right now. He had enough on his mind without all that.

Bobby had barely launched into Danny Kaye's "Melody in 4-F," complete with his own take on Kaye's scat singing, when the rest of the band came in. Nobody had told him there was a practice this afternoon. His fingers hammered the keyboard with an aggression he didn't know he had in him.

"I didn't know you could scat like that," Booker said. "We'll have to put that in the act."

Bobby wished no one had heard him singing. It was something he liked to keep to himself.

"Any news?"

"I'm working on it, Booker," Bobby barked.

"That means you got no leads."

"I have some. I'm following them up." Bobby made a sour face.

"You can't be following those leads sitting here at the piano."

"I can't follow them every minute of every day."

"Why not? James's in jail getting his ass whooped." Booker

smashed his palm on the piano keyboard emitting a sour chord. "You might be getting a gig with the band."

"Might. And nobody told me there was a practice now."

"You musta missed the call. What's really bugging you?"

"I'm not a detective, Booker. I'm doing the best I can."

"You're keeping something from me?"

"I just have a bad vibe. I have a feeling this is bigger than just a simple murder."

"And where does this feeling come from? White boy's intuition?"

Bobby kicked the piano bench out from under him. Stormed past Booker and off the stage. He'd heard stories about Booker. And Leach had also put a bee in Bobby's bonnet, and now Booker was all over him.

"Seems to me someone's sending a message, hanging him out to dry the way they did," Booker shouted.

Bobby halted. "Could be, but what's the message?"

"That's your job, Bobby, if you want a gig with the band. Remember, James is rotting in jail."

"I remember."

Bobby turned on his heel the way a soldier would and high-tailed it out of there. He slammed the Olds' door so hard the windows rattled. He was glad the glass didn't crack because with all the war rationing, he might not have been able to replace it. Shaky fingers pulled the pack of smokes from his pocket. He had a hard time lighting the cigarette.

"Screw you, Booker," Bobby said. Bobby shot out into traffic, car horns berating him for cutting them off. The Olds left deep black rubber marks on the pavement. He drove up to Hollywood Boulevard, barely looked at the marquee as he entered the theater but was glad to find Robert Benchley in a Joe Doakes short. Those always made Bobby laugh and he needed to laugh right now. Bobby bought a huge tub of buttered popcorn and a Coke and settled in for the night. Screw Booker. Screw James, who treated Bobby like crap anyway.

Bobby laughed through Joe Doakes. He laughed through *The Great Dictator*. And he laughed through *To Be or Not To Be*. And then he did it all over again, sitting through each flick twice. And before each one started he made another trip to the candy counter and the restroom. Restrooms in places like this were always tricky as Bobby never stood to pee. But he managed as long as there were doors on the stalls and this theater had them. *Thank God.*

Bobby's mother had warned him—her—about all the crappy food one found at movie theaters and amusement piers and the like. He had never heeded her warning, and as he lay in bed after a night of stomach discomfort from all that theater food, he thought maybe next time he'd listen. Or at least eat a little less of the garbage. That's what he said now. When the time came, he knew it would be different.

He woke up at noon, stole his first smoke of the day. Showered, dressed, and blew out of there, heading for the Bradbury Building and IBM's offices. All night long he'd said screw you to Booker, that he wasn't going to follow through. But even as he was saying it, he knew it wasn't true.

"I'm sorry, Mr. Stinson's—" the receptionist said.

"—Busy, yeah I know."

"Well, he is a very busy man."

"I can wait."

"There's really no point."

"I know that too."

"You're a very smart fellow."

"And you're a—" Bobby flung the door closed behind him without finishing the sentence. He looked at his watch. He could hang around till Stinson left, but he was antsy. Wanted to be on the move, doing something. Anything but hanging around. He drove to MGM studios in Culver City, the studio that boasted "more stars than there are in heaven." And with a roster that included Gable and Garbo, Garland and Rooney, Crawford and Loy, and a galaxy more, it was true.

Bobby knew he'd have a hard time getting in and he did. He had the guard call up to Leland Russell's office. After hearing Bobby was there about Dietrich, Russell let him come on the lot. Russell's office was nothing special. He was an associate producer and production manager. Bobby's first impression was of a regular guy. No jodhpurs or riding cane. Just a middle-aged man in khakis and a tie. But a man, nevertheless, who ranked high on Margaret's list of Dietrich's associates.

"All's I can say is that Hans was a good guy. We were drinking buddies. You know how it is."

Bobby didn't but played it as if he did. "Where'd you do your drinking?"

"A bar up on Sunset called The Backlot of all things, especially since it's not really close to any of the backlots."

"So why'd you go up there?"

"I live near there, on Mansfield, a few blocks south of the boulevard."

Russell was very forthcoming. Maybe too much so. Bobby thought about one of the most clichéd lines in the movies: "It's too quiet." And, of course, seconds after that the Indians would come whooping and hollering and ready to scalp. In a similar way, Bobby wondered if Russell's openness was a ruse. Pretend to be a nice guy, throw Bobby off track. Could Margaret have set him up, tipped Russell off to say, or not say, certain things?

"How did you know him?"

"What do you mean, you know people?"

"Yeah, but you're in the movie business and he's in the import-export business. German on top of that." It seemed like something Bogart would say.

"Lots of Germans in show biz."

"German-Jews?"

"Yes, exiles. Look, I have to get back to work."

"One more thing, do you know why—or who—might want

to kill Dietrich?"

"No, I think he was pretty well-liked."

"Germans aren't too well-liked these days."

"He was. He was a good guy. Mild."

Bobby knew "mild" was sometimes only on the surface. Sometimes they were the really crazy ones when push came to shove. And how mild had Dietrich been on the Apollo? "Do good guys harass colored people?"

"What're you talking about?

"Your friend was going after a colored band member on the Apollo like he was a member of the Ku Klux Klan—or maybe the Nazi Party."

"That couldn't have been Hans."

Bobby continued to pump Russell. Did he know any of Dietrich's friends, business associates? Did he know anything about his business or his partner or his receptionist? What about IBM and Stinson? Russell's stream of resounding "no's" seemed to ricochet off the walls.

It was exciting for Bobby to be inside the Dream Factory. Though Bobby didn't get to see much of it as the standing sets were on various backlots throughout Culver City. He might have been able to wander on to a soundstage but wanted to get on with his investigation and the soundstages were harder to get into than a military base. Still he would have liked to see Joan Crawford in action.

Next stop, Chavez Ravine. About a mile from downtown Los Angeles in distance, light years in lifestyle and culture. Locals called it Palo Verde, a barrio for people, mostly Mexicans, who couldn't afford to live anywhere else, or weren't allowed to. Its steep terrain was filled with goats and chickens. In its early days the area had been a potter's field, a smallpox infirmary, and a TB sanitarium. But it had also held Southern California's first botanical garden, the Chavez Ravine Arboretum. He just hoped Maria del Toro would be home.

Several brown-skinned children and one white boy batted,

fielded, and ran bases in the middle of the street. Bobby had to wait for an RBI to be played out before he could park. Maria del Toro, a middle-aged woman with an aristocratic bearing, stood framed in a doorway that badly needed painting. Flecks of withered green paint blew off the doorjamb, riding the wind to who knew where. In the window to the right of the door hung a service flag. One gold star, one blue star. One son lost in the war, another in the service.

"*Sí?*"

"Maria del Toro?"

"Who is asking?" she said, with the slightest hint of an accent.

"My name is Bobby Saxon. I wanted to talk to you about Hans Dietrich."

"You are with the police?"

"I'm a-a private detective."

"*Sí*, like Charlie Chan. Humphrey Bogart—*Maltese Falcon.*"

"Yes." Bobby couldn't help smiling. His smile brought one in return from Mrs. del Toro. "I understand if you don't want me to come inside, but can we talk?"

Slowly the chain came undone.

"I think it is okay, you come in. I want to help find who hurt *Señor* Dietrich." Mrs. del Toro looked around. Bobby wasn't sure what she was looking at or for.

He followed her inside.

"Ah, *Señor* Dietrich, *pobrecito.*"

The living room reminded Bobby of a stateroom on a ship. Aside from the Apollo he'd never been on a ship, but he'd seen movies. Everything compact, a place for everything and everything in its place. A picture of FDR graced the fireplace. Photos of her boys in uniform, one in the Marines, the other a sailor. Which one was the gold star for? There wasn't much else in the way of decoration. He removed his hat. She offered him strange-looking bread she called monkey bread. He'd never seen it or tasted it. He didn't want to be rude, so he took a piece. It was good.

"*Cervesa?*" She understood the blank look on Bobby's face. "Beer?"

"Yes, thank you." Not only did he hardly ever drink hard liquor; Bobby also almost never drank beer. But he didn't want to turn down her hospitality.

She brought the beer and smiled again. "How may I help you?"

"You were Mr. Dietrich's cleaning woman?"

"*Sí*, I was his maid."

"For a long time?"

"I think for *tres años*, three years. He is only in this country a little over three years."

"You have a good relationship with him?"

"*Sí*, he is very nice to work for. I work for others before him. Not so very nice, especially those from Hollywood." She anxiously kneaded a piece of monkey bread between her fingers.

"Leland Russell?"

"He is a friend of Mr. Dietrich. I meet him several times."

"What was he like?"

"Very, how do you say, *apasionado*."

"Passionate?" Bobby hadn't gotten that impression. "About what?"

"I don't stick my nose where it don't belong." She wrenched off a piece of bread, wedged it into her mouth. "They always talking. Argue. But *amigos. Entiende?* You understand me?"

"What'd they argue about?"

She shrugged.

"And Dietrich?"

"Everything very proper—he is very nice man."

"You worked in his apartment in the Bryson building?"

"*Sí*, but sometimes I do errands for him."

"Errands? What kind of errands?"

"Anything he needs. I shop, sometimes I—"

"Did you ever do business errands for him?"

"Sure I do. I pick up packages that arrive at the Union Station.

Sometimes I take things he needs to send, when not too many, to the Railway Express office."

"Did you ever go to a company called IBM, International Business Machines?"

"Yes. Many times."

"Many times?"

"I go to pick up envelopes," she said, walking to the mantel. She straightened the photos of her boys. Ran a small feather duster over them.

"Envelopes? Do you know what was in them?"

"No, I no open them."

"Do you know a man named Stinson?"

"I drop things off for him from *Señor* Dietrich, but I don't know him. Never meet him."

"Is there anything else you can think of?"

"I think that is all."

"If you know of something, please let me know." Bobby wrote his number down on a piece of paper. Someday he'd have business cards made up. If not for a musician then for a private detective. Or both.

He headed for the door. "Did you ever see Margaret Lane at Mr. Dietrich's?"

"Yes, all the time. Poor girl. She is so serious all the time."

"Serious? About what?"

"I not knowing. The war I think. Yes, maybe the war."

"The war? Did she lose someone?"

"I'm thinking not. It is her work with *Señor* Dietrich."

"What kind of work?"

"She is always bringing clothing and blankets."

"For what, who?"

"I do not know. Maybe for soldiers or poor people, *yo no sé.* I don't know."

"Thank you. You've been very kind."

"*Momentito, por favor.* One moment, please."

Mrs. del Toro disappeared into the kitchen. Bobby couldn't

figure out what she was doing. Was someone going to come out blasting? Had he seen too many Warner Brothers gangster movies? She came out a moment later with a large grease-stained paper bag.

"Some things for you to eat. A single man, you probably don't eat so good." She patted his flat stomach.

"Thank you. *Gracias.* But you really didn't have to."

"You find *Señor* Dietrich's killer."

"I'll do my best." He picked up his hat and started out the door. "One more thing. Do you know if Mr. Dietrich knew or did business with a man named David Chambers?"

"I am sorry, I do not know this name."

Bobby thanked her again. Left. He felt like he'd done pretty good for a tenderfoot.

CHAPTER SIXTEEN

Mrs. del Toro had confirmed and strengthened Dietrich's ties to IBM. And what was Margaret Lane so serious about all the time? Who were the clothes for? What made Leland Russell so intense? Or was it just plain tense? He'd seem very relaxed when Bobby met him, at least at first. After the obligatory time, he'd wanted Bobby out of there. Then there were Maria's trips to Union Station and Railway Express. Of course, someone in the import-export business would probably do a lot of business at those places. She'd said that Dietrich was very proper. Nice. Nobody had a bad word to say about the man. Maybe he was the nicest, most decent Nazi in the world or maybe they were all covering for him, the "honored dead," as Bogey referred to the two German couriers in *Casablanca*: "They got a lucky break. Yesterday they were just two German clerks. Today they're the 'honored dead.'"

Bobby wanted to go to Stinson's home to wait for him. Still too early. He could have gone to the club to practice. Instead, he went home. He couldn't wait to shake off his shoes and throw himself on the couch and sleep and sleep and sleep.

After an hour's catnap he felt refreshed, decided to go to the club. He parked on Central a few doors up from the Alabam. It was one of those glorious Los Angeles days, crisp, clean air filled his lungs. Blue sky with silver-lined clouds everywhere. Warm sun telling him that no matter what was going on in his life, no matter what was going on in the world, things weren't that bad and even if they were they'd get better someday. Bobby hummed Irving Berlin's "Blue Skies."

A ham-sized hand, maybe a paw, reached out and grabbed Bobby's shoulder. His heart did double time as he spun 'round, ready to be mugged. Staring him down—literally, as the man was almost a foot taller than Bobby—was Sam Wilde, Lois' sometime boyfriend. Wilde gripped Bobby's shoulder, holding him at arm's length. As if Bobby would or could do much else, though he was pleased to see the bandage on Wilde's hand.

The surprise of seeing Wilde was second only to the fear that hit Bobby like a lightning streak. He wanted to be tough, like Bogart; he wanted to be urbane, like William Powell. Right now he just wanted to get the hell out of there.

"Hold up, pal."

Bobby stuffed his fear down, not wanting to let it show. He had bested Wilde the last time out. He didn't know if he could score a doubleheader.

"What do you want? And how the hell did you find me?"

"Like you found me. You have your ways, I have mine." Wilde lit an unfiltered Camel. "You really looking for Lois?"

"Yeah."

"But you're a musician."

"Don't bust my chops. What do you want?"

"She can be a real ball buster. But I give a damn about the broad. Let's go."

Bobby looked around. He didn't want to go with Wilde; it could be a trip to nowhere that he'd never come back from. Several colored people talked and joked outside the Dunbar Hotel next to the Alabam. He didn't know if he could count on them for help. They might not want to get involved with two white men. It would only mean trouble for them one way or another. Wilde guided Bobby in an about face and they walked back to the Olds.

"You drive. Might as well use up your gas ration as mine. 'Sides, I drove down here." Wilde scratched at his side.

Bobby got behind the wheel, Wilde in the passenger seat.

"Head south."

"Where're we going?"

"Long Beach. The Pike."

"That's a long ways. Why the Pike?"

"Drive."

Long Beach was a navy town south of Los Angeles, the Pike its oceanside amusement quarter. Bobby knew there'd be lots of sailors around, if they ever actually made it to the Pike. They'd have to pass through the Wilmington oil fields on the way and that was as good a place as any to dispose of a body. The oil fields were a well-known dumping ground. Bodies were always bobbing up through the greasy black muck that leached to the surface.

Bobby white-knuckled the steering wheel, gripping as hard as he could, mostly so Wilde wouldn't notice his shaking hands. They passed through the oil field, with its forests of towering derricks—supplicants reaching for the sky. Safely past the dumping grounds, he loosened his grip on the wheel.

"You bested me good in that pool hall, kid."

Bobby's knuckles turned white again.

"You're small, but wiry and fast. You know how to move. So what are you, a musician or a detective?"

"I guess I'm a little of both right now."

"Who wants you to find Lois?"

Bobby knew that Bogey would never divulge his client's name. He didn't have a private detective's license and he didn't have Bogey's scruples either. He told Wilde the whole story, from James and Dietrich arguing to Booker's dangling carrot of a gig with the band, and everything else.

"So you got no real interest in Lois?"

"You mean as competition for you?"

Wilde nodded.

"Strictly professional and mercenary."

"Good." Wilde lit another Camel off the one in his mouth.

"You ever ride the Cyclone?"

Bobby shook his head. Every kid growing up in Southern California knew about the Cyclone, but Bobby had never been to the Pike. "Well, you're in for a treat then."

Why the hell did Wilde want to take him on the Cyclone? Was he going to push Bobby out the car at the top of the tallest hill, claim it was an accident? They parked the car, so he'd know soon enough.

A warren of tangled streets and narrow alleys, the Pike reminded Bobby of the Casbah in the Charles Boyer/Hedy Lamarr movie *Algiers,* with its bewildering labyrinth of streets and passages, dead-ends and mystery around every corner. Colorful buildings with turrets and domes, like movie sets, screamed out at every turn down here.

"If you ever get lost here," Wilde said, "just listen for the waves, point yourself toward the ocean, and walk. Sooner or later you'll get your bearings again."

Bobby could barely hear the waves over the din of the crowds and the screaming of the rides. He'd heard that Main Street at the Pike was called "The Walk of a Thousand Lights." And now he was dizzy just looking at the maze of streets and lights and people. They were in the middle of the midway and he had no idea which way the ocean was. Wilde walked fast. Bobby jogged to keep up.

"Let's eat. Best barbecue in the world's down here."

Bobby trailed Wilde to Lee's Barbecue. He followed Wilde's lead and ordered what he did, including a beer. Bobby's mind raced as fast the coaster cars in the distance behind Lee's. He still had no idea what they were doing at the Pike. It seemed like another good place to lose someone—forever. Bobby didn't plan on getting lost.

The barbecued pork sandwich satisfied Bobby's hunger but not his need for answers. "What are we doing here, Mr. Wilde?"

"Call me Sam." Wilde slurped barbecue sauce from his lips. "Y'know, Lois is a nice kid. I don't want to see her hurt."

"You think someone's trying to hurt her?"

"I haven't heard from her in a while. Neither has her mother. It's not like her."

"So what does the Pike have to do with any of this?"

Wilde chugged beer, nodded. "Dietrich used to send her down here, sometimes with a package to drop off, sometimes to pick something up."

"What did she pick up?"

"Envelopes mostly, sometimes packages. And no, I don't know what was in them. But sometimes I'd come down here with her, y'know, to sort of protect her. It's not a great place for a girl alone, sailors, seedy people always on the make."

"Where did she make these pickups and drop offs?"

"Let's go." Wilde grabbed Bobby's arm, jerking him forward.

Bobby looked up and down the midway. It must have stretched a mile, smeared with arcades, tattoo parlors, dance halls, and bars that Bobby didn't think he'd want to find himself in. Sailors from the nearby base trolled for girls, sometimes brawling with marines or soldiers over a girl. The Cyclone Racer towered above everything, like a stairway to the heavens. The side-by-side coasters raced and chased each other up and down rickety wooden hills and mountains, coiling through steeply banked curves, as he and Wilde sprinted along the midway.

They sped past an octagonal wooden booth with a huge sign proclaiming *Esmeralda, Psychic Seer to the Stars*. Wilde glanced at the woman in the booth; she didn't seem to notice them. She wore what looked like a gypsy fortune teller's outfit from what Bobby could see. Peasant blouse, beads. Head scarf. Wilde dragged Bobby past the Davy Jones' Locker attraction to the Mirror Maze. He bought two tickets and in they went. Bobby was surprised Wilde didn't make him cough up. He had no idea what the hell they were doing in the maze and still didn't trust Wilde. Lighted mirrors glowed golden. Curved mirrors made them look fat and skinny, tall and short. Upside down. Bobby had heard that houses of mirrors were inspired by the palace of

Versailles. Some day he would like to find out for himself if the Nazis didn't bomb it into oblivion.

Two little boys in cowboy hats, chaps, and Hopalong Cassidy holsters and cap pistols, charged by them, laughing. A sailor and his girl smooched in the recesses of the maze. Wilde led Bobby through the brightly lit halls. They were nearing the end of the knot of intertwining corridors. Wilde stopped, looked around, making sure no one else was there. He reached his hand to the strip of small lights outlining one of the mirror panels. He stared at them for a few seconds, put his hand on one, and turned. The mirrored panel clicked open. Wilde pushed his way in, followed by a reluctant but curious Bobby. Once inside, Wilde closed the door. They found themselves in a dreary room cluttered with boxes and work benches. A handful of flimsy chairs.

Bobby looked behind him. The mirrored panel they had come through was a two-way mirror; he could see people walking by outside, staring into the glass, making faces. Trying to figure out which way to go in the incredible maze.

A man and woman entered by another door. She looked like a gypsy fortune teller in flowing skirts, sparkling with bangles— Esmeralda.

The scrawny man's sunken cheeks and hollow eyes gave him an eerie, skeletal look. Spooky. Wearing only a tank top undershirt, no top shirt, and grimy dungarees added to the graveyard effect. He slicked back his thinning hair, then ran his hand over three days' unshaven growth.

"Who the hell are you and what're you doing here?" the man said in a voice that could slice gravel.

"Remember me?"

"Don't."

"I came here with Lois. Lois Templeton."

"Who the hell is that, some tramp?"

Wilde moved on the man. The smaller man didn't back up. "Don't talk about her that way."

"Okay, all right. But who is she?"

"She come here to drop stuff off for Dietrich. You know Dietrich."

The man planted his feet wide as Wilde loomed over him. He looked like he was about to swing on the man. Bobby wanted to change the subject before they came to blows. He wasn't sure what to say.

"I just had drinks at the Sunset Tower with Mr. Tony Leach—you've heard of him," Bobby blurted. It sounded silly, but it was all he could come up with. "And the subject of Mr. Dietrich came up."

"What does a gangster like Leach care about any of this?" The man glared at Bobby.

"That's Mr. Leach's business. All I can say is that it would be to your benefit to talk with us." He turned to the woman.

"Esmeralda's not your real name, is it?" Bobby said, remembering her name from the booth outside, and trying to change the tone of the encounter before it got ugly.

The woman turned to Bobby.

"You're too pretty to be an Esmeralda," he said. "Surely that's a stage name for your fortune telling or whatever you do down here."

Esmeralda smiled. "My given name is Katherine, with a *K*."

"Shut up," the man shouted.

"But, Jerry, maybe we should—we don't need no trouble."

"Like Katherine Hepburn. Pretty name."

Wilde watched with amazement, as Bobby put on the charm.

"Don't fall for his smooth line," Jerry said.

Jerry lit a cigar. Bobby almost choked. He wasn't used to the heavy, blue smoke. "We need to get back to work, so whadda you want?"

Bobby looked to Wilde. Wilde nodded, Bobby continued, "We want to know why Lois Templeton came down here."

"Several times," Wilde said.

Esmeralda—Katherine—started to speak. Jerry cut her off. "That Dietrich guy. He's in the import-export business, something like that. But he's also from Germany. Mail and all of that's been cut off from Germany since the war. Sometimes we can get a letter or something through on a ship—"

"Navy ship, from Long Beach?"

"Mostly on commercial freighters or somethin'. Maybe get a letter to or from his family in the old country. It don't go straight to Germany, of course, but it gets there eventually."

"Sometimes there were packages," Wilde said.

"Sure, care and comfort packages. They got little comforts over there these days."

"Makes sense," Bobby said, looking straight at Katherine. She blinked rapidly, a tell.

"So you just sort of act as the middleman for Dietrich and his family?"

"Yeah. That's all it is. And Lois, well, if you was Dietrich, would you be wanting to drive all the way down here? So he sends his girl."

Bobby saw Wilde's hands tighten into hard balls. He was waiting for him to interject something. Was glad when he didn't.

"How did you know Dietrich—how did he know you could help him get the stuff to his family?" Bobby said.

"Friend of a friend if it matters to you."

"Did he ever do any illegal importing or exporting?"

"The guy's a square. Not hep."

Jerry kept talking about Dietrich in the present tense. Didn't he know the man was dead? Bobby thought it best not to bring it up.

"When was the last time Lois brought something?"

"Hmm, dunno, maybe two, three weeks ago, give or take."

"And it was—"

"The usual."

"Packages?"

"Maybe just some comfort things for the family. Blankets maybe. Stuff like that."

Bobby wondered if this had anything to do with Margaret

bringing blankets and clothing to Dietrich.

The conversation continued in the same vein for a few minutes. Bobby and Wilde finally left through a door in the back so they didn't have to fight their way through the Mirror Maze again. Bobby's eyes watered in the bright sun. He wondered why they hadn't used this door in the first place. Maybe Wilde had wanted the element of surprise.

"So what do you think?" Wilde said.

"I don't think they're telling us everything."

"Ain't that the truth. And did you notice that he still thinks Dietrich's alive?"

"I noticed. It could be a ruse. Did you see how he filled up every hole with talk so Esmeralda couldn't get a word in edgewise?"

"Yeah," Wilde said. "You did good in there, kid. Subtle. Just like you did with me at the pool hall. 'Course we done it my way, he'd be bleeding, but maybe we'd know more."

"There's plenty of time for that. We have to move strategically, like MacArthur."

"All right, let's go."

"Where?"

As promised, Wilde took Bobby on the Cyclone Racer. Shooting up and down, twisting around banked curves, nearly flying off into the ocean, Bobby thought he was on a roller coaster in more ways than one.

They swooped down the tallest hill. Bobby's stomach swooped up.

"Criminy!"

CHAPTER SEVENTEEN

What was Wilde's story? He looked fit and the right age for the service, so why wasn't he in uniform? Could he be trusted? He had kept his volatitility in check at the Pike. His silence on the way home gave Bobby time to think about the Gordian Knot this case and his life had become. Nobody could figure out how to undo the original Gordian Knot until Alexander the Great did the simplest thing of all. He cut it. Bobby wasn't sure where to cut.

"You don't think it's what they said, that Dietrich was trying to get some comfort and aid to his family?"

"Not even close."

"Then what?"

"I don't know. What did Dietrich do, importing and exporting. Before the war, he imported German toys, cuckoo clocks, and business machines. According to you nobody seems to know what he exported, if anything." Wilde bashed his elbow on Bobby's car door. "Damn. Wait'll I get my hands on the SOB that took Lois."

Bobby didn't want to mention that Lois might have gone off voluntarily. He turned onto Central, pulled up behind Wilde's beatup 1940 Ford Deluxe Tudor convertible.

"Nice car," Bobby said. "I like the V8. Lots of pickup, lots of speed."

"Belonged to a buddy of mine. He don't need it anymore."

"The war?"

"Wake Island." Wilde stared out the window. "Hey, I want to help. Work with you. I want to find Lois." Bobby saw the eager but distant look on Wilde's face. "And I can help. I can do things you can't. I know you're tough and wiry, but I'm also tough and big. People get scared. I can do strong-arm if necessary. I don't have to be involved minute by minute, just keep me posted. I'll do what I can."

"All right."

Wilde shook Bobby's hand, clamping down with enough pressure to turn a steel girder into slag. Bobby was surprised his fingers were still intact. He liked Wilde's firm grip. There was something about Wilde, a real man's man, that stirred something inside him. And it scared the hell out of him. "Keep in touch," Wilde said, getting out of the Olds. He scribbled his phone number on a scrap of paper, pressed it into Bobby's palm.

"I will."

"We'll make a good team." Wilde walked off, stopped, turned, and leaned back in the window. "You're not all you seem, are you?"

He winked and was gone. *What did he mean?* Did he know more than he was letting on? Bobby took Wilde's parking space, popped into the Alabam to get in a few practice licks, but mostly to unwind. He was glad the only people there were Lawrence, the barkeep, and Gaby, the janitor. He didn't want to talk to Booker.

He threw himself into a rendition of "Stormy Weather" and thought about Wilde.

The mail sat half in Bobby's mailbox, half on the hallway floor. The usual assortment of bills and flyers for sales you could pay for with the help of rationing coupons. What stuck out was a fragment of paper that looked like it had been ripped from a notebook. The scrawl on it read: "Watch your back. The nigger's playing you."

A threat? The word *nigger*, glaring off the page, shocked Bobby, even though it was common enough to hear it. What the hell did the note mean? Booker? Playing Bobby? How? Maybe James *had* killed Dietrich and Booker wanted to throw suspicion elsewhere? What if Booker himself was involved? Bobby's mind spun like the Cyclone Racer as he walked to the kitchen sink. His eyes were red and sore, his feet hurt. His bones ached. Even his skin burned. He splashed water on his face, then headed out again. He could have used the phone but thought it better to face people in person.

Bobby had driven to the Malibu sheriff's station in half the time hoping to catch him there. If he wasn't, what would Bobby have done, gone to sleep in his car? Not after getting that note. He wasn't ready to confront Booker about it. He couldn't ignore it either. Someone didn't want him digging around and didn't want him talking to Booker.

"Nicholai's out, kid," the desk sergeant said. Taking pity on the *kid*, he told Bobby that Sergeant Nicolai was at the Shark's Tooth, a bar a couple miles up Pacific Coast Highway. That's where Bobby found him, drinking rye and Canada Dry ginger ale highballs, under an array of tacky fisherman's nets hanging from the ceiling and walls festooned with swordfish and a variety of seashells and other debris from the ocean.

"Hey, kid, find out anything? Where you been?" Nicolai said, his breath sour with whiskey.

"On a wild goose chase to the Pike—"

"The Pike?"

"But I don't know any more than I did when I saw you last time. Lois Templeton and Harlan Thomas are still missing. I haven't connected with Stinson from IBM. James is still in jail—"

"—And Dietrich's still dead." Nicolai guzzled the highball. "And I'll drink to that."

"Are you drunk, Sergeant?"

"Not yet. But I plan to be before I leave here."

"Have you found out anything?"

"Nope. Guess I'm not trying very hard."

"Why not?"

"He's just a dead kraut. The enemy. Nobody cares." Nicolai scratched at the table.

"What if an innocent man's in jail?"

"Nobody cares about that either."

Bobby already figured that. "In your extensive detecting have you found out anything about Booker?"

"'Boom-Boom' Booker?" Nicolai slurred his words.

"I think you're a little more drunk than you think you are."

"Only a little. What about Booker?"

"What's his background? Where does he hail from?"

"Hail from? What kind of a word is that? Next thing you know you'll be wanting to play 'Hail to the Chief' to him."

"I think we're getting off track, Sarge. Does he have a record?"

"Far as I know he's got all the usuals those people have."

"Usuals?"

"Petty crimes, some dope dealing. The usual. Oh, and suspicion of murder but there wasn't enough proof and no one would talk. He *hails* from out of state. I haven't dug that deep into his background to know all the details." He grabbed a fistful of peanuts. "Hell, all those people have the usual in their background."

"Those people?"

"Then he got successful as a musician and his record's clean, at least for a few years, though I'm sure if we tried, we could get something on him."

"Sergeant, didn't you once tell me you didn't care what color a person's skin was, you just wanted to get the bad guy? And now you're talking about *those people*."

Nicolai swigged his highball down to the last drop. Nodded to the bartender for another. "Far as the sheriff's office is concerned the *clase* is *cosed*."

"And what about you, Sergeant?"

"Far as I'm concerned, it's closed."

"What about justice?"

"Boy are you naive, kid. Besides, it's not my call."

"Then whose call is it?"

"Deputy Hardin's, the mayor's, the sheriff's. God's. It's an act of God, that's what it is."

The bartender set an amber-hued highball glass on the counter, leaving Nicholai's dirty glass in place.

"So now you think James is guilty?"

"That's the party line."

"I thought you weren't a member of any parties, Sergeant."

"I'm a member of the drunkard party." He lifted his fresh glass.

"A citizen of the drunk world," Bobby muttered. Nicolai looked up, like he wanted to understand but couldn't. "Where do you live, Sarge?"

"What for?"

"I'm taking you home. You can't drive like this."

"What are you, one-a them homos?

Bobby wanted to slug him. Instead, he gathered Nicolai up, pulled him to the parking lot. Nicolai wanted to drive his own car home. Bobby wrestled him to the Olds Six.

They ended up at the beach, in a one-room dive kitchenette-apartment in a pay-as-you-go motel.

"Criminy," Bobby mumbled, looking around the joint. *Black Mask* detective and girlie magazines littered every flat surface, from floor to tabletops. A Gypsy Rose Lee stripper calendar hung on the back of the door. Surprisingly, the kitchenette and bathroom were spic and span. Thank God for small favors. He set Nicolai on the couch. Bobby flopped on a large armchair. He looked out the picture window, the sea bobbing in and out of shore. His last thought before nodding off was that this would be a nice apartment if Nicolai just kept it up, like he kept the kitchen and bathroom clean.

He woke to the smell of eggs and hash browns, the smells of home. At least they reminded him of growing up on Poinsettia, the good parts.

"What time is it?" Bobby said.

"Three in the morning. And you thought I was drunk. What're you still doing here?"

"I was tired. And I didn't want to go home."

"Why not?"

Bobby didn't want to say that he was avoiding Booker. Avoiding everyone. "How would you get your car?"

Whether or not Nicolai bought it he didn't say anything. They ate at a small table next to the picture window. The full moon glowed silver on the waves. Even so it was very black out there.

"I thought you were married with a family?" Bobby said.

"I don't wear a ring. What made you think that?"

"You just seemed the married type."

Nicolai stared out the window into the dark. "I remember everything we said at the Shark's Tooth. I'm the kind of drunk who never forgets, no matter how hard I try."

"What are you trying to forget?"

"That I was married with a family, once. Let's leave it at that, okay."

"Sure." Bobby poured ketchup on his eggs.

"Find out anything new, kid?"

Bobby filled him in on Wilde. The Pike and the carnies. "But I feel like I'm spinning my wheels, Sarge."

"Sometimes you gotta do that, then something clicks, like out of the blue." Nicolai scratched at his temples, rubbed, as if to work out the hangover knots. Ran his fingers through his hair. "So'd you find out about that Thomas character or Lois Templeton?"

"They're both still missing, that's all I know. But surely they're separate cases, so even if the case is closed on James Christmas, these two should still be open, right?"

"There's a war going on. People go missing. We got espionage to worry about."

"So normal everyday people go missing and the police don't

care."

"The police don't have enough manpower to care."

"I believe you care, Sergeant Nicolai."

"So you were asking about Booker." Nicholai scooped up half his hash browns in one bite.

"Yeah, but right now I'm more interested in what turned you so cynical."

"Let's leave that alone too."

"Sergeant, you've done a one-eighty on this case."

"I got other cases."

"Someone's telling you to back off."

"Happens all the time. It's just the way of the world, kid. You'd best be dropping it too."

"And what if James Christmas is innocent?"

"And what if he ain't? And even if he is innocent-a this he's probably guilty-a somethin' else. You should just get back to your music, your band."

"I don't have a band. And Booker wants me to find out—"

"Last night you were asking a lot of questions about Booker. What gives?"

Bobby hesitated, finally pulling out the scribbled note, sliding it across the table to Nicolai.

"Watch your back. The nigger's playing you," Nicolai read out loud. "Good advice kid. Watch your back and get off the case. You ain't no detective, though I admire your pluck."

"I thought you had it too. Was I wrong?"

CHAPTER EIGHTEEN

Bobby no longer knew who his friends were. His enemies. Compared to what the boys in the army, navy and marines were going through, even Howard Gibbon and Phil Bartel, Bobby's problems seemed insignificant.

He might have wanted to be a private dick—if he couldn't be in a band—but he was still going in circles, still not sure what a real private detective would do at this point.

"Back to square one."

A blade of orange sky peeled over the crest of the Hollywood Hills behind George Stinson's Los Feliz house. Bobby parked across the street. He didn't expect anything. Stinson surprised him a few minutes later, pulling into his driveway in his cream 1941 Packard Clipper.

Bobby fumbled for the ignition key hiding in his pocket. Fired up the Olds and pulled into Stinson's driveway behind him. Very clever, he thought.

"Who the hell are you?" Stinson's crimson face shouted, the veins in his neck protruding. Scared to death, Bobby's heart pounded a driving beat, like a Gene Krupa riff. But he also felt a surge of power, getting this reaction from Stinson.

"Mr. Stinson—"

"You know my name?"

"I need to talk to you."

"Make an appointment with my secretary."

"I'm afraid I've tried that. You're harder to see than General

Eisenhower." Bobby stuck his hand in his pocket, as if he had a gun. Oldest trick in the world; he laughed on the inside. He didn't know what made him do it, maybe seeing *The Maltese Falcon*. Maybe just trying to be a man, like Bogey or Autry.

"What, you're going to pull this tough guy stuff on me?" He looked Bobby up and down. "How tough can *you* be?"

"Tough enough to find you." *Tough enough to go down to Central, tough enough to get a gig with Booker, tough enough to confront Leach. Tough enough to go face to face with Sam Wilde. And tough enough to get beat up by my old high school classmates and not whine about it. Tough enough.* "Let's go inside and have a talk. Maybe we can even make it friendly?"

Stinson's kitchen had all the latest gadgets. Bobby wondered what he was sacrificing for the war effort.

"You'll excuse me if I don't offer you a glass of champagne or invite you into my living room."

"If I want your champagne, I'll find it and take it," Bobby said.

"What do you want?" Stinson clutched his briefcase.

Bobby played off Stinson's impatience, hesitating. Stinson set the briefcase down, began drumming the countertop. Bobby noticed the ring on his finger—the same skull and bones 322 that David had. That certainly seemed to tie them together, though Stinson had to be twenty years older than David.

"Nice ring."

"It's a school ring, why do you care?"

"Yale?"

"Surely you didn't come here to discuss jewelry with me."

"Tell me about your relationship with Hans Dietrich."

The drumming grew louder. "Who?"

"Dietrich. Don't BS me." Bobby could see the machinations taking place in Stinson's mind.

"Ah, him. I had no relationship with him. And who the hell are you?"

"I was on the Apollo. So were you."

"You don't know anything. Regardless, it's none of your damn business. Now, I'm tired. I work for a living. I'd like to relax a little, if that's all right with you?" Stinson set his briefcase down, closed the gap between him and Bobby, towering over him. He looked around for something to use as a weapon, if it came to that. "Listen you. You come to my house, you invade my privacy, you—"

Bobby held his ground. "Someone you knew is dead. Don't you care?"

"I hardly knew him."

"How *hardly* did you know him?"

"He wanted to export some of our products to Europe."

"There's a war on. What could he export and where?"

"That's what I told him." Stinson backed up a step.

"Did you do business with him?"

"Hardly. Like you said, there's a war going on. Now get out of my house before I throw you out."

Bobby tried to use the gun-in-pocket ploy again. Stinson laughed.

"You've seen too many movies, kid." Using his weight and height advantage, Stinson shoved Bobby toward the back door. "Now I have a question for you. How come you're not in the service? You a sissy?"

He didn't wait for an answer, instead shouldering Bobby out the back door, slamming it behind him. Bobby's face flushed with humiliation. He had wondered why Stinson so easily let him into his house. Now he knew: Stinson was playing Bobby, not the other way around. He wanted to see what Bobby knew. Chalk one up for the other side—this time.

"Creep," Bobby said to the empty street, getting into his car. Driving off.

Humiliated by Stinson, he was more determined than ever to uncover every clue. He swung by Lois Templeton's duplex. Mrs.

Templeton still hadn't heard anything from her daughter. Worry showed in her eyes and the droop of her mouth. She had contacted the police. They gave her lip service—didn't really seem interested. Would Bobby help? He said he would, but she had no new info to give him.

By the time he reached Harlan Thomas' Hollywood Hills house, streetlights sprayed splotches of light everywhere, leaving barely a shred of sunlight. That's what he wanted. Bobby pulled all the way down the driveway, parking in front of the garage, near the incinerator. A lot of houses in the hills didn't have long driveways. Thomas' did, as he had a large lot, which suited Bobby fine. He grabbed a flashlight, closed his car door without a sound, looked in every direction, especially at the neighbor's house on the driveway side. No one around. He walked back to the front door, rang the bell. Waited. Rang again. No answer. He walked to the back of Thomas' house, slipped his younger brother's Boy Scout jackknife from his pocket—"always prepared," he thought—slid the blade under the window and pried it open. Bobby pulled himself up, climbed into the window.

The flashlight cast coarse shadows in the room which, at first glance, looked like an office. As it wasn't late and the house was dark, Bobby assumed no one was home. He did a quick tour to make sure. Mail lay piled on the floor below the mail slot by the front door. So, where was Harlan Thomas these last few days?

A huge portrait adorned the curved wall that followed the entry hall stairs. A woman of regal bearing, with piercing dark eyes and flowing black hair. Judging by the clothes maybe from the twenties. Thomas' mother? Sister, wife? Just some painting he liked? Bobby continued up the stairs.

He moved quickly, hoping he wouldn't trip over any dead bodies. A hall sprouted off the landing at the top of the stairs. Three doors opened off it. On the other side of the hall a railing overlooked the foyer below. Bobby hit the first door. A bedroom with nothing in it. Not a bed, not a chair, not a dresser. Only venetian blinds on the window casting harsh, striped streetlight shadows to the hardwood floor. He flipped on the light, the shadows vanished. A layer of dust covered the floor. Bobby knew if he went in the room he'd leave his mark on the dust. He went anyway. Threw open the closet door. Empty. He opened the door to the Jack-and-Jill bathroom. Flicked on the light—a red light bulb. At first glance, just more dust. And a funny-looking machine of some type sitting on the built-in cabinet of drawers, all locked. He tried to open the medicine cabinet. Locked. A taut clothesline stretched from one side of the bathtub to the other, several shiny metal clips attached to the line.

Bobby walked through the open door on the other side. Another bedroom. This time with the requisite furniture. All the bureau drawers hung open. The closet door was askew, as if flung open instead of being opened normally. The drawers were empty, not so much as a lone sock or spare piece of change. What the hell?

Bobby's breath quickened. He darted through the second bedroom, out the door to the hall. He hadn't looked under the bed. Was that where the body was?

The last door on the hall had to be the master bedroom.

Bobby inched toward the door, one hand trailing along the wrought iron rail.

He opened the door expecting to find—what? As far as he could see it was a normal master, large bed, brocaded draperies, the usual assortment of dressers and such. Two things seemed slightly out of place, a deco martini bar, similar to Dietrich's. Was that significant? He got up to see what record was on the player on the dresser. Sidney Bechet's hit version of *Summertime—and the livin' is easy*. Maybe for someone; not for Bobby. Not for the millions of boys overseas. Not for their mothers and fathers. Not for the people still reeling from the Depression. So who the hell was the livin' easy for? He opened the closet door: shoes, suits. He even looked under the bed. No dead bodies. Now that Bobby was sure he was completely alone, he could do a more thorough search of the house. Since he was in the bedroom he started there, opening drawers, rifling through socks and underwear. He looked in the closet, picking up each Florsheim wingtip, sticking his long piano-player fingers in each to see if something was stuffed inside, coming up empty every time.

He went through every cigar box stuffed with old family photos, trinkets from travels, boyhood memories. He pulled out a photo that he assumed was Thomas—dark hair slicked back on a balding head, deep set eyes and a thin moustache—put it in his pocket.

He sat on the edge of the bed, his eyes fighting to stay open. He hadn't slept well since becoming a detective. He drifted off, picturing Thomas in his mind—where the hell was he? What had happened to him?

Bobby woke up bleary-eyed, but not for long. The sight of a man standing over you with a pistol aiming at your gut will wake you up damn fast. The tachometer of Bobby's heart revved up; his breath coming short and quick. He palmed the bed post to steady himself. Sucked in deep breaths to calm his pounding heart, said a quick prayer to a God he'd long forgotten to help him get through this.

When Bobby's vision cleared he saw it was the man from the photo in his pocket.

"Who the hell are you?" the man said.

CHAPTER NINETEEN

"Harlan Thomas?" Bobby honed in on the black hole of the barrel, aiming point blank at his chest.

The man's slicked-back hair, what there was of it, surrounded his silver dome. His deep-set eyes stared down at Bobby, while his sharp nose pointed accusingly at him. A thin moustache graced his upper lip, like Tyrone Power's in *The Mark of Zorro*. The man wore a button-down dress shirt and slacks; his outfit looked like half a suit in search of its better half. With his sharp features and solid body, he cut a striking figure.

"You haven't answered my question."

"My name's Bobby Saxon." He eyed the man's finger twitching inside the trigger guard.

"What're you doing here?"

"You wouldn't believe me if I told you."

"Try me."

Bobby shifted on the bed. The long snout of the pistol shifted with him. He thought better than to try to get up. What would Bogey do in a situation like this? Gene Autry? Or Hoppy? They'd know how to finesse it. Bobby had no idea.

"I'm a musician—"

"And you just came by to play my mandolin?" Thomas snorted out a laugh.

"I'm investigating Hans Dietrich's murder." He wondered if he might be staring Dietrich's murderer in the face.

"What's your interest in his death?"

"Don't you want help finding his killer?"

"Who says I need help?" Thomas sounded tough. Looked tough. But his hands were shaking ever so slightly, the pistol bobbing up and down. He was putting on the bravado act as much as Bobby. "Why're you so interested in him, or me?"

Bobby filled Thomas in on the gig with Booker. On Dietrich's getting killed and hanging from the rafters, which Thomas already knew about. And on James being pinched for it. Thomas pursed his lips. His eyes seemed to lose focus for a split-second. "It's just wild enough that it might be true."

"It is true."

Thomas lowered the gun. A thousand years of tension seemed to drain from him. His whole body sagged, face seemed to fall. He sat on the bed near Bobby. "Get me a drink, will you?"

"I've never made one before. It won't be very good."

"As long as it's heavy on gin it'll be fine. But we have to keep our wits about us. One drink only."

Bobby fixed a drink for Thomas, declining one for himself. After one long swallow, Thomas wanted to go downstairs to see if there was anything edible. He paced the kitchen, munching on stale bread from the bread box. Bobby sat at the small table. He also nibbled the stale bread.

"What's going on? Why was your partner killed—James Christmas didn't do it."

"Probably not. Unless he was getting paid by someone."

"Who?"

"How do I know I can trust you?" Thomas shook his head. Tapped his feet. His fingers twitched. With those nervous trigger fingers, Bobby was glad he wasn't aiming the gun at him anymore. "I gotta get outta here before they get me too."

"Do you have any idea who might have killed Dietrich? And why in such a public place?"

"They're warning me off. This has gotten way too out of hand."

"What are they warning you off of? And where've you been,

why are you on the run?"

"Isn't that obvious, I might be next. I've been hiding out, I have a cabin up north, just came back here to get a few things."

"What're you and Dietrich involved in? And what's that funny-looking machine in the upstairs bathroom?" The words shot from Bobby's lips in a machine-gun staccato.

"That, that's an enlarger. Let me go out to my car. I have something I want to show you."

Before Bobby could respond, Thomas was out the door. Before Bobby could choke down another piece of hard bread a loud shot cracked the silence of the hills.

Bobby charged out the door. Thomas had barely hit the driveway, lying just outside the back door. The shooters' car blocked the driveway entrance at the street, several yards off. Another shot cracked the air, Bobby instinctively dropped to the pavement. He tried to get a look at the shooters, but their large four-door sedan sped off. It all seemed like a scene from a gangster movie, where the bad guys fly by in their big car firing Tommy guns, bumping somebody off. Bobby was glad these guys weren't using a Tommy gun.

He noted the killers' car: 1941 maroon Mercury. It squealed off. He low-crawled to Thomas' body. The hole in Thomas' chest oozed. He gurgled up blood. The death rattle? Sweat beaded Bobby's forehead. He reached his hand out to touch Thomas, checking to see if he was still alive. He didn't think so. Shaky hands pushed him up to his knees. He watched Thomas' body for several minutes, unable to turn away.

"Oh my God," he whispered.

Thomas didn't move. Bobby assumed he was dead. He ran in the house, dialed the police. Didn't want to be there when they showed, headed outside to his car at the back of the driveway.

"Shit!" Bobby said, realizing that his car was blocked by Thomas'. He thought about moving Thomas' car and leaving. Looked inside—something caught his eye, an alligator briefcase on the passenger seat. Bobby reached in through the open window, grabbed the briefcase. He was dying—though he would have preferred another expression—to see what was in the case. As much as he wanted to see what was in it, he made sure it was closed tight and threw it as far as he could down the canyon behind the back wall, not willing to take a chance of it being found in his car when the cops came. It was his to check for clues, not the cops.

"Criminy." A shiver of guilt—or was it fear?—shocked him. Hiding evidence from the cops. Was he crazy? Regret crept in. Not for long. The cops didn't give a damn, Nicolai had said as much. Screw them.

Neighbors might have seen him throw the case over the hill. Hopefully not. And since he had called the cops, he wouldn't look so guilty. Someone else must have called them too because they were there in less than five minutes from Bobby's call. The officer blocked the driveway with his black-and-white prowl car, same as the shooters' car had. Another cop drove up on a motorcycle, strode toward Bobby, tall black motorcycle boots slapping the pavement, a nervous hand resting on his still-holstered revolver.

"Oh shit!" Bobby muttered seeing Officer Daley, the cop who'd ogled the feminine Bobbie but let her out of a ticket, march toward him. Daley seemed twice as big as he had the last time. And his breath had twice the alcohol on it.

"Step back," Daley said. "Let me see your hands."

Bobby held his hands out. "I'm the one who called—"

"That's fine. We'll get to that. Right now, lean against the car. Spread out."

Bobby knew Daley wouldn't find a gun. He hoped the officer didn't find his taped-up breasts or other secrets as he frisked him.

"All right, what happened here?"

Bobby explained that he and Thomas had been talking in the house and that Thomas had gone to his car to get something.

"What?" Daley asked.

"I'm not sure. He just told me he was going—"

"All right, so what were you doing here?" Daley asked again, maybe trying to see if Bobby would give a different answer.

Bobby wasn't sure how to respond. He told the partial truth, that he was trying to find out who killed Dietrich and had come here to talk to Thomas. That Thomas was scared and wanted Bobby's help.

"Some help." Daley stared at Bobby. "Have we met before?"

"I don't think so."

"Did I ever give you a ticket maybe?"

"No. I don't have any tickets." *God, I hope he doesn't recognize me.* Daley gave Bobby the once over from head to toe, asked for his license. Scrutinized it carefully when Bobby handed it over. Bobby was saved—maybe—when two other patrol cars pulled up, along with an unmarked car. Two men in suits and hats took their time getting out of the detective car.

The lead detective introduced himself as Lieutenant Michael Paine. Daley handed Paine Bobby's license. Bobby had to go through all the basics again for him, from working with Thomas to seeing the sedan drive off. Paine's expression never changed so Bobby couldn't tell if he was buying the story or not. He wished that Sergeant Nicolai was here, but he was a sheriff and this wasn't their territory. He just wanted to get in his car and get the hell out of there. He asked Paine if he could leave.

"Until we clear the scene your car is part of it. And we're going to have to go through it."

"Deputy Sergeant Ed Nicolai can vouch for me."

"This ain't sheriff's territory," Paine said.

"No problem, Lieutenant." Bobby had visions of being dragged down to the police station, put in a small room with a single bulb hanging from the ceiling and being interrogated.

Paine told Bobby to sit on the low wall at the back of the lot, keep his hands out of his pockets. Had one of the uniformed cops stand guard. Bobby hoped the cop wouldn't look over the wall to see the briefcase down the canyon. He wanted to make small talk, thought better of it. A few minutes later a black Ford panel van pulled up. Two men in white coats, like doctors, got out, carrying little black bags. They walked down the driveway. Paine spoke to them. One came over to Bobby.

"Lemme see your hands," the lab man said.

"What for?"

"Paraffin test."

"What's that?"

"To see if you have gunpowder residue on them."

"I didn't shoot any guns."

"This will tell."

Bobby tried not to pay attention to the lab man as he poured warm wax on his hands. He just let him do whatever he needed. He watched Paine check Thomas' body. He ordered someone to photograph the body and the skid marks the sedan had left on the street.

"Smile," a voice said.

Bobby looked up. A camera flash exploded in his eyes. The photographer snapped his picture. "What's that for?"

"We just like your face," Paine said. "Paraffin test says you didn't shoot anyone. We have all your info. You can go now."

"What about my car?"

"No car. Come back tomorrow. It'll still be here." Paine turned. "Daley."

"Yo, Lieutenant."

"Take this man down the hill. He can take a bus from there."

"Thanks," Bobby said.

"All I got is my bike, Lieutenant."

"He can sit on the back. We ain't a limo service."

"Yes, sir."

Bobby jumped on the back of Daley's motorcycle.

"Your car looks familiar too. Okay, maybe I didn't give you no ticket, but I'm sure we've met."

"I don't think so, Officer. Where would it have been?"

"You play softball, maybe in the league?"

"Sorry, no."

"Maybe I come to see your band play somewhere?"

"Not unless you saw me on the Apollo before they closed it down—"

"Naw, never been. Maybe I just seen so many faces bein' a cop they all start to look alike to me. Sooner or later everyone starts lookin' like a criminal."

"That's a comforting thought."

"What?"

"Nothing. Thanks for the ride."

"Don't mention it."

Bobby hopped off the bike on Sunset Boulevard, took a gander around.

He walked to Dolores' Drive-In a couple blocks away, went inside to the eat-in part, ordered a cheeseburger and Suzy Q fries with a malted. Stared at the walls. What the hell had he gotten himself into and how the hell would he get out of it?

CHAPTER TWENTY

Bobby picked up a bus, headed home. It dropped him off a few blocks from his place. He quickly covered the three blocks to his apartment, being careful to avoid cracks in the sidewalk— step on a crack, break your mother's back. Mrs. Hazelton stood on the lawn with a man in a dark suit and fedora. He handed her an envelope. Bobby headed for his apartment.

"Mr. Saxon, it seems that you're bringing in a bad element to my building, which is against the terms of your lease. I thought you were such a nice young man too. But it seems you go with an undesirable element."

"Mrs. Hazelton, I just got home. I've had a rough day, I'm tired. Can we talk about this another time?"

"There's nothing to talk about, young man." She pulled a piece of paper from her pocket. Handed it to him. "I don't think you understand, Mr. Saxon. I'm evicting you."

"Criminy."

Mrs. Hazelton gave Bobby three days to get out. She probably thought she was being generous. B-I-T-C-H. The man nodded at Bobby, walked to his car across the street and drove off. Bobby saw the driver give a two-fingered salute up to Mrs. Hazelton. He headed inside.

Bobby collapsed on his sofa and slept like the *big sleep* that Raymond Chandler had written about. He woke in the morning feeling cheery and happy, though he wasn't sure why, until he remembered his car was in the hills, his apartment wouldn't be his in a few days, he had no job and, oh yeah, there was a war going on. He'd blown a wad of money on makeup and girly clothes. And his savings were dwindling by the day.

After a quick shower, he squeezed four oranges on the glass juicer, felt the blood drain from his face as he watched the juice drain from the orange. He drank his breakfast. His nerves were shot to hell. He patted his cheeks to bring the color back, made sure he had his wallet and was out the door, walking north to Sunset. There he hopped on an electric trolleybus heading for West Hollywood. He could hear the electricity spark as the bus' wire contactors rode along the overhead wires. He got off at Laurel Canyon, hiking the rest of the way up to Thomas' house, thinking about who might have shot him and why.

Bobby halted in front of Thomas' to catch his breath. Yesterday the house and Thomas had given him so much hope. Today only the shell of hope was left, nothing more real than the facade of a movie set. Bobby examined the black tire marks embedded on the street. He couldn't tell anything from them. He'd seen the shooters' car and he couldn't even tell the cops what the men in the car looked like, the whole encounter whizzed by so fast. He looked at the house—no sign of the cops. No sign of life. Should he go inside? An overwhelming hopelessness submerged him so instead he walked the driveway to his car. Thomas' car was gone. Towed by the police so they could work it over? The Olds didn't look any the worse for wear. He slid in, pulled out the choke, shoved the key in the ignition, depressed the clutch, and started to back out, not so easy in the narrow drive. Slammed on the brakes. Slapped his palm against his forehead.

"Criminy." He'd forgotten all about the briefcase.

Bobby killed the engine. He didn't want the neighbors hearing it idling for several minutes. He gently closed the door, headed to the end of the driveway, climbed over the low stucco wall. Jumped into the brush on the other side—started rolling down the ravine. His pant leg snagged on a dead root, ripping from thigh to calf. He grabbed a gnarled tree branch and stopped himself.

It's never this hard in the movies. Brushed himself off, cursing his torn pant leg—a nearly new pair of pants from Alexander and Oviatt down on Olive Street. *Just what I need now.*

Bobby crabbed down the hillside, stopping every few feet to scan for the briefcase. It was about sixty feet down, which didn't seem like a lot until he looked up the steep slope he'd have to climb to get back to the car, only now carrying the briefcase. He steeled himself for the climb. Something caught his attention—mattresses, maybe a dozen. All moldy and mildewed, the stuffing spilling out of some. What were so many mattresses doing down here? Maybe somebody had used the ravine as a dump. If they had, they'd have to have done it from Thomas' yard or one of his neighbors. What the hell, it probably wasn't important. He jostled the case a few feet above him on the hill, climbed to it. Repeated the action till he reached the low stucco wall. Set the case on top, pulled himself over. He desperately wanted to rest. More than that, he wanted out of there, so he grabbed the case, dashed to his car.

Bobby's heart raced, thinking about what was in the alligator case. He could have gone home, except that it wasn't home anymore. Just a place to sleep for a few more nights. He wound the car around the twists and turns of the hilly streets until he came to Mulholland Drive, found an overlook, pulling in under a pepper tree that acted as an umbrella from the sun. He ran his hand down the tear in his pants, felt the chafed skin of his leg. He paid eighty-two fifty for those tailored pants from Oviatt, ten times what he could have paid in a thrift store. *Damn!*

He steadied the case on his lap. Locked. Taut thumbs pushed the locks as hard as they could. No dice.

He jerked open the car door, snatched the case, swinging back, ready to heave it against the trunk of the pepper, hoping it would pop open. Thinking better of the idea, not wanting anything to go sliding down the slope on the valley side of Mulholland, he set the case on the ground, rummaged his trunk until he found a tire iron, wedging it into the case until the locks popped.

A stack of rubber-banded photos filled the main compartment. Bobby retched seeing the black-and-white picture on top. A man, no more than skin on bones, wearing striped pajama-like pants, sliding a tray—a human-sized tray—out of something that looked like a huge brick oven. The charred remains looked like they might once have been human. Once. A long time ago and in another world.

The rest of the photos were similar. Bobby had to close his eyes, brace his hands from shaking. He didn't know what the pictures really were. He knew it couldn't be good. And he knew he'd have to come back to the pictures, but first he probed every cranny and compartment of the case. He wrote down everything he came across:

Keys. Seven keys on a ring.
Small photo of Thomas and Dietrich.
Photo of Thomas with a woman. Who?
Photo of Dietrich and Thomas with a third man. Who?

Bobby stared at the last picture. The man looked slightly familiar. Bobby couldn't place him. Probably just a coincidence.

An inventory list of what looked like items to be exported or imported, clocks, toys, typewriters. Nothing unusual.

A to-do list:
-buy bread
-fix car brakes
-dispose—Bobby couldn't make out the rest of this line; whatever had been here was crossed out so many times there was no trace of it left.
-renew life insurance policy
-7 Seas
-Apollo
-brad bl
-storehouse
-Hans: 211

-ML

-present for Laurie—don't forget!!!

The list made Bobby's head spin. So many things. ML—Margaret Lane? Who was Laurie? The 7 Seas—did that refer to the restaurant on Hollywood Boulevard? The Apollo—where Dietrich died and where Leach hung his hat. And who was Brad? What about Dietrich at 211—was that a time 2:11, a date, February 11th? And what about that line that started out *dispose*, with the rest crossed out? The list gave Bobby more questions than answers. He turned back to the contents of the case.

What looked like the remnants of a saltine cracker.

A small, tightly sealed bottle of some kind of liquid.

Maps of Los Angeles, western Los Angeles, central, southern, eastern. Long Beach. The guy wanted to know where he was going—as did Bobby.

And a single key on a chain with a rabbit's foot.

The rest of the case was filled with the things you'd expect, pens, pencils, note paper, loose paperclips. Nothing out of the ordinary.

Bobby didn't want to go back to the stack of rubber-banded pictures but he did. Each one was more unpleasant than the one before it. At the bottom of the pile were pictures of Germans—officers?—smiling, laughing. Most taken in what appeared to be offices, with secretaries and typewriters, filing cabinets and the other things one would find in an office.

Bobby put everything back in the case. Closed it, surprised the latch still held after the way he had popped it open. What did it all mean? And what was an enlarger? He stared out across the San Fernando Valley, with its orange groves, ranches and farms, and a few streets of homes and businesses dotted here and there.

Europe was to the east, ten thousand miles away. Bobby imagined he could see all the way to Europe and Germany.

* * *

Time ticked by slowly. Bobby wondered if it ticked by as slowly for the soldiers and sailors in the European and Pacific theaters of war. After an hour of sitting and staring and thinking, he still had no idea what, if anything, the things in the briefcase had to do with the deaths of Thomas and Dietrich. Thomas' murder seemed like a gangland killing. He didn't know what to make of Dietrich's unusual end.

He packed everything in the car, headed for Malibu. Nicolai wasn't at the sheriff's station. Bobby drove up the road to his beachside apartment. No Nicolai. Driving up Pacific Coast Highway, heading for home, he passed the Shark's Tooth, yanked the wheel hard, swerving into the lot. Dark and cool inside, with Frank Sinatra coming from the juke. Bobby found Nicolai at the bar. Not drinking. Instead of handing money over, money was being shoved in his hand.

Nicolai looked up.

"Oh shit."

Bobby left two stools between him and the sergeant. Nicolai pocketed the dough, slid down the bar.

"Don't look so wide-eyed, kid."

"You're on the take—is that what they call it?"

"That's what they call it." Nicolai lit up. Puffed perfectly round smoke rings into the air. "Everybody does it."

"Doesn't make it right."

"Hell, what's right and wrong anyway?"

"If you think that way, why be a cop?"

Nicolai exhaled. "Good question. Now what're you doing here?"

"Do you keep all the money? How many places—"

"What does it matter?"

"I just want to know how the world works."

"Read the papers."

Bobby didn't respond. Didn't light up. Declined a drink when the barkeep offered.

"Don't be so disillusioned, kid. Grow up."

"I'm working on it."

"Good. You wanna know how it works. I hang around a joint like this, bad guys see cops around, they don't come, not often anyway. I keep half and give the other half—" Rather than finish, Nicolai sucked in smoke.

"To who?"

"What the hell? To Leach. Leach runs half this town. Good name for a bloodsucker, don't you think?"

"I guess everybody's a bloodsucker in their own way."

"Guess so."

Bobby turned to the bartender, "I'll have that drink now. Scotch."

The barman nodded.

"So Leach told you to back off the James Christmas case?"

"Told me to go easy. He wants to get his gambling boat open again. Sooner more than later. And he's not the only one."

"The brass?"

"It doesn't matter, kid. There's nowhere to go with it. You're still trying, though, huh?"

Bobby nodded. The bartender set Bobby's scotch on the long, scarred bar. Bobby took out his wallet. Nicholai nodded. "Drink's on the house," the bartender said. Nicholai wouldn't let Bobby protest.

"You came here for something and now, now you're disillusioned with me. I'll help you if I can."

"And go straight to Leach with whatever I tell you."

"No, kid. I collect his protection money from the happy businessmen. I get free drinks or free burgers and whatnot. But he doesn't own me."

"That's not the way it is in the movies."

"This ain't the movies."

"I wish I could trust you."

CHAPTER TWENTY-ONE

Bobby could feel the sand creep into his shoes and between his toes as he and Nicolai walked on the beach. They settled at a splintery wooden picnic table. Bobby opened Thomas' briefcase, slid it across to Nicolai. He trusted Nicolai as much as he trusted anyone—he had no one else he could trust, so he might as well trust the sergeant. He was learning that you had to temper that trust with vigilance.

Bobby filled Nicolai in on how he got the briefcase and Thomas getting shot.

"You must want that job with Booker's band awfully bad."

"I did. I'm not sure anymore. That aside, this case's gotten under my skin. I want to find out what's going on because *I* want to find out."

"Ever thought about becoming a cop?"

"I don't think I could pass the physical."

"You look fit enough to me."

"I'm not tall enough, besides I've got hidden obstacles." Bobby hoped Nicolai would leave it at that.

"Well, let's see what we have here." Nicolai rummaged through the case. "Looks like the usual stuff."

"Look at the pictures." Bobby had set them in the case face down. He watched Nicolai's eyes grow wide, then narrow to slits.

"Jesus!"

"Do you know what they are?"

"Can't say for sure, but my guess would be they're from

those concentration camps the Germans have. I don't know much about them, but I've heard mention of them."

"How can one person do that to another?"

"That's not so hard to figure. Man's been doing it for a million years. Ain't never gonna change. The question for us right now is why the hell does an ordinary businessman have pictures like these in his briefcase?"

"Maybe he's not an ordinary businessman." Bobby fumbled for a Viceroy. Tried to light it. The onshore wind blew out his lighter. He cupped both in his hand, finally got it going. "Do you think the pictures have anything to do with Dietrich's death?"

"Think about it, kid."

"Dietrich's German. These are pictures of German concentration camps. There's got to be some connection."

"I'd say so." Nicolai scrutinized the pictures more closely. "Some are indoors. Some are out. They're all pretty disgusting. But what do they have in common?"

"They're all from concentration camps."

"What else?"

"I, I'm not sure." Bobby tried blowing a smoke ring. It came out a formless blob.

"I think we need to look at them closely to see."

"What about the rest of the stuff in the briefcase?"

"We need to look at that too." Nicolai ran his fingers over the case's alligator leather. Fanned the photos on the table, placed his handcuffs on them to keep them from blowing away.

"I thought you were off the case?"

"I am. But I'll help you as much as I can."

"Teach me the ropes of being a detective? I'd like that, Sergeant. Should I turn the case over to the Los Angeles Police?"

"You can if you want. But it'll get quashed just like it did at the sheriff's."

"So why, Sergeant? Why do you let them quash it? Why do you follow their BS orders?" Bobby glared. "Why are you—I'm sorry to say it straight out—on the take?"

Nicolai thought a moment. He moved his hand to rub his chin; Bobby was afraid he might swing on him. Instead he said, "I've been humbled by life, kid. It doesn't compromise my job...much."

"Why'd you become a cop in the first place?"

"What's the point? Let's get back to the stuff in the case."

"So Leach, the sheriff, the chief of police, they're doing the quashing? Why do they care?"

"I suspect they each have their reasons and they might not all be the same. You know why Leach wants it hushed up, business. And the cops, both departments, they got a colored boy for it, they're happy, don't want to waste the manpower. Don't worry about it, we'll do an end run and figure it out. Let the big wigs think they've got it under control."

"Whatever *it* is." Bobby watched a seagull dive for food in the ocean. If only it was that easy.

"Exactly."

Bobby finished his cigarette. Pulled out another Viceroy, cupped it in his palm. Flicked the lighter at it. It wouldn't catch. Too much damn wind. He tried again. No go.

Nicolai took the cigarette from him. "Like this," he said. He pulled two matches out of a matchbook, holding them very close to each other. Cupped his hands. Struck the first match. The second match ignited a split-second after the first. He lit the cigarette, took a puff and handed it to Bobby. "The two matches give you a long enough time to get the butt lit before the wind blows the flames out."

Bobby took the cigarette, inhaled. "Learn something new."

"First thing we need to find out is who's in these pictures with Thomas. But I'm thinking the real key is in the concentration camp photos." Nicolai thumbed the snapshots.

"Why?"

"Because there's so damn many of them. You don't have this many pictures of the same thing for no reason. And how the hell did he get them? This ain't the kind of thing the German govern-

175

ment is putting out to show the world what nice guys they are."

"Maybe it's not *in* the photos, just the idea of them or the camps?"

"Could be. On the other hand, lots of people are pissed off that Roosevelt won't bomb the tracks leading to the camps. Maybe it has to do with that."

"Or remember, there was that ship of German Jews came to Florida fleeing the Nazis, and Roosevelt and the State Department refused them entry." Bobby dragged on his Viceroy.

"Yeah-yeah. Nineteen thirty-nine I think it was."

"The St. Louis. The boat was the St. Louis. Sent them back to Europe and eventually a lot of the passengers ended up in concentration camps."

"Camps a lot of people don't believe exist."

"Maybe the pics are just to show us that it's real. Like you said lotta people don't believe it's happening."

Nicolai grabbed his handkerchief, pulled every item from the briefcase. "What's wrong, kid? Your expression says you just ate mom's apple pie before she could serve it at Thanksgiving."

"I, I didn't use a handkerchief. My fingerprints must be all over everything. Maybe even covering up other ones we might need."

"Don't worry. We're not sending this out to the FBI laboratory, at least not yet. But yeah, let's be a little more careful with this stuff from now on."

Nicolai picked up the rabbit's foot.

"What do you think he has that for?" Bobby asked.

"If you were worried about concentration camps, you'd carry a rabbit's foot too."

"I don't think a rabbit's foot will protect you from Nazis."

They spent forty minutes going through the case. Examining every object.

"Nothing jumps out at me, kid. Except for the stack of concentration camp pictures, it's all the normal stuff a businessman might have. Of course maybe something that looks innocent isn't quite."

"What about the to-do list?"

"Some normal items, buy bread, fix the brakes. Some questionable, 'dispose'—what'd he want to dispose of? So here's what you do, you track down who the people in the personal pictures are. There's a laundry list—you check out his laundry. There's seven keys, figure out what they're to. That kind of thing. First you have to figure out what the questions are—like what is the 7 Seas—then you can figure out the answers."

"Sounds impossible." Bobby tried blowing out a smoke ring again. The wind obliterated it before it could form. Nicolai cracked a smile. "What's in the bottle?"

"I've been wondering that myself. Kind of wary about opening it up."

"You don't think it's nitroglycerin do you?"

"You watch too many movies, kid."

"Probably."

Nicolai slowly twisted the bottle top off. Sniffed. He screwed up his nose. Passed it to Bobby, who sniffed it and could taste the acrid vinegar on his tongue as well as smell it.

"Smells like vinegar. What is it?"

"It's not vinegar and it's not nitro. Other than that, I'm not sure, kid. But don't drink it." Nicolai screwed the cap back on. Slipped the bottle in his pocket.

"You're taking it?"

"I'll have the lab boys do me a favor. Call you when I find out what it is."

"Thanks, Sarge."

"Listen, the keys are probably to the normal things: house, key to the office, maybe to a desk in the office—now there's a good place to look. Maybe a key to his folks' house. Car keys. Seven ain't very much. And you can start eliminating—"

"Yeah, but if I try to use one to go into his office or house and someone sees they might call the cops."

"Chance you gotta take if you want to be a good detective,

y'know, like that gumshoe in those novels by Raymond Chandler. I like him. He's pretty good for an amateur."

"Chandler or his gumshoe?"

"Both. Chandler's a good writer. The gumshoe, Marlowe's a good private dick. You might read one some time."

"I'd think you'd have enough with detecting in your job."

"Yeah, but in my job sometimes the bad guys get away with it. With Chandler and Marlowe they get caught and everything gets wrapped up nice and neat. Makes for a pretty universe, unlike the real thing." He slapped his hand down on the stack of concentration camp photos. "Wish he'd write another one already."

"Sergeant, what's an en-enlarger?"

Nicolai scratched his five o'clock shadow. "I think they use them in film labs."

"Like movie films?"

"No, still pictures. Photographs. To blow up pictures."

"Like the ones in Thomas' briefcase."

"Could be. Where'd you hear about enlargers?"

"Thomas has one in his house."

"I'd follow up on everything in the case, especially those pictures." Nicolai gazed out to the ocean—what did he see? "Wanna come in for a beer?" Nicolai invited Bobby into the Shark's Tooth. It was like being invited into his house.

"I really want to get started tracking down these clues." Bobby shut the briefcase, turned the locks as best he could.

"Be careful. Two people are dead already. And one's missing."

"My mother would tell me to forget it altogether."

"I ain't your mother." Nicolai saluted Bobby, strode through the swinging doors of the Shark's Tooth the way a sheriff in a Hopalong Cassidy Western would.

The wind died down. Bobby tried again, blowing the perfect smoke ring. No one around to see it. He flicked the butt to the sand, swung the briefcase onto the passenger seat, and followed it into his car.

He floored the gas pedal, pushing the Olds up Sunset, toward town. Two women, decked out in riding costumes, rode stunning Arabian horses along the bridal path in the center of the road. There were plenty of leads to follow in the briefcase and it looked like Bobby would be on his own. Nicolai would coach from the sidelines. Bobby liked that—he wanted to do this on his own. Not for Booker. Not to have a spot in the band. Not even to help James Christmas. He just wanted to do something good on his own and if it helped in those other arenas so much the better.

His immediate problem was finding a place to live. He only had two days left in his apartment.

Bobby's eyes widened, blood pounded his temples. He had a slow fuse, but it was about to explode as he pulled up in front of his apartment building or should he say Mrs. Hazelton's building? His clothes, his photo albums and yearbooks, his sheet music, even his underwear was piled high on the sidewalk. The damn bitch hadn't even waited the two days he was still entitled to. Bobby stormed past the wreckage of his life like the marines storming ashore at Guadalcanal. He sprinted to his apartment, slipped the key in the door.

"Criminy, the bitch changed the locks."

Bobby took a step back, raised his leg, kicking it into the door with a loud crash that brought Mrs. Hazelton out of her nest.

"What's going on here?"

"You locked me out of my apartment."

"It's my right."

"You gave me three days. Besides, I didn't do anything worthy of getting evicted anyway."

"You can't go in there."

"Stop me."

"Fresh! I'll call the cops."

Bobby glared. "Why don't you call whoever gave you the money to kick me out?"

"What money—what're you talking about?"

"The money in the envelope. I saw it."

"You're crazy. In fact you're worse than crazy, you're a degenerate; I found women's clothes in your apartment. You know having women over is against my rules. And how come you're not in the army?"

"How come you're such a bitch?"

"How dare you!"

Bobby about-faced, walked through the busted door into his apartment—his former apartment. Even if she'd let him, even if she paid him, he wouldn't live here anymore. He searched the apartment, grabbing anything the bitch hadn't put on the street. He stuffed everything into a couple of pillowcases, then pounded his way down the hall. The bitch stood rigid by the front door to his place.

The phone in Bobby's apartment rang. He thought about walking on, screw whoever it was. Decided to go back.

"Hello." He surveyed the wreckage of his apartment—his life. "Yes, hi David. I'm glad you caught me 'cause I won't be at this number any longer."

The bitch watched from the door. Bobby tried to talk in a voice somewhere between his male and female tones. He hoped David wouldn't notice. He didn't care what the bitch thought now. Or maybe he did because he tried to keep his side of the conversation discreet. He hung up the phone, yanked the cord out of the wall. Pushed past the bitch back into the hallway.

He briefly considered asking her—or beating it out of her—who had given her the money. Who had hastened his departure from his home? He wouldn't give the bitch the satisfaction. He was too proud.

She puffed up as he walked by. He stopped. Looked her in the eye. She wasn't about to give ground, wasn't about to retreat into her lair.

Bobby stared her down.

Her eyes showed nothing but contempt. Bobby slapped her

in the face. Paused, while it registered and her skin turned pink.

"How dare you?" she said again. "You're certainly no gentleman, Mr. Saxon."

Bobby grinned and walked out. He piled his things in the car and drove off quietly, somehow content. Even happy.

CHAPTER TWENTY-TWO

Bobby parked on the street. He had driven by this house several times in the last few days. He'd been chasing after bad guys and killers, but he hadn't had the courage to walk up this walkway. He inhaled deeply, steadying his nerves, crossed the street, and headed to the front door. He could have used his key—he didn't think they had changed the locks. Instead, he rang the bell.

The seconds dragged on. He looked at his watch. Bobby pivoted on his heel to leave. He heard humming—"Long Ago and Far Away"—and footsteps on the tile floor inside. He turned to face his mother in the open doorway. She hadn't changed. Same permed hair. Same sad eyes, which she tried to pump up into happy eyes, but that only made them look all the more sad. Same smile lines, or were they frown and crying lines? Guilt surged through his body because he wanted them to be crying lines—crying for the loss of her relationship with him.

"Roberta."

Awkward silence bounced off the walls. Bobbie didn't look much like a Roberta today in his double-breasted suit, hat, and Florsheims, but his mother still called him Roberta. He could have corrected her. She looked so sweet and innocent that he couldn't do it.

"Hi Mom."

"It's nice to see you, dear." Emily drank in Bobby's male attire, hair, his look. Said nothing.

"I'm sure, Mother."

"It is, really." Emily pulled Bobby inside, hugged him close. Bobby wanted to sink into his mom's bosom and just hide from the world there. He knew that was impossible. But it felt good for the moment. He wondered what his mother was thinking. He felt a tear form in the corner of his eye. Willed himself not to let it fall. They unclenched. He couldn't read his mother's expression. Her face had that imperturbable look that she put on when she didn't want people to know what she was thinking. But Bobby could usually figure it out.

"You're looking good, dear. Would you like some tea—do you still drink tea, it's been such a long time I'm not sure."

"Tea is fine."

The kitchen looked the same. Light, cheery curtains blowing on the soft breeze. Optimistic yellow paint that looked fresh. The smell of roast turkey in the oven; you'd never know there was a war on except for the radio ringing out war news between songs, many of those about longing for the people who were away doing the fighting. Emily filled the kettle, set it on the stove.

"So, darling, how are things going?"

"They could be better." Bobby fidgeted with the salt and pepper shakers on the table.

"Hmm," is all Emily said. Her eyes said a lot more, taking in Bobby from head to toe. He knew that his mother still saw Roberta and only Roberta, despite how Bobby looked or dressed on the outside. His cheeks and ears burned.

Why had he come here?

"What's wrong? Work not going well?"

"I got a gig with the Booker 'Boom-Boom' Taylor Orchestra—a big band."

"I'm sorry, dear, I'm not familiar with them. I do like Guy Lombardo though."

"Yes, I know. Booker's is a hot swing band."

"Booker? Are they colored?" Emily's voice was measured. Her eyes squinted almost imperceptibly. Bobby knew what that meant.

"It's a good gig, pays well." Bobby wished. "I'm sort of on a provisional basis. If things work out, they'll take me on permanently."

"Oh my. How will you travel with them? Most bands travel, don't they?"

"I—I'm not sure. I haven't got that worked out yet. But right now it doesn't matter. We were playing a gig on that gambling boat, the Apollo—"

"I've heard of it. Didn't that man die there?"

"Yes."

"Now I remember. They suspect someone in your band of the murder, don't they?"

"Yes, and Booker, the band leader, has me investigating that. He doesn't think James is the killer."

"That's what everyone says about the people they know, dear."

"I know."

Emily poured tea into the Fire-King Jadeite cups that Bobby remembered so well. "Are you sure this is what you want, dear?"

"All I've ever wanted to do was play music."

"I know, but this—" she said, gesturing toward Bobby's outfit. "Why do you do it?"

"This is who I am, Mother."

"But you're a girl. I don't care so much, you know that. But society, other people. I think you're just asking to be hurt."

Bobby rubbed the lingering bruise on his chin, sipped his tea, mainly to avoid having to respond. He changed the subject. "How are Tommy and Johnny?"

"Your brothers are fine. Tommy enlisted in the marines." Emily's voice cracked ever so slightly.

"Good for him. I wish I could."

"And John-John's going to enlist in the navy. He wants to fly airplanes off ships, imagine that."

"He's too young."

"He wants our permission. They'll take him if we sign."

"What're you going to do?"

"I don't know. Isn't giving one son to the war enough?"

"What does dad want to do?" Bobby said.

"He's ready to sign. He thinks it will make John-John grow up."

That sounded like Bobby's father. "What do you think?"

"I don't know. He wants to serve his country. Who am I to say no?"

"I wish I could join the marines," Bobby reiterated.

"I think you'd make a better soldier than John-John."

"I'm not sure if that's a compliment or not, but I'll take it as one." Bobby sipped his tea. It was on the bitter side. "I need help, Mom."

"What kind of help?"

"I just got evicted from my apartment."

"Because of...this—" Emily pointed at Bobby's attire again.

"No. Because Booker came to see me."

"A colored man? Well, no wonder."

"You're better than that, Mom."

"I guess maybe I'm not, dear." Emily sighed with resignation.

"I need a place to stay. Just till I can get back on my feet."

Emily's face wrinkled up, showing those frown lines. "He won't like it. Not if you insist on, on being this way."

"Don't you have a say?"

"Your father is the king of his castle. You know how he feels about your—your dressing or whatever you call it. He's constantly complaining about that woman we hired to teach you piano—blames her for everything. That's when he'll talk about it at all."

"Don't you mean when he'll talk about me at all? And she didn't make me this way."

"Your father's not a bad man. He's just—"

"What about Tom and John?"

"They'll always love you. You'll always be their big sister to

185

them."

"And what will I be to you?"

"You're my daughter, Roberta. My daughter who I love."

Bobby stifled back a sob. "When will they be home?"

"The boys are at a movie, but your father will be home for dinner. Soon." She looked at her watch. "I—You—"

"You don't have to say it. I'm leaving. Tell Tommy and John that I wish them luck. Wish I could join them."

"I will."

Emily closed in on her *daughter*, hugging her tight. She blinked, quickly covering for the tears that were starting to form.

"Do you need any money? I can help you with that."

"I'll see myself out." Bobby needed the money. He wasn't about to take it from his family if he wasn't good enough to spend a few days at home.

Emily collapsed onto her chair, picked up her cup of tea. It was as good a place to hide as any Bobby supposed.

On his way out, he paused under the high living room arch, peeked in. Saw the piano where *that woman* had taught Bobby to play. Saw the family photos bedecking the piano and mantle. One big, happy family. Smiling mother. Beaming father. Two sons. And a daughter.

How many other families lived in pain under the smiles and Norman Rockwell normalcy they presented to the world? Did he really hear his mother sobbing softly before he left or was it all in his head?

Bobby walked across the street to his car. Two boys that he recognized as living on the block, whom he'd babysat for, sat on a low brick wall. He hoped they wouldn't recognize him, though he was sure they knew all about him. Somehow the whole neighborhood seemed to.

"Agfay," the first boy said in Pig Latin.

"Dyke," said the second boy.

Bobby turned toward them, staring them straight in the eyes.

They stood. They were about Bobby's height, though probably not done growing. Bobby quick-stepped right up to them. He spread his legs, clenched his fists, ready to fight. They might have been stockier, but he'd had enough crap for one lousy day.

"Ooh, I'm scared," said the first boy.

They stared at each other for several seconds, or several minutes, or maybe a lifetime.

"You're not worth it." Bobby turned, heading back to his car. Turned to face the boys again. He tossed them a quarter. "Go down to East L.A. and get a blow job—assuming they can find your little peckers."

"At least I have one."

Bobby wasn't going to give them the satisfaction of reacting. He slowly, deliberately walked to his car, his words to Emily echoing in his head: *This is who I am, Mother.*

He got in the car, not glancing back at the boys, though he could feel their presence a few yards away in the hairs standing up on the back of his neck. He took out his keys, made himself comfortable. Started the engine.

He drove by another car whipping its way toward him on the opposite side of the street. He saluted the other driver, who stared straight ahead, completely oblivious to Bobby.

"So long, Dad," Bobby said.

CHAPTER TWENTY-THREE

Bobby absent-mindedly stopped for gas, as he reflected on the call from David Chambers. David had asked him—her—out again. Why did that excite her so?

He didn't want to break his few lowly bills, so he fished in his pocket coming up with two bits. With that he could buy two and a half gallons of gas, glad today was his ration day 'cause he was running on empty. Where now? He had no place to sleep or hang his hat. He could have gone to a movie. Instead he drove up to Pickwick Books on Hollywood Boulevard, a three-story emporium of books. Bobby walked the length of the store, stopping every now and then to check out a book or a customer. He had the pleasure of checking out both men and women.

He walked to the second and third levels and back to the first. He found the book he was looking for, Thomas Wolfe's *You Can't Go Home Again*. He didn't really know if it was the right book in terms of content, but the title said everything to him. He took the book to the counter.

Bobby stared at a substantial, dark-haired man looking at books on magic. He looked familiar.

"Orson Welles," the salesman whispered.

"What?"

"That's Orson Welles, you know, Mercury Theatre, *War of the Worlds*, *Citizen Kane*. Don't stare."

Bobby looked away.

The clerk looked at the book Bobby had set on the counter.

"Thomas Wolfe. No, you certainly can't go home again."

"Neither you nor me."

The clerk finished wrapping Bobby's book in brown paper, tied it with string. He handed it to Bobby with a wink. "Here's your change."

Bobby nodded, walked into the glaring sunshine of Hollywood Boulevard. Except for the rationing stickers on car windshields, he would hardly have known there was a war on. He walked up the Boulevard to Musso and Frank Grille. Not a lot of money in his wallet, but why not splurge? Hell could freeze over tonight, the Japs could bomb L.A., but Bobby would go out on a full stomach. He noticed two men in overcoats, hats pulled low over their foreheads. FBI? Or maybe Leach's goons—what would they be doing here?

Midafternoon, plenty of empty tables. That didn't mean the service was particularly good. Bobby looked at the "Buy War Bonds" posters on the walls and thumbed through Thomas Wolfe, while waiting for his lamb chops.

He devoured everything on his plate, reached into his pockets. Seeing a piano in the corner he had another idea. He approached the maître d'—asked if he could play for his supper.

"You crazy, bud?"

Maybe Bobby was. Crazy enough to have talked the maître d' into it. Every penny saved was, well, a penny saved.

Bobby came out of Musso's, spotted the two FBI men leaning on a car. *They must be after some German spy.* If nothing else, Bobby had a great imagination. Bobby walked to his car. The sun hid behind theaters and buildings on the boulevard throwing sharp, elongated shadows across the sidewalk. The men fell in behind him. Was it coincidence? Bobby stepped into the street. A brawny hand grabbed him, driving him down into the dirty water flowing in the gutter. He put his hand out, trying to get up. The man shoved him back down, soaking his pant legs. The Wolfe book slipped from his hands, splashing into the foul gutter water. The other man just watched with the slightest of smirks on his face.

"What do you want? I don't have any money." Bobby tried to reach for his wallet.

The man grabbed Bobby's arm, yanked him up, slugged him in the gut. Bobby exhaled more wind than he thought he could hold. The man rammed Bobby into the Olds' fat fender, doubling the wind-sucking effect on him. Bobby bounced back, kneed him in the groin.

"Shit, you little fuck," the man grunted as he fell to his knees. Bobby tried to run. The second man caught him.

"Take it like a man, you little shit."

The first man held him, while the second man pounded him until he couldn't take it anymore and slumped back to the filthy gutter. He looked around. Pedestrians scurried by, barely noticing the scuffle in the street.

The men let go of Bobby. If not for the fender of his car, he would have crumpled into a pile right on Hollywood Boulevard.

"Mind your own fucking business," smirk said.

The men walked off, laughing. All in a good day's work. Bobby looked up, the men were gone; he saw the cartoon-like drawing of Kilroy staring down at him from the wall of Pickwick Books. He pulled himself up, tried to catch a glimpse of their car as they sped off, got a little of their license plate. Was it the same car that was at Mrs. Hazelton's? His head was too filled with stars to tell. He leaned on his car, surveyed his torn suit, his scraped-up shoes, his scratched and cut hands and arms. He didn't even want to think what his face might look like. He sucked in air. It felt like a cannonball had whomped his solar plexus. He looked down, saw his book in the gutter—soaked through. He picked it up, shook it off. He groped his way around the car to the driver's door, opened it, and collapsed on the seat.

"Autry wouldn't cry—and neither will I," he muttered. He sat there for ten, maybe fifteen, minutes before he turned the ignition. But he never looked in the rearview mirror to see his face.

* * *

There's nothing as dark and lonely as a nightclub during the day, but the darkness of the Alabam felt good to Bobby. He didn't know where else to go. He couldn't go home; could have gone to Marion's. Nah. So here he was.

A young dude sat noodling at the piano, playing a bluesy ditty. Not a complete song, something he was trying to work out, get the music down and the lyrics to go with it.

Bobby leaned on the bar. That only made his bruised stomach ache more. Lawrence nodded, brought him a drink. Something bitter and alcoholic. Bobby didn't care. It tasted good. He downed it in two gulps.

"Here man, have some more. Looks like you could use this." Lawrence filled the glass again.

"Thanks, Lawrence." He knew he looked like a mess. He could see his face in the mirror behind the bar—the streaks of dried blood, the slightly closed left eye. Luckily no cauliflower ear.

"Looks like you got run over by a train."

Bobby didn't have the strength to respond. Lawrence nodded, walked to the far end of the bar. Bobby watched him dial the phone. He caught a snatch of the piano man's lyrics.

The blues don't care who's got 'em,
The blues don't care who cries,
And the nights don't care who's lonely,
Or whose tears are in whose eyes.

The guy tried various combinations of words, but he kept coming back to these. Bobby got lost in the music and the alcohol. His gut didn't hurt quite so much.

"Bobby," Booker yelled, coming through the front door, his voice echoing in the near-empty room. "What happened to you, man? You look all in."

"I ran into a wall."

"Looks like a five-fisted wall to me, or maybe a brass knuckle wall. Cops?"

"I don't think so."

"Something to do with James?"

Lawrence brought Booker a drink, as Bobby and Booker lit up at the same time.

"Yes, no, I'm not sure." Bobby exhaled a plume of smoke. "I don't know, Leach maybe. Stinson. The guys who shot Thomas."

"Whoa! Shot Thomas—who's Thomas?"

"Dietrich's partner." Bobby filled Booker in.

"Maybe this means you're getting close to something."

"Too close." Bobby lit up again, even though he'd barely smoked the first butt. "Too close and I still don't know a whole lot more than when I started."

"You know. You just need to put it all together."

"I can't. I don't even have a place to stay. I can't think about it now."

"Whatd'ya mean?" Booker inhaled. Exhaled. "Maybe I shouldn't put all this on you. You're just a kid, white kid at that. Don't know about the mean streets."

"I'm not a quitter, Booker. I never quit anything in my life."

"What're you talking about, you don't have a place to stay?" Booker changed the subject back.

"I got evicted."

"It's all those wild parties you young white boys are having. Your landlady's just jealous 'cause you don't invite her."

"Yeah, the parties. Jealous. Yeah. She really didn't like the guests."

Booker's eyes narrowed. "Me?"

Bobby's look must have registered on him.

"You got evicted 'cause of me? 'Cause I went to your lily-white, all-cracker neighborhood."

Bobby wasn't sure how to respond. He didn't want to hurt Booker's feelings. Maybe if he was a real man he wouldn't care. But he did. On the other hand, he wanted to strangle Booker. Bobby's whole life was like a hurricane ever since that first night with the Booker Boom-Boom Taylor Orchestra. And now he had no home. No job. Was Booker just leading him on, playing him like the note said? He said nothing.

"We'll find you a place. Maybe you can book with one-a the band."

"I need a place by myself."

"Don't wanna room with no *nigger*?"

Bobby couldn't tell if Booker was serious or not. "It's not that. I just need privacy. It's been a hell of a week."

"Like that all the time for a black man."

"I'll find a place on my own."

"You got kicked outta your place on my account. I'll get you a place to hang your hat till you're back on your feet."

"Thanks, Booker."

"I know things ain't swingin' your way, but stick with the case. Think about it. Put the pieces of the puzzle together."

"It's like mercury."

"Mercury?"

"Yeah, the case, it's silver and shiny and slides and glides all over the place. And when you try to *catch* it, it splinters into a thousand little pieces and then you have to catch each of them. And then they splinter—" Bobby sucked deep on his cig. "And I don't think my white skin is helping me get anywhere."

"I bet if we knew who beat on you, we'd know something."

"I can't make it work. Every lead I follow ends up a dead end—literally. Lois is missing and probably dead. And now Thomas is dead."

"I'm beginning to think you're right, Bobby. It's all just mercury slipping through our hands."

"Mercury," Bobby said. It came to him in a flash.

"Yeah, mercury. Slippery. The case—"

"—No, Mercury!"

"I think that knuckle sandwich you got shook some screws loose."

"Booker, their car was a Mercury, the guys who beat me

up—so was the shooters' car at Thomas'. A late model Merc. So I have that and part of the plates. I can have my friend at the sheriff's run it."

Bobby's head cleared; he remembered the car well. He knew part of the license. He might be able to get help from Nicolai with that. And now it came back to him. The car on Hollywood Boulevard was the same car the man had driven off from Mrs. Hazelton's after she evicted him. Had they given her the envelope with the money? Who were they working for? His blood pounded through his veins. He could go back to Mrs. Hazelton and put the fear of God in her. Or he could tell Booker everything and imagine Booker and several large Negroes going to put the fear of God in her and get her to tell everything she knew.

Booker put his arm on Bobby's shoulder. "You want a doc?"

"Nah, I'm okay. Looks worse than it is." Bobby wasn't sure about that.

"Okay, now let's get you a place to get your beauty sleep. 'Cause I want my boys to look right pretty when they're up there onstage." Booker stood.

"Any idea when we'll start giggin' again? I might have to take a square job in the meantime."

"I know you, Bobby, you'd die in a square job."

"I'm starting to think I might die in this job."

"The music's in your blood. The Apollo's still on ice, meanwhile I'm trying to find some gigs till we can get back to the Alabam. Now let's skidoo."

Booker helped Bobby off the barstool. "I'm okay, Booker. Really."

They headed for the door.

"Who's that guy?" Bobby whispered, pointing at the dude at the piano.

"Vic Abrams. From New York, I think. Likes to come in and tickle the ivories when he's in town sometimes."

They headed out the door to another refrain from Abrams' song.

When someone's heart is broken,
The blues are not to blame,
'Cause the blues don't care who's got 'em,
So they just added my name.

CHAPTER TWENTY-FOUR

"The Dunbar?"

Booker walked Bobby to the squat four-story brick building next door to the Alabam. The Dunbar Hotel was *the* place for colored royalty to stay in segregated Los Angeles. Duke Ellington kept a suite there. Everyone who was anyone in the black community stayed there one time or another.

"I, I can't stay here."

"Why not?"

"They won't let me. They don't have whites—do they?"

"Oh, you mean the Dunbar's segregated like the rest of L.A.? Well, I hate to disappoint you but you won't be the first honky staying here. That honor goes to W.C. Fields. Won't be easy to get you a room, but I know people and people owe me favors."

Bobby didn't think he wanted to know what kind of favors. They went through the double doors and Bobby knew he was in another world. It wasn't a world totally foreign to him. He'd been hanging around the Alabam and other clubs on Central for some time. He was comfortable around colored people, but not necessarily when he was the only non-colored. Bobby had never been inside the Dunbar before, considering it off limits. He figured that, just as whites wanted their places to themselves, coloreds did too. It was different at the clubs, but this was more intimate. People lived here, slept here, made love here. Bobby felt out of his element, surrounded by the art deco lobby, Spanish arcade windows, and tile floors, and a lot of colored folk. Booker nudged him toward the front desk.

"Wait here," Booker said. He turned to the desk clerk, nodded; walked behind the counter and disappeared. Bobby felt several sets of eyes staring at him.

Booker came out a few minutes later, laughing, smiling. All that turned to concern when he saw Bobby's face. "What's the matter, you look like you seen a ghost."

"No ghost, just Cab Calloway and Billie Holiday. Jee-zus!"

"Maybe I'll introduce you some day. Right now you need to get up to your room and get a bath and some sleep."

They went up to the room. Bobby looked around. "Looks like the last guest hasn't left yet," he said.

"The last guest don't have no use for this room at the moment—he's in the county jail."

"James? This is James' room?"

Booker grinned. "Sweet irony, isn't it?"

"Yeah, real sweet." Bobby checked out the room. A huge poster of Marcus Garvey in full pseudo-military regalia nearly took up one entire wall. It made sense to Bobby that James would have a picture of the recently deceased leader of the Pan-African movement.

"Ain't all bad. You're close to the club. Got some room service even. Just keep working the case." Booker peeled a couple of sawbucks off a stack of bills. "This enough?"

"It'll help. That's for sure."

"And be glad you got a bath. Not all the rooms have them."

"I saw the sign. *115 rooms, 75 with bath.*"

"What I said. You're a lucky man."

Bobby wasn't sure about that. He guessed maybe he was as he lay down in the tub to soak after Booker left. Had Josephine Baker or Lena Horne sat in this very tub? He couldn't help but notice the purple bruises on his stomach. He was glad they hadn't hit him in the breasts. He would have been more glad if they hadn't hit him at all.

Bobby fell asleep in the tub. He woke, starving, to jivin'

sounds from the Alabam next door. He figured he'd have to put on his torn suit to go down and get his things from the car. They were sitting in the bedroom with a note from Booker saying he had the bellboy bring them up. Bobby's whole life to this point had barely filled his car up and now it was spread on the floor before him. The note also told Bobby not to worry about tipping or charging meals with room service or in the restaurant. And it reminded him, gently, that James was rotting in jail.

Bobby felt too uncomfortable to go down to the in-house restaurant. Why was it that he always felt out of place wherever he was, whoever he was with? Bobby just wanted one place to call home. One group of people to call family. One good friend. Right now he had none of that.

He ordered room service, dressed in a fresh shirt and slacks, and waited. He explored James' room, feeling like the ultimate voyeur. A stack of *California Eagle* papers as tall as the dresser stood in the corner. Next to it a stack of Marcus Garvey's *Negro World* and *Blackman* newspapers. Several Good Humor wrappers were left on the bureau. Reeds for James' sax, but no sign of the sax itself. In a small, wooden box were several hand-rolled cigarettes. Nothing unusual. A lot of people still rolled their own. Or were these reefer? Bobby picked one up, sniffed. Reefer, definitely. Several pieces of Double Bubble gum, two Sky Bars, and a handful of Tootsie Rolls. Bobby popped one in his mouth. He was starving.

A bottle of Pluto Water stood out. Bobby chuckled as he read the slogan for "America's Laxative" on the bottle: *When Nature Won't, PLUTO Will.* Bobby had heard it was Louis Armstrong's favorite laxative. James was in good company.

A soft knock on the door startled Bobby—room service. The porter laid the food out on the table. Bobby started to pull money from his jacket.

"That's all been taken care of, sir."

"Thank you."

Bobby enjoyed the best Porterhouse he'd ever had, while listening to some of the best music ever made—Louis Armstrong himself drifting over from the Alabam. If only he could capture this moment in a bottle and live in it forever. But sooner or later bottles break. And sooner rather than later he knew he'd be back on the case.

Bobby couldn't get "Long Ago and Far Away" out of his mind. It was one of those songs that stuck with you. Now even more so because his mother had been humming it the other day. He flipped on James' Zenith radio—war news. Cleared his head with steaming coffee, a fresh breeze from the open window, and a cool, crisp, sunshiny L.A. day. But on every sunshiny day lately the same thought occurred to him: what were our boys overseas doing? Were they doing it in sunshine or snow? And did it make a difference? It was hell either way.

Where to start? Clues. Start thinking like a detective. He wasn't getting anywhere on the Dietrich angle. But if he worked the Thomas side of things it might come back around to Dietrich anyway. Follow up on the various items in Thomas' briefcase. Try to find out who beat the hell out of him. He was starting to form an idea of who might have been behind the beating.

Bobby left the Dunbar feeling relatively calm. On the way to the Sunset Tower, his gut ached more every minute he sat in his car. Bile rose until it was an explosion waiting to happen.

Adrenalin pumping, he went straight to the bar. Leach sat at the same table as last time. Bobby lurched across the room. A large man in a dark suit jumped up from a nearby table—someone Bobby had seen on the Apollo? The bartender bolted across the room. Both charging to intercept Bobby. Leach looked up.

"What goes on?" he said.

Bobby stood over him. Dark suit grabbed his lapel, yanked him back a foot. Bobby tried to pull his ham-hand off. Leach nodded. Dark suit let go, with a hard jerk. He stood by, just in case. The bartender returned to the bar.

"You're the kid with chutzpah, from the band. What happened to your face?"

"Same as happened here." Bobby wrenched up his shirt, showing his bruised purple belly to Leach. While Leach looked, Bobby eyed his dark-suited thug, trying to ascertain if he was one of the men in the Mercury. He didn't think so. But Leach had a lot of thugs at his disposal.

"You think I did this to you?" Leach's voice crescendoed.

"I, I don't know what to think. But you have people—"

"Let's go for a walk, kid."

Dark suit pulled Leach's chair out, trailed several yards behind Bobby and Leach as they walked along Sunset.

"Y'know, for things like this, accusing me, I've had people smashed. I like you, kid. You've got guts. My boys didn't do it and it hurts me to think that you think they did. Why?"

Bobby knew he should probably keep his mouth shut. Pissed off, he couldn't hold back. "You want me to stop investigating so the cops'll close the case and you can reopen the Apollo."

"Nobody talks to me the way you do, kid. And somehow I let you and you don't end up getting accidentally pushed into traffic."

Bobby looked to the traffic whizzing by on Sunset. Hoped he wouldn't end up under the wheels of a speeding car.

"Of course I want to open up the Apollo, but my guys got better things to do than beating up piano players. At least for now." He winked at Bobby.

"I'm caught up in this cyclone, spinning, and I can't see which end is up anymore." Bobby wasn't sure why he was spilling to Leach. Maybe because there was no one else to spill to.

"So because you've heard I'm a gangster, you figure I had my boys...Wasn't my boys. I told you, I'm on your side, kid. But you gotta trust me. I'll ask around. See if I hear anything."

"Thanks, Mr. Leach."

"In over your head, huh?"

"Yeah."

"Sometimes that's the best way to learn. Sink or swim. That's how I did it. You make mistakes. Long as you learn from them, you're doing good. Now what'd these guys look like?"

Bobby filled Leach in on the two men, their car, even the partial license.

"Watch your back," Leach said before striding back into the Sunset Tower.

Bobby remembered the anonymous note he received, *Watch your back, the nigger's playing you.* The thought crossed his mind that Leach could have sent that. He shooed it away, made up his mind to trust Leach. *You gotta trust somebody. Might as well be a gangster.*

He wanted to call the license in to Nicolai. But hadn't Nicolai been the one to tell him to watch his back also—that it was good advice. Had he sent the note? After all, he was on the take. Bobby had trusted him, had shown the contents of Thomas' briefcase to him. Now he wasn't sure that had been a good idea.

Bobby had his work cut out for him. No gig. A little money and a place to stay. His ration books and coupons. His moxie and determination. Besides, now it had become a game to him. And Bobby liked to win.

Bobby walked to a gas station phone booth. It wasn't far and why waste gas, especially on a day when his ration sticker wouldn't allow him to fill up. He used a nickel to call Sam Wilde. When he'd left Wilde after their trip to the Pike, he wasn't sure if he would call him again. He didn't know who else to call. And if there were any more thugs in Mercurys, Wilde would come in handy.

CHAPTER TWENTY-FIVE

Bobby set a meet with Wilde for the next day. The rest of today would be spent getting ready, preparing for her date with David tonight. She was confused. Very confused, on a multitude of levels. Right now she was also excited about her date with David and that made her even more confused. She still didn't know who she was, what her sexual desires were. Did she like men or women? Did she dress as a man simply to get ahead in her field or were there other reasons? She knew how Marion would answer that question. She wasn't sure how Bobbie or Bobby would.

She pulled down the blackout shades, stepped into the tub, slid down into the warming water. Totally naked, with her breasts exposed, she felt a little shy, as if James might be there watching her. *What a silly notion.* She luxuriated in the comforting water longer than she needed to. Then she got down to business, washing, shaving her legs, shampooing her hair. She stepped out of the tub, stood in front of the full-length mirror on the back of the bathroom door. Now she didn't mind seeing her breasts and hips and a woman's soft, round shape. In fact, she wished her breasts were larger, just a little and just for today.

Bobbie applied her makeup, carefully, to cover the bruises on her face. Luckily they weren't as bad as they had first seemed and her eye didn't look swollen anymore either.

She slipped into her Bullock's Wilshire outfit, checked herself in the mirror. Did the best she could with the short hair she had to work with.

"Not bad, lady. Not half bad for someone who doesn't know what the hell she's doing. Though it does seem a little more natural each time."

She lifted a lipstick to her mouth—applied it carefully. Pursed her lips. *Perfect, hope it stays that way.* Now, just one more worry. How the hell would Bobbie get out of the Dunbar dressed as a woman?

Criminy!

She could have climbed down the fire escape. That would have been suicide in this outfit. Besides, someone could see her there too. No, she would have to go down through the lobby, take her chances and run the gauntlet.

Bobbie walked down the stairs as fast as her heeled feet would take her. She started across the lobby, marching for the front door. A loud cat whistle echoed. She didn't dare look to see who or where it came from. She flew through the lobby like a P-51 Mustang. A large, black man in a natty suit held the door for her. Tipped his hat.

"Thank you," she said. *He thinks I'm a chippie.*

She made it to the street. To her car.

Could the people on the street see her heart pounding through her chest?

She turned the ignition. Drove off.

She would worry about getting back into her room later. Right now she worried about how to approach David. He had wanted to pick her up at her place. She'd told him she was moving and didn't know where her place would be. They decided to meet at his office on Beverly Boulevard. Low in the sky, the sun glared off her windscreen as she pulled to the curb to park. David, looking sharp in a navy blue suit, waited for her on the sidewalk. He walked to the Olds, opened the driver's door for her. She stepped out.

"You look terrific," he said, pecking her cheek.

"It's the same dress as the other day. The war, you know."

"Hey, stick with me. I can get all kinds of things. Dresses.

Nylon stockings."

"Nylons?" Bobbie knew theywere in short supply. Women had taken to painting a black pinstripe on the back of their legs and using makeup to give them color to simulate the look of stockings. She had opted for the bare leg look this time. "Black market?"

"Nah. I just have some friends—"

They walked to his 1942 black Caddy convertible coupe. She was relieved it wasn't a maroon Mercury. He opened the passenger door for her, walked around, and got in behind the wheel.

For some reason the Cadillac logo stayed in Bobbie's mind, juxtaposing itself with the Canada Dry ginger ale logo. She didn't know why or where it came from. Then she remembered Sergeant Nicolai drinking ginger ale highballs. Well, either way, she didn't drink the stuff and she couldn't afford a Caddy. *Enough of this nonsense*, as her father would say.

"Where're we going?"

"Someplace nice. Let it be a surprise."

He drove leisurely down to Wilshire, headed east. They joined the smooth flow of traffic. Reminisced about old times some more. Talked about which bands they liked. He was a Benny Goodman man. She liked Ellington. She wanted to ask if he liked The Booker "Boom-Boom" Taylor Orchestra, decided not to.

They passed the Ambassador Hotel and the Cocoanut Grove.

"Ever been there?" David asked.

"No, but one of these days."

"One of these days I'll take you."

David pulled up to the Brown Derby's valet.

"I've never been here either."

"Great place. Might even see some movie stars."

"I've heard this place was inspired by Bat Masterson's derby."

"Or Al Smith's. Who knows?"

Valets opened both car doors for them. David came 'round, took Bobbie's hand and led her inside the giant-sized hat. They were seated immediately. David ordered a Manhattan, Bobbie a martini; it seemed so William Powell-elegant.

"You should try the Cobb salad. It was invented here and it's their specialty."

"Do you come here often?" Bobbie asked.

"Often enough that they know my face. Not often enough to order 'the usual.'"

She chuckled in a most girlish way. Just the thought of being that girlish made her cheeks hot. She tried to maintain a feminine composure and posture. *Man, this is hard.*

She enjoyed reminiscing. Enjoyed looking into his deep green eyes. Feelings swirled in her that made her anxious. She didn't understand them, didn't know what they meant or what to do with them. Feelings for David? She still considered him a suspect, but she'd dropped him way down the list. Coming to the Derby had moved him back up a notch or two. Now she was sure it was him who she'd seen with Stinson. That still didn't necessarily mean anything. And David was so nice. Should she bring up the Apollo, James, IBM, Stinson? Should she wait for him to do it? What if he didn't? What if she didn't—heck, she was having too good a time; didn't want to spoil it.

"Where'd you end up moving?"

"I—I'm just staying with a friend. Still no permanent place to hang my hat."

"I might have some friends with vacant rooms you might be able to rent."

"Good thing this isn't Washington."

"Huh?"

"Like in *The More the Merrier*. Not a room to be had these days."

"I don't get to the movies much. Maybe we can go. You can fill me in on what I've been missing."

"That would be nice. It'll be different from our first movie experience. Do you remember going to *Robin Hood*?"

"How could I forget?"

The waiter brought their drinks, took their dinner orders. Bobbie ordered the Cobb salad. She told David she had a line on a more permanent place to stay but if it didn't work out, she might take him up on his offer. She guessed James' room at the Dunbar would be free for a while, maybe longer if she didn't find out who really killed Dietrich, and why.

"Did your girlfriend go for that job at IBM?"

"I'm not sure. I haven't talked to her since I told her what you'd said."

"Good company. She could do a lot worse." He sipped his Manhattan. "You know, when you came to me before, I thought you were playing an angle."

"Angle?"

"Yeah. I thought maybe you wanted something—"

"Besides finding out about IBM for my friend?"

"Yeah."

"Well, that was a ruse. You know, I pass Fairfax High sometimes and, of course, it makes me think of you. The old gang. So—"

"You don't have to explain. I'm just glad you got in touch."

"Me too." Bobbie sipped her martini. It was good, though she still didn't think she'd become a drinker.

The waiter brought their food.

"I always felt like we had something in common," David said "Maybe that we were just a little above the other kids. Special, you know."

"They all thought the drama kids were a little weird."

"I guess we were, but not in the way they thought. Besides, with Hollywood at our back door, why not do the drama club thing?"

"But you're a lawyer and I'm a—"

"Sure. But in a way we're both still acting."

That was for sure, Bobbie thought. She knew she was. Whether as Bobby or Bobbie she was constantly acting. She guessed other people were too. "I'd like to see you again."

"You said that last time."

"And now this time."

"Well let's make it happen. Maybe we can go to the Apollo?"

"The gambling ship?" David seemed surprised.

The waiter brought their check. David peeled off several bills, leaving a more than generous tip. He pulled Bobbie's chair out for her, escorted her outside. They decided to make it an early evening as it was their first date, drove back to his office. He pulled up behind Bobbie's Olds, opened her door for her. They stood in the foggy halo of a streetlight. *Just like in the movies.* He put a hand on each of her arms. She wasn't sure how to react. He gently pulled her closer, brushed his lips on hers. Then held her tighter and gave her a deeper kiss. She responded—after all, it did sort of come naturally, as they say.

She felt her cheeks turning hot again. She didn't want David to know she was staying at the Dunbar, so she promised to call him at work or at home. They kissed again. He opened her car door and made sure she got off okay.

Bobbie drove down Beverly Boulevard, her head as foggy as the street. She didn't know if she was coming or going.

She tried to put it all together. David on the boat, David at the Brown Derby, probably with Stinson, though she was beginning to doubt herself on that now. Not that he wasn't there, just that he might not have been with Stinson. After all, David went there on a fairly regular basis. Too much of a coincidence?

And did David know about Bobbie's male alter ego? There had been some hints in high school—after all, he knew she was "weird"—but she'd done nothing overt. Not even with close friends like David. He knew she'd been a tomboy. Did he think she'd outgrown it?

She had feelings for him. But she also had feelings for Margaret Lane, though she was unsure about her too. And for Loretta, the canary in Booker's band. She thought of Oliver Hardy's famous line, "Well, that's another fine mess you've gotten me into." This mess was of her own making. One way or another she'd find her way out, find out who she was. What she was interested in. Who she wanted to be. And who she wanted to be with. Right now there were more pressing issues. Like getting back into her room at the Dunbar. Getting out was probably easier than getting in would be. The Dunbar really came alive at night. It was midnight now and the place would be hopping.

She was right. Cars jam-packed the street in front of the hotel. People crowded the sidewalk, waiting to get into the Alabam next door. Or the hotel's nightclub. She circled the block three times and still wasn't sure what to do. A single white woman here alone at midnight. Was she afraid because she was white and most of the people colored? She didn't think so. She'd have the same feelings up in Hollywood or Beverly Hills, especially at this time of night.

Central Avenue was bright with lights. East Forty-second less so. She found a parking place there, slammed her door, and scurried around the corner to the hotel. She felt every eye on her. She dashed through the propped-open front door, making a beeline for the stairs before anyone could even think of saying anything to her. They probably all thought she was a hooker—is that what they called them?—heading up to someone's room. Her purse weighed heavy as she fumbled for the room key. Dropped it from shaking hands. But finally fit it in the lock and went into her—into James'—room.

She closed the door, collapsed on the bed under the watchful gaze of Marcus Garvey.

CHAPTER TWENTY-SIX

Bobby walked determinedly through the May Company, Wilde trailing.

"Bobby," Margaret said, looking spiffy in her fashionable cream Ike jacket.

Mrs. Ford, Margaret's supervisor, looked up from what she was doing, her eyes giving a very good impression of an evil temptress from some B movie that Bobby might have seen on a lazy Saturday afternoon before the war. Except that Mrs. F was hardly a temptress. Margaret on the other hand interested Bobby in many ways. Though now wasn't the time or place.

Bobby noticed Wilde noticing Margaret. Competition?

"I need your help, Margaret." Bobby looked toward Wilde. "This is Sam Wilde. He was a friend of Lois Templeton's—"

"—Hans' secretary?"

Margaret stole a look at Mrs. Ford.

"What's with the Wicked Witch of the West?" Wilde said.

"Ssh."

"When's your break?"

"I'm overdue." Margaret walked to Mrs. Ford. "I'm going to take my break now."

Mrs. Ford looked in Bobby's and Wilde's direction. "Take the rest of the day off, Miss Lane."

"Thank you."

"Without pay."

"No thanks. I'll just take my break." Margaret wheeled on

her heel, walked out with Bobby and Wilde.

"She's something," Wilde said.

They stood in the parking lot, the raw L.A. sun beating down on them, broiling the hood of Bobby's car. He set Thomas' briefcase on the hood, scorching his hand on the hot metal. He wanted to cry out in pain; didn't want to show weakness and bit down the desire.

"This is Harlan Thomas' briefcase."

"How did you get it?"

Bobby ignored her question, plowed on. "We need your help identifying the people in the pictures."

"I'll do what I can."

"You knew Thomas, right?" Bobby said.

Margaret nodded. "Not well. But yes."

"And you know he's been murdered."

Margaret gasped loud enough for two dowagers to turn their heads.

"I'm sorry, I thought you knew."

"It just keeps getting worse and worse."

"Do you want to do this another time?" Bobby asked.

"No, let's get on with it."

"Let's start with these." He pulled out all the photos except those of the concentration camps. He held up the small photo of Thomas with the other man.

"That's Hans." Margaret pointed.

"That's what I thought. Do you know where or when it was taken?"

"I'm sorry, I don't."

Margaret took the photo of Thomas with the woman. "I think that might be his wife. She died before I knew Hans or Mr. Thomas. But I can't say for sure that's who it is."

Bobby stared at the photo. Something came to him. "That's the same woman that's in the painting in his house. Younger, but the same."

"I, I wouldn't know."

Why is Margaret hesitating?

"I met Thomas, you know." Bobby filled Margaret in on his short acquaintance with Hans' partner. *Does that brief twitch of her eye mean anything?*

"Do you know what happened to Mrs. Thomas?" Wilde said.

"He didn't say much about her to me." Bobby tapped the photo on the car hood. He liked Margaret, but as he'd told Wilde, he didn't trust anyone completely and he needed to see what she knew. "When, how did she die?"

"I believe she died in a concentration camp." Margaret held her purse close to her chest. A gesture of reassurance or security, Bobby figured.

"No wonder he has a briefcase full of those pictures," Wilde said.

"What're you talking about?" Margaret looked Wilde in the eye.

"Was she Jewish?" Bobby's hand accidentally slid against the sizzling hood of the car again. He swallowed the pain, like a man.

Margaret winced. "I think she might have been, but Thomas wasn't. That much I know."

Wilde unbuttoned the top button of his shirt, fanned the heat. "Well, that gives us a little background we didn't have before."

Bobby handed her the photo of Dietrich, Thomas, and the third man. She squinted, trying to see who it was in the black-and-white photo. "I'm sorry. I don't know who that is." She fussed with her earrings. "I didn't know Thomas well, more or less in passing."

"Let's try some of these other things." Bobby pulled out the ring of keys. Margaret examined them, shook her head. The same routine followed for the rest of the items in the case. He reached for the stack of concentration camp photos, which lay upside down in the case—hesitated.

"More pictures?" Margaret said.

"I don't know if I should show these to you or not."

Margaret looked puzzled.

"They're very ugly. Pictures from the war."

"Let me see."

Bobby spread the pictures on the closed briefcase. The first picture started to curl in the heat.

"These are terrible."

"But you've seen pictures like them before. Tell me what's going on."

"Mr. Thomas was concerned about his wife. He tried to get her out of Germany, but—"

"Do you know why Thomas—or Hans—might have had these?"

"All I know is that they were trying to get her out of the country since they had connections there before the war from their import-export business. And Hans also had family there."

"What about Dietrich—he Jewish?"

"No, but he was trying to help Mr. Thomas," Margaret said.

"I thought Hans was a Nazi. He sure talked like one on the Apollo." Bobby scanned the pictures, still not sure what to look for.

"Maybe he was playing both sides," Wilde said. "Maybe he's the one who got Mrs. Thomas killed."

"Murdered," Margaret blurted, looking like she regretted doing so. "Hans was a Nazi before he left Germany. He had no choice if he wanted to do business."

"Was he still?"

"No. But even if he was, he was trying to help Thomas get his wife out. They were friends."

"It sounds very complicated," Bobby said.

Margaret looked down at the pictures. *What was she thinking?*

"Were they blackmailing someone?" Wilde said.

"I don't think so."

"But you're not sure."

"How sure can you ever be? A couple weeks ago I would have been sure Hans would be alive today. But I guess with all that's going on in the world, well, who knows?" She pursed her lips. "I have to get back to work or Mrs. Ford will have me fired for taking too long a break." Margaret scurried off.

"Did she seem like she was in a big hurry to get away from us?" Wilde said.

Margaret couldn't—wouldn't?—help them, but Bobby had the feeling she wasn't coming totally clean. He said nothing about it to Wilde. He also had other feelings about Margaret, which he didn't mention. As soon as they popped into his mind, David Chambers' face superimposed itself over Margaret's face. Bobby was searching for a hell of a lot more than Dietrich's killer.

"Where to now, boss?" Wilde said. Bobby liked the sound of it. Maybe one day he would be a boss, leader of his own band.

"The briefcase. We go through the contents on our own. See if they lead us anywhere."

"Cops don't know you got the briefcase?"

"Nicolai knows."

"He's on your side, right?"

Bobby nodded, though his look was distant.

"And the rest of the cops, they don't know about it?"

"Uh uh."

"I guess what they don't know won't hurt them."

Bobby drove to Thomas' house in the hills. He pulled down the driveway, shielded from the neighbors by the hedge. He and Wilde walked up the drive to the house. "Now you're cookin' with gas," Wilde said.

"This one looks like a house key," Bobby whispered, trying one of the seven keys on the ring in the back door. "Criminy, if it's not a house key, what is it?"

He tried several more keys. Nothing.

"He probably had his house keys on him," Wilde said.

Bobby signaled for Wilde to follow. They walked to the window Bobby had previously pried open. It hadn't been fixed and was easy enough to slide up and for them to climb through. He switched on the light, illuminating the office.

"Some of these smaller keys might be to the desk or file cabinets." Bobby took half the keys off the ring, gave them to Wilde. They started trying them in desk and file cabinet drawers.

"Hell, all these drawers are unlocked anyway."

"Still, see if any of the keys fit."

Of the seven, one key worked the two file cabinets, which were already unlocked. Each of them took one cabinet, began rifling through them.

"Nothing unusual," Wilde said after an hour. "Just what I'd expect to find, tax receipts, Jeez, he made a good living—until the war."

"I guess he'd have to to live here."

"Medical records, service records, he was in the Lafayette Escadrille in the First War." Wilde threw a stack of papers on the floor. Sighed.

"Maybe that's where he met his wife?"

"Or doing the import-export stuff with Germany before this war." Wilde pulled a fat cigar from a drawer. Struck a match off the wall, lit up. "Looks like he had a dog fight with the famous Red Baron himself, plane crashed, but he walked away. Lucky guy."

"I think his luck ran out a few days ago."

"We all gotta go some time."

"True. But I'd like to know why he had to go right now."

"I guess that's why we're here." Wilde blew out smoke, tried unsuccessfully to make a smoke ring. Scratched at his side.

"I can't find nothing."

"Me neither."

"At least we know what one key does, it opens the file cabinets. Let's move to another room." Bobby knew which room he wanted to get to. But instead of rushing headlong to the bathroom with the enlarger machine, they methodically made their way through the house, enjoying *man talk*.

"Whoa! I think I hit the jackpot," Wilde said. Bobby's heart nearly exploded. He rushed into the den.

"What is it?"

Wilde pulled a stack of magazines from a rosewood secretary. Bobby had envisioned secret files, secret plans, or a secret decoder ring like Little Orphan Annie or Captain Midnight had, but a real one. Something that would give away the secret to Dietrich's and Thomas' deaths, Lois being missing and all the other mysteries that were enveloping and choking Bobby. He was surprised to find stacks of *Photoplay* and *Modern Screen* magazines, pinup pictures of Rita Hayworth, Betty Grable, Lana Turner, Veronica Lake, and others.

"I thought you found something."

"I have. This is a treasure trove. Now we're really cookin' with gas." Wilde held up a picture of Betty Grable, all legs. "Va-va-va voom!"

Bobby's face dropped.

"Don't you like what you see? You're not queer, are you?"

"I like. I like." But now wasn't the time or place, as his mother used to say. He tried the six remaining keys in the secretary. Voilà! One key worked. Two keys down.

"I know, you want to get your mystery solved and play in that colored band. So let's move out." Ash from Wilde's cigar fell to the floor.

They continued their meticulous search of the house, not really knowing what they were looking for.

Wilde went on and on about what he'd like to do with Grable and Hayworth and the others.

"What about Lois? Don't you want to be loyal to her?"

"What kind of man are you? You mean to tell me if you got that job with the band and Rita Hayworth came up to you with those long legs of hers and that fiery red hair and said, 'Hey baby, buy me a drink,' you'd turn her down?"

"No. No I wouldn't."

"And then what if she wanted to go back to your place?"

"I'd tell her not to cheat on Orson Welles."

"Okay. But better yet, she wants to go back to her place and lay on those satin sheets of hers from the *Life* magazine cover." He held the magazine up. "You'd turn her down because your girlfriend, say that mousy Margaret from the May Company's, got you pussy-whipped. I'll bet the mouse won't even sleep with you till you're married."

"Margaret isn't mousy."

"Hey, you got it bad for her, don't you? I was just using her as an example. No, she ain't mousy. She's really kinda hot in that dark-haired, exotic, Hedy Lamarr way."

"You know you're right, she does look like Hedy Lamarr."

"Well, maybe if Lois doesn't come back—"

"How can you say that?"

"I'm a man."

He was at that and there was something about him that Bobby found attractive. Not the salaciousness, but something strong and virile. Something very masculine. David Chambers popped into his mind again. He was the kind of man Bobby wanted to be—Wilde was the kind Bobby wanted with him in a dark alley. He was confused. Until this interaction with Wilde he had been thinking about Margaret. Wondering if she might want to go on a date with him. Wondering, if she did, how he would play it. In a way he was glad for the diversion of trying to find Dietrich's killer. It kept him from having to examine himself.

CHAPTER TWENTY-SEVEN

Wilde lit up another cheroot. Immediately the downstairs hall filled with pungent gray smoke. Bobby stifled a cough.

"Do you think we should be smoking in here?"

"Why not?"

"They'll know someone was here."

"They won't know who. And Thomas won't care."

Bobby couldn't argue with that logic. They moved upstairs.

"Are they all like this?" Wilde asked, entering the empty bedroom.

"No, the other two bedrooms have furniture."

"And so does the rest of the house. This is strange."

Bobby watched dust flakes dancing in the filtered light.

"Why wouldn't he have furniture in here?"

"Maybe he hadn't had time to buy any. Or he had more space than he needed."

"Could be. But wouldn't you at least use it for storage, have some boxes in it? There's nothing in here either," Wilde said, opening the closet door. He looked to the ceiling, "No attic access." He got down on his knees, skimmed his hands across the wooden closet floor.

"What're you looking for?"

"I don't know. Some kind of secret compartment. Does that sound stupid?"

They felt along the entire bedroom floor. Looked for a button that might open a doorway to a secret passage. Nothing.

"Maybe it's what I said before, he just didn't need the space."

"When I was in China—"

"—You were in China?"

"With the China marines."

"I've heard of them. That was one tough outfit. That's why you're not in the service now?"

Wilde pulled up his shirt, revealing a chest and belly full of dull pink scars. He scratched at them. "You should've seen 'em a couple years ago. Bright red."

"What happened?"

"That's for another time. Anyway, when I was in the mysterious Orient we had a situation where this marine was killed. Some kind of jealous triangle between him and a Chinese girl and her Chink boyfriend, or he thought he was, but he wasn't. Anyway, the so-called boyfriend killed the gyrene, so now whadda they do with the body? They've got money, soes they've got a nice house— for China you understand. Now they got a house with a dead marine in it. And my buddy, John Wayland, and I are coming to find him. He's AWOL and we know he wouldn't do that.

"Soes, we go to the house and everyone's very polite. They're polite, we're polite. We ask to see the daughter. 'Oh yes, yes, come see Ah-lam'—name means 'like an orchid'—and she was a delicate flower. Very pretty. Pretty name, pretty girl. My pal was head-over-heels for her. Soes they invite us in for tea, all very genteel-like in the garden behind the house. We're trying to ask questions about Bud, that was his name, Bud Lambert. Soes I ask to use the head—they got indoor plumbing which is rare— but I'm really checking out the house. And I see there's a room with nothing in it—just like this room here. I think it's odd, but what am I gonna say?

"Well, me being me, I gotta say something. Soes I ask what they're going to do with that empty room. Ah-lam starts to cry. She tries to hide it, but she can't. To make a long story short, the boyfriend killed Bud in that room, they stuck him in some kind of hope chest and hauled it out, cleared out the whole damn room, washed the blood off the floor."

"So you think someone was killed here?"

"All I'm saying is an empty room might be an empty room, then again it might be something else." Wilde walked to the window.

"You should be a cop."

"I don't know what I wanna be when I grow up, daddy. Right now I'm happy being a bum."

Wilde checked the whole room, inch by inch. "There was something here. Hard to tell what. But there's some scratches on the wood. Might be something, might be nothing. But without a Flash Gordon magic camera to take a picture of this room in the past, I don't think we're gonna know."

"No secret compartments here, that's for sure."

They moved down the hall, Wilde tamping the floor with his heel to see if there were any hollows. Nothing. Bobby was saving the Jack-and-Jill bathroom, with its weird enlarger machine, for last.

Wilde searched the second bedroom while Bobby did the master.

"Hey, I've got another key solved," Bobby called out.

Wilde joined him. "A martini bar, and the key fits it? I might just take this home with me."

"Last time I saw this bar a man was murdered."

"Thomas?"

Bobby nodded. "But if the key fits."

Bobby slipped the ornate, old-fashioned skeleton key into the cabinet door.

"So now we know what three of the keys are for. The file cabinets downstairs, the secretary, and the martini bar. Pretty mundane stuff."

"Maybe one of the four things left won't be so mundane. Find anything in the second bedroom?"

"Nope."

"Ditto for the master. Nothing of interest."

"So let's go for the interesting bathroom with the strange

machine."

The bathroom looked the same as when Bobby was there last. "That's it, Thomas called it an enlarger."

They examined the odd-shaped machine, with its long neck.

"Somebody wanted it dark in here, lightproof," Wilde said, tugging lightly at the blanket over the window. "This is what they call a darkroom, for developing photographs. See the red lightbulb in the fixture. They hang the pictures to dry; that's why he has this clothesline over the tub. This enlarger machine is to blow the pictures up."

"Yeah, that's what Sergeant Nicolai thought." Bobby fidgeted with the machine's arm. "You think he was making dirty pictures?"

"More likely concentration camp photos."

"That's like smut, isn't it?"

Bobby tried a key in the medicine cabinet. No go.

"Try another key," Wilde said.

Bobby tried the four remaining keys. "Voilà!"

It was filled with dark brown bottles of no medicines Bobby had ever heard of: fixer, ferrotype. Toner and stop bath. The same key opened the built-in cabinet of drawers. Tin pans that looked like baking pans. Things that looked like drums. Rolls of film. Boxes of photographic paper.

"Four keys down. Three to go."

"But no damn pictures," Wilde said. "He's got this whole set up, but no photos other than the ones in the briefcase and we can't even be sure he developed those here."

"Maybe the photos are somewhere else in the house?"

"We've been through it."

"Let's do it again."

They combed the house again, looking for photos and things to put the keys in. Nothing fit and no photos. They wound up in the ground floor office, where they'd started.

"You'd think there'd be something in here," Wilde said. "Some paperwork that would give us a clue to something. Anything."

"Yeah, why have all this equipment and no photos lying

around?"

"You tell me, kid. You're the detective."

"I still think we're making some progress," Bobby said, trying to rally their falling spirits. "Maybe there's something at the business."

"Weren't you there?"

"Never alone to search it."

They gave Thomas' home office another going over. Found nothing, headed outside.

"Did you check the garage when you were here before?"

Bobby hadn't. They walked to the back of the driveway. The double doors were closed but unlocked. They chucked them open. Yellow late afternoon sun filtered in, casting eerie shadows. Not much to see, a couple old tires, a set of suitcases, all empty.

"Try the keys in the door."

Bobby tried the three remaining keys and the rabbit's foot key in the side door. None worked.

"Let's blow."

Instead of walking toward the car, Bobby strode to the incinerator, began clawing through the char. "Maybe something didn't burn all the way."

Wilde watched.

"Don't want to muss up your lily white hands?" Bobby said.

"No sense both of us turning colored."

Bobby sifted through the blackened remains of paper, cardboard boxes, and what looked like photographs, blistered and curled at the edges. He lifted the photos out, laid them on the incinerator's sloped edge.

"Can you tell what these are?"

"This one, can't tell a thing. This one here, looks like your empty bedroom upstairs. See the window curtain. But in the picture, there was something in the room."

"I can't tell what it is."

"Neither can I. Not enough of the picture left."

Wilde started sifting through the ashes. "No dice. There's

nothing else even looks like anything but ashes." He walked to the garbage cans. Rummaged through them. "Nothing."

"There goes my last lead. I feel like I'm on one of those rides at the Pike where you're spinning in a circle and the bottom drops out and you're glued to the wall. Just spinning in a vortex with no end."

"It's just a false bottom. Believe me, every time you think you've hit bottom, a trap door opens and you fall again."

"You're even more cynical than me."

"I've seen more than you, kid."

"Why does everyone call me kid?"

"'Cause that's what you are, half-pint." Wilde laughed.

"Criminy." Bobby grabbed what was left of the burned photos, headed for the car. Spread them on the hood. "There."

"What?"

"That's the bedroom right? And that's a mattress. A bunch of them on the floor. See."

"So?"

Bobby tugged on Wilde's sleeve, realized what he was doing and quickly removed his hand. *Too much of a girlish gesture. I'll have to watch that.* But it did the trick. Wilde followed him to the ledge overlooking the canyon. Bobby pointed down. Wilde couldn't see what he was pointing at. Leaned over the edge.

"Mattresses," he said.

"About a dozen of them. That's where I threw the briefcase so the cops wouldn't get it. I wondered what they were doing down there but I figured someone just dumped their trash over the hillside."

"Someone with a big family?"

"Yeah." Bobby exhaled. "A big family. What was Thomas doing with a dozen mattresses in one room?"

Wilde snatched up another photo. "This looks like one of the concentration camp photos. What's that?"

Bobby scrutinized it. "A machine. Looks like a typewriter or something, but not exactly."

"I can't tell. The photo's too frayed."

"Something else for us to figure out," Wilde said.

"The bottom just dropped out again."

"How we doin' on gas?"

"Okay. I put in two bits' worth. I guess we're okay if we don't go far."

Wilde looked at Bobby's ration sticker on the windshield. "Today's your day. I'll fill it up for you."

They hit a gas station. Wilde paid the full freight.

"Can you top it off?" Bobby said to the attendant.

"Sorry, can't."

"Don't you know, you're not s'posed to?" Wilde said.

"I was hoping he'd make an exception."

"I know. Murder investigation."

Bobby couldn't tell if Wilde was pulling his leg or was really annoyed, after all he was a former marine. Maybe he didn't think Bobby should be topping off his tank when the troops needed gas for planes and Jeeps.

They pulled into a parking space near Dietrich's office. "I don't feel comfortable doing this while it's still business hours," Bobby said.

"Just go in like you own the place."

"What if none of the leftover keys work?"

But Wilde was already marching through the marble lobby. The lobby glowed in the golden hour sun. Almost on fire. Wilde bounded two steps at a time to the second floor. By the time Bobby joined him, he was trying the knob. Locked. Bobby tried the three remaining keys and the rabbit's foot key again. No dice, as Wilde would say. He even tried the other four keys just to be sure.

"Snake eyes."

Wilde pushed Bobby aside, looked both ways down the hall. He fished in his pocket, bent down in front of the knob. Metal-on-metal scraping. Seconds later the door was open.

"I've only seen that done in the movies."

"It's easy. The lock was just your basic pin-and-tumbler." Wilde flashed a set of tools that looked like dentist's instruments to Bobby. The tools disappeared into Wilde's pocket and they disappeared inside the office, closing the door behind them.

"It's like a tomb in here. So musty," Bobby whispered.

Wilde picked up a framed photo on from the receptionist's desk. Stared at it. Bobby came 'round to see. Wilde and Lois arm in arm. Smiling.

"Happier days?"

"Maybe one day I'll be able to say 'happy days are here again.'" Wilde let out a wistful sigh, set the picture down. "Let's get to work."

He yanked open the top drawer of Lois' desk. Bobby started trying the leftover keys in every keyhole he saw.

"Don't we need to wear gloves or something?"

Wilde paid no attention. Began checking out every item on and in the desk. Bobby opened a file drawer. Empty. Another. Also empty. Three file cabinets, four drawers each—all as barren as Eliot's *Waste Land*.

"There's nothing here, not even a scrap."

"Cleaned the place out. Somebody didn't want something known."

"The cops?"

"They're not that thorough."

"Let's check the other rooms."

Dietrich's office yielded more of the same. A few knick-knacks here and there. Nothing of interest.

"Goddamn!" Wilde shoved the desk and chairs aside, yanked up the rug.

"Looking for secret compartments?"

"Anything. It can't be this damn hard. It's like they never existed." Wilde wrenched open an armoire, found only a raincoat inside. "Must be his slicker." He tore it off the hanger, clawed through the pockets. "Nothing. Damn nothing and more of it."

He charged out. Bobby followed him to Thomas' office, feeling as if he'd lost control of the situation. This was his case but now he was being carried on the wind, a Wilde wind.

Thomas' office was no different. Wilde tore it apart, top to bottom, carpet to crown molding. "Except for a little gimcrack here and there it's like no one was ever here." He slid down a wall to the floor. "Like Lois never even existed."

Bobby had never expected Sam Wilde to be so vulnerable.

"Maybe the office is already leased and someone, the new tenant or the landlord or somebody, is just clearing things out."

"It's too easy. Too damn easy. No. Somebody doesn't want us, or maybe the cops, finding out what's going on here. Did you try the keys?"

"Yeah, they don't fit anything."

"They got a warehouse somewhere?"

Bobby shrugged.

"They're in the import-export business. They must have a place where they store whatever it is they import and export."

"Did you ever talk to Lois about it?"

"We didn't talk shop much. What products did they—"

"They imported toys, clocks. Office machines. I'm not sure what they exported."

"You don't know? How long you been working this case?"

"I'm as green as they come."

"That's the understatement of the century."

"The century is still young."

"Maybe Margaret knows. Let's vamoose." Wilde charged the door.

"Why don't you take the picture with you?"

"That would just kibosh everything."

"What do you mean?"

Wilde stopped, faced Bobby.

"If I take the picture...that means that Lois isn't here anymore. Get it?"

CHAPTER TWENTY-EIGHT

"So, where to now?" Wilde said.

"We still have three regular keys, plus the one on the rabbit's foot, that we don't know what they open."

They got in Bobby's car, slipped into the Beverly Boulevard traffic flow.

"I'm just reaching, but I keep going back to that empty room. The mattresses. Do you think maybe Lois and Thomas—"

"She wouldn't truck with a guy like that."

"Maybe for business?" Bobby said.

Wilde's jaw set like a clamp. Bobby shot him a look. "Hell, even if she did, she'd only need one mattress."

They laughed, breaking the tension.

"It's got to be here, in this damn briefcase," Wilde said. "The answer has to be in here."

"But we've been through it how many times."

"And his house, and office. Zip."

"Well, where to now? I can't be driving around wasting gasoline, even if it is my ration day."

"Him." Mrs. Templeton said, opening the duplex's door to Bobby and Wilde. "What's he doing here?"

Bobby clenched his fists waiting for Wilde to detonate.

He smiled at Mrs. Templeton, hoping she wouldn't complete her thought, which he assumed was that Wilde had killed her daughter. Bobby didn't think so, not anymore.

"He's trying to help, Mrs. Templeton. Won't you let us in?"

The rolling of her eyes said she didn't believe it, but she let them both in anyway. Nothing had changed since Bobby had been here before. The same chintz curtains, the same still air, with the filtered light of the blinds shimmering on millions of dust diamonds.

"What can I do for you boys?" She didn't offer them tea or even a place to sit.

"We've been through everything. Through Dietrich's office and house—the police have too," Bobby said. "Through Thomas' house. He was going to help me before he got killed."

"He's dead too? I hadn't heard about that. What does that mean for Lois?"

"You have to have hope, Mrs. Templeton."

"Hope fades a little more every day when the sun comes up. It's worse than the nighttime. Everything's the same. The sun shines. The birds sing. The days get longer, even without daylight saving. At night you expect to be lonely. But during the day—"

"I'm sorry. But if you'll let us, we might be able to help."

"And how can you help?"

"Mrs. Templeton, I know you don't like me." Wilde spoke for the first time. "But Lois did. And I like her. I want to find her."

"What if you find her and she's, she's dead?"

"Then I want to find the people that hurt her and hurt them."

Bobby knew that was true. And he knew Wilde was more than capable, both mentally and physically. From the look in Mrs. Templeton's eyes she knew it too. It was a look of recognition, but maybe a glimmer of hope too. Hope that they would find Lois, but that if they didn't...

She led them down a hall, past a small den and arched telephone alcove, to Lois' bedroom, done up in lavender and lace.

"I'll just leave you boys alone. I guess I can trust you." She muttered the last line under her breath, but loud enough for Bobby and Wilde to hear.

"I don't know where to begin," Bobby said.

"Never been in a girl's bedroom?" Wilde winked. Bobby wasn't about to tell him that he'd grown up in a *girl's* bedroom. Wilde was a good guy under the sandpaper exterior. But Bobby doubted he would understand his situation.

"Of course I've been in a girl's bedroom." That was neutral enough. And true.

"But not while the girl was there." Wilde laughed. "Don't look so glum, chum."

Wilde playfully hit Bobby on the arm. It was something men did. Their way of showing affection. Bobby was still perfecting male protocol. Should he hit Wilde back? He gave him a little closed-fist tap on the arm and knew it didn't hurt nearly as much as Wilde's tap on him had.

"I been in lotsa girls' rooms, but never this one. Mrs. T don't like me."

"I couldn't tell." More bonding, Bobby thought.

"I'm surprised she let me into her house at all."

"She's desperate. Her husband's overseas and her daughter's missing. Los Angeles can be a mean town, damn mean town."

"Whoever named this place the City of the Angels musta been nuts," Wilde said.

Bobby gingerly pulled open a desk drawer. A pink pad of paper with cute puppies on it stared up at him; something he, or even Roberta, would never in a million years have. Wilde slid open a nightstand drawer.

"Are you from L.A.?" Bobby said.

"Me? Nah. Just sort of landed here after separating from the service."

"I think that's how a lot of people end up here, they just sort of land. Me, I was born here. Not too far from this house."

"A native; that's a rare bird."

"Not as rare as this." Bobby held up a single key. "It looks like our mysterious key, the one on the rabbit's foot."

Wilde took it, stared at it. "All keys look alike."

"I found it under a pad of girly writing paper, taped to the bottom of the pad."

"That makes it more interesting."

Bobby jogged from the room, leaving Wilde riveted on the key. He returned a moment later with the briefcase, had it open before he set it on the bed. Wilde reached in, grabbed the rabbit's foot with its mystery key—held it flush with the key Bobby had found.

"The cuts seem to line up."

"Cuts?" Bobby said.

"The teeth. But a lot of keys look like the cuts line up when they don't really. Only way to know for sure is to see if both keys work the same door."

"Or go to a locksmith."

"You're a genius, kid."

"Criminy."

Mrs. Templeton entered carrying a tray. Bobby hoped she hadn't thought his last remark had to do with her, hoped his face wouldn't turn red. She set the tray on her daughter's desk. Poured tea from a white porcelain teapot with a huge, smiling yellow sunflower on it.

She handed a cup to each man. "Sugar? Lemon? I also have milk. I know the English like milk in their tea but I don't understand why."

"Lemon and sugar will be fine," Bobby said. Wilde nodded.

"There's some cookies on the tray. Help yourself."

"Thank you," Wilde said, in a quiet, almost subdued voice. Mrs. Templeton hesitated a moment, as if she just wanted to be in her daughter's room with two living, breathing people.

"Would you like to join us?" Bobby said.

"Oh no. I was just thinking about Lois. I don't want to interrupt." She retreated.

Bobby and Wilde finished their snacks quickly and searched the rest of the room. They put things back as best they could so as not to upset Mrs. Templeton. But they were anxious to get to the locksmith.

* * *

Wilde held onto his hat as Bobby floored the Olds.

"There's a locksmith on Melrose near La Brea. It's just a few minutes from here," Bobby said.

"The way you're going it'll only be a couple."

"As long as we don't get pinched by a cop."

Armetta's Shoe Repair and Locksmith filled a tiny ramshackle storefront. Walking from the car, Bobby and Wilde had to dodge an organ grinder with his little white-headed monkey.

"Reminds me of a Shirley Temple movie I saw once," Wilde said.

Bobby gave him an astonished look.

"I was dating a woman with a kid. Whaddaya want from me?"

There were no customers in the modest store and Armetta seemed glad for a little business.

"Gentlemen, how I help you?" he said, in a thick Italian accent that reminded Bobby of spaghetti and that Shirley Temple movie Wilde had mentioned.

Bobby held up the two keys. "Can you tell us if these are the same key? Open the same door?"

The grin on the old man's face faded. He wiped his hands on his not-so-white apron, took the keys, pressed them together. Slid his specs up onto his chrome head. Squinted.

"Same."

"You can tell just by looking? You don't need to put them in a machine or something?"

"Same. I been this business forty year, more. Same key. Same lock."

"Thank you," Bobby said. Wilde said it more concretely. He slapped a fin on the counter.

"Hey. Don't need. Didn't do nuthin'." The old man's voice fell on a closing door.

Walking past the organ grinder and his monkey, Wilde slipped him a buck.

"You're pretty loose with the money today."

"Spread the wealth. Eugene V. Debs and all that."

"You're not a socialist, are you?"

"Naw, just today. I think we're a step closer with those two keys matching."

"Closer to what? We don't know what they open."

"But when we find out, we'll blow this whole case wide open. Don't look so glum, kid. It'll come together. It always does."

"This isn't the movies, Sam. Everything doesn't always come together."

"It does for me."

Bobby wished he felt as sure as Wilde.

"Let's go have some fun."

"The Pike?" Bobby said.

But Wilde had something else in mind. Bobby's heart pumped as the Olds hugged Mulholland Highway above Beachwood Canyon. Was Wilde taking him back to Thomas' house? He watched the OLLYWOODLAND sign loom larger, as he drove farther up the hill.

"That's it. Park over there."

Bobby followed orders, parking across the road from a Georgian-style mansion that reminded him of the White House. A gracious middle-aged woman in a long black dress met them at the door. Her warm smile made him feel at home, almost.

In the parlor—she called the living room a parlor—she told them to have their pick of the women there. Bobby counted six of them of various shapes and sizes. Wilde told him to choose anyone, it was on him. Slugged him in the arm. *What the hell am I doing here and how the hell am I going to get out of it?*

He wasn't sure how he ended up in an upper rear bedroom, overlooking a blue pool filled with dead leaves. The girl sat on the bed, her fingers caressing Bobby's thigh. He didn't know what to say, what to do. Felt his cheeks burning and a trickle of sweat run down his back.

The house was old but didn't show its age much. Bobby had expected a worn bedspread. It looked new. Clean carpet. The curtains gauzy white. A lilting breeze blew them in on a stream of sweet fresh air. On the other hand, the girl was young, no more than twenty-two Bobby figured—just slightly younger than him. But she looked tired, frayed around the edges. Dull eyes. She tried to spark them alive.

"What's your name?" Bobby figured that was as a good an icebreaker as any.

"Whatever you want it to be. You like exotic—Francesca maybe. Normal, Jane. Maybe—"

"Your real name."

"What's yours, sailor?"

"You call everyone who comes here 'sailor'?"

The girl smiled coyly.

"Bobby. My name's Bobby."

"Bobby, cute. So hon, do you want to talk or do what you came here to do?"

Bobby wasn't sure what he had come here to do. He knew what Sam Wilde was here for. He knew what he was supposed to be here for. But he didn't know what *he* was here for.

There was a certain vulnerability to the girl. It reminded him of his own vulnerabilities. The soft underbelly that every animal tries to protect. Bobby liked her—he liked girls. Whether he was Bobby or Roberta, he liked girls. Men were alright too. But he didn't think he was as drawn to them. Still not sure about that, but when he fantasized himself in romantic scenes from the movies, he was Clark Gable romancing Myrna Loy. He was Tyrone Power kissing Linda Darnell. Errol Flynn rescuing Olivia de Havilland from evil Basil Rathbone. He looked in the mirror over the vanity—saw a man, Bobby Saxon. Robert. Not Roberta. But what would this girl see if he took his clothes off? Would she go screaming from the room, blow his cover? Or worse, would she laugh and ridicule?

The girl's eyes opened wide, china blue saucers in a face older than its actual years. Was this for real or just another cliché Bobby had seen in the movies or read in a book? He looked at her and she at him. What did she really see? Were his eyes wide with fear or did she see below his suit to the same-sex person as she underneath it?

"My name's Vivian La—" She pulled a pack of Kools from her garter belt. Bobby reached into his pocket, pulled out his black-and-chrome Mastercase lighter. Lit her up. "Thanks."

She drew on the cigarette, offering one to Bobby.

"My name's not Vivian at all. That's what they call me here. It's Irene."

"That's a nice name."

"I hate it. It's old-fashioned. Too old-country Europe."

"Irene Dunne uses it pretty well."

"She's a movie star. She can afford a dreary name."

Bobby lit the cigarette. "Menthol. I've never smoked a mentholated cigarette before."

"They're more mild." She blew a perfect smoke ring. Bobby wanted to move closer to her. Stayed where he was. "Listen, if all you want to do is talk, that's fine. I get paid the same and no one has to know."

"What makes you think—"

"What I think doesn't really matter. But if you want to know what I think it's that you're young, innocent, and inexperienced."

Bobby felt his face burn with fire.

"But if you want—" The girl snuggled closer to Bobby on the bed. She let one hand slip onto his knee again. A spark ran up his thigh. "—maybe I can teach you a few things. Then you'll be experienced when you do find a girl."

"You're a girl." Bobby didn't know what else to say.

"Damaged goods."

"Why don't you get out of here? Do something else?"

"Like what?"

"I don't know. But with the war on women are doing lots of things they couldn't do before."

"The money's good here. Better than anything I could make in the war industry."

"You'd be helping the war effort."

"I'm helping it here. Believe me, hon, generals, colonels. Senators. Admirals. Even a cabinet member or two when they've been on the West Coast. I'm helping the war effort as much as Rosie the Riveter."

"I'll bet you are at that."

"My goal is to someday *help* FDR himself."

"The president. He would never—"

"Don't kid yourself, hon. He's a man, ain't he?"

"But he's the president."

"Listen, hon, you seem like a nice guy. What'll it be, talk or—I gotta ask you know."

"I—I'm not sure. Like you said, I've never done this before."

"You're not a homo, are you? I hear they have weird diseases." She pulled her hand from his leg.

"No. Not a homo." Bobby didn't think of himself as a homosexual male or female. When he was Bobby he was a man, all man. Well, almost. He saw himself as a man and as a man he liked women. When he was Roberta, which he was as little as possible, he was more, what was the word? He knew he'd heard it: a-sexual.

A soft knock on the door woke him from his thoughts. "Time," the madam's voice said.

Rescued—for now.

"I guess that takes care of that," Irene said. She stood. Bobby followed her lead.

"Maybe sometime we could get a bite to eat or something?"

"I don't date the customers, hon."

"I'm not really a customer, am I?"

"You got me there. Still, I'm not sure it would be a good

idea." She opened the door. "But come back some time. I could initiate you, know what I mean. I'd like to see you again."

"As a customer?"

Irene took Bobby's hand. "Listen, Bobby, you wouldn't want to get to know me. I'm really not a nice person."

"You seem nice en—"

"This business makes you hard. You get jaded. It wears you out." And just in saying it, her face, her whole body seemed to sag. Bobby felt sorry for her. What a way to make a living. "What do you do, Bobby?"

"I'm a musician."

"Really. Long hair music?"

"No, hot jazz."

"Swing. That's my ticket. You in a band?"

"The Booker 'Boom-Boom' Taylor Orchestra."

"I don't think I've heard of them. You play around town?"

"Down at the Club Alabam."

"On Central. I know the place. I'll come see you some time."

She walked through the door. Bobby hoped she would come down one night. He also hoped he'd have a spot in the band, something that seemed more and more remote with each day.

Wilde was waiting for him in the foyer. He tipped the madam and they headed for the car.

"You were up there a long time. Having fun, kid?"

"Too much fun. Didn't want to leave."

Wilde slapped Bobby on the back.

"How was it, really?"

"Great."

The grin on Wilde's face as they got in the car was worth the price of the lie. It was great, but not the way Wilde took it.

Bobby stared at the OLLYWOODLAND sign as he turned the ignition. The sign stared back, inscrutable.

CHAPTER TWENTY-NINE

Bobby lounged on the bed of his Dunbar Hotel room, trying to put the events of the last few days in some kind of perspective.

He liked Wilde. If he was going to be pals with a guy, he wanted it to be a man like Wilde. Bobby couldn't fathom how Wilde would respond to Bobby's secret. He wasn't sure it was worth it to find out. And still, David Chambers lurked in the back of Bobby's mind.

His room service chops came and hit the spot. *What kind of food is James Christmas getting in jail?*

There was no point going to the Alabam. If he ran into Booker, he'd have nothing concrete to report. He closed his eyes and drifted off.

Bobby woke from a dream where he was chasing Stinson in his car. Stinson put his hand out and grabbed the fender and lifted it like he was Superman—the wheels of his car kept spinning as Stinson hoisted the car off the ground and laughed at him. Bobby knew Stinson was behind everything, he just had to find out how. He grabbed a cup of coffee at the diner on the corner and headed to Stinson's office.

Bobby sauntered up to Pop, tipping his hat up high up on his head.

"Oh, it's you. Didn't rec-a-nize you before. Still interested in that Stinson fellow, eh?"

Bobby nodded.

"What is it you want from him?"

"I don't know."

Pop's eyes opened wide. Before he could ask the obvious question, *Then what the hell are you following him for?* Bobby pulled out some of the pictures that had been in the briefcase. He'd left the case in the car and most of the photos, including the ones from the concentration camp. But he spread a handful of pictures on the newsstand counter. Pop bent down to look at them. He slid his glasses up on his forehead, squinted. Pulled them back down. Went through this routine three, four times, then finally turned to Bobby.

"Do you recognize any of these people?"

"Seen him. Several times. Don't know his name though." He was pointing at Thomas. Bobby felt his heart skip.

"Do you know who he came here to see?"

"Can't say. All's I can say is it wasn't someone on the first floor. Took the elevator each time, but after that I lost track what floor he went to, let alone what office."

That was good enough for Bobby. It had to be more than co-incidence that Thomas would show up here where Stinson had his office. He still couldn't tie it all together, but something felt closer.

"What about the woman?" Bobby showed him the photo of Thomas' wife.

"I'da remembered her."

"And him?" Bobby pointed to Dietrich.

"Mmm, might've come by. But I can't say for sure."

"Think. He spoke with a German accent."

The old man shook his head.

"What about this third man? Who's he?" Bobby picked up the photo of Thomas, Dietrich, and the third man, placed it in Pop's fingers. The old man moved it close to his eyes, farther away. Back and forth.

"Nope."

"Thanks, Pop. You've been a big help."

"Hey, you want a paper?"

"Sure, I might need it to look for a job."

The phone booth caught Bobby's eye. He dropped a nickel in the slot. Dialed Sam. After a brief conversation, he jammed back to his car. He'd thought about trying to see Stinson again, but had other things he wanted to pursue right now.

Bobby shot down Broadway, heading south to Pico. He was going to pick Wilde up at the pool hall. Wilde didn't want him coming by his apartment or wherever it was that he'd received the phone call. Bobby wondered why Wilde wouldn't want him to know where he lived.

Before leaving the Bradbury, Bobby had looked at the building's directory to see if any of the names of the firms or people that occupied the upper floors rang a bell. Nothing did—except for Stinson and IBM. That didn't one hundred percent mean Thomas had gone there to see Stinson, but the odds were good. Bobby put the pedal to the metal, flying down Pico.

Even this early in the morning, the balls flew across the tables at Brownie's.

"Don't you see what this means? It ties Stinson and Thomas together."

"Didn't we already know that? Know that Dietrich knew Stinson." Wilde banked a shot. "More English."

"But this confirms it."

"Well, like you said, it's not a hundred percent."

"Close enough. At least it's something."

"So where do we go from here?"

"You could brace Stinson."

"Brace?" Wilde said. "You watching more of those Bogart movies?"

"What's gotten into you? Did someone get to you?"

Wilde's head jerked up from the table, fierce eyes glaring at Bobby. "Don't you talk like that in here. People can hear you.

"Don't you want to find out what happened? What about Lois? You seem to have lost your fire."

"No, kid. The only thing I've lost is my English." He chalked his cue.

"But that shouldn't stop you, us."

"It won't. I'm just tired. Let's get outta here." Wilde threw down his cue. Headed for the door.

"And go where?"

"Just drive."

Bobby pulled into traffic on Western. Turned onto Pico heading west again. "I can't be driving around with no place to go. We'll run out of gas."

"Let's eat, I'm starving. Got a craving for this little joint in the Farmer's Market."

Bobby cut up to Wilshire, continued heading west.

"I don't think there's any point going back to Stinson's office. Least not yet. Okay, maybe there's a connection there," Wilde said. "And you say this Pop couldn't identify the woman or the other man in the pictures."

"No, but maybe Stinson can."

"Sure. But is he going to talk to us?"

"That's where I thought you might come in."

"I think it's too early for strong-arm stuff. Not that I'm against it, mind you. I like my fun as much as the next guy. But I think if we hit him too soon and too hard, he'll fold his tent and slither away."

"He's got a job. A house."

"Yeah, but if he's the bad apple you seem to think, that won't matter. He'll take his money and run."

Bobby wondered why Wilde was so reticent to take strong,

direct action. Wilde had already answered that and probably didn't want to be probed further.

"Okay," Bobby said. "But even if he runs maybe we can follow him and see where he goes. That might tie it together."

"You got any money to follow?"

"No. But maybe I can go to Booker."

"You think that nigger's gonna trust you with his money?"

"I wish you wouldn't talk like that."

"What am I now, your husband? It's just a word, leave it be."

"He's already trusted me with money and his friend's room at the hotel."

They drove past the May Company and the La Brea Tar Pits.

Bobby slid the Olds up to the whitewashed clapboard of Farmer's Market on Third and Fairfax. "I'm hungry. And you're treating."

"That's fair since we're using your gas—that I bought. But who's counting, I'll treat."

They bought skirt steak sandwiches on french rolls at a small stand.

"We could eat over at the park by the Tar Pits."

"No way. That place gives me the willies. I mean, all those dead dinosaurs stuck in that tarry muckety muck." Wilde shivered. "And how many dead bodies you think are in there too?"

"Guess we'll be eating here."

They sat at a nearby table. Bobby'd been coming here since he was knee high to a grasshopper, as his grandfather always said. He took a bite.

"It's nice and all sitting here breaking bread with you, but we gotta think what to do next," Wilde said. "We got two keys that match up."

"But no idea what they go to. You and me or me alone has been through Dietrich's apartment, Thomas' house, their office. We've shown one of the keys to Margaret—"

"—We haven't looked through Stinson's house or office, have we?"

CHAPTER THIRTY

People shuffled back and forth, with coffee and sandwiches and donuts. Mostly older folks, the young men off to war or working in war-related factories. Women and kids too. Bobby looked around the white clapboard buildings of Farmer's Market. He used to love coming here, with its throngs of people and varieties of foods. Now it was like a ghost town.

"I'm surprised we could get steak sandwiches with the war and all, chewy as they are. I guess it's hit or miss. Though I did have a pretty decent Porterhouse at the Dunbar." Bobby finished off the last half of his sandwich in one bite that he chewed and chewed and chewed.

"I'm surprised you're avoiding the subject."

"We can't just break into the guy's house. Or office."

"Why not? We went into all those other places."

"Yeah, but they're all dead."

"Correct me if I'm wrong, but Thomas wasn't dead when you first went into his house."

"He was a few minutes later. Besides, that was different."

"Grow up, kid. It wasn't different and you know it."

Bobby did know it. Still, there was something holding him back from wanting to break and enter Stinson's house or office. Fear? No, something more than that. What if they found the key and it led somewhere he didn't want it to lead? Like back to Margaret.

He should have been thinking about how to get into Stinson's.

Instead he was thinking about where Wilde lived. Why he was so secretive about it?

"Saddle up, kid."

The drive back to Los Feliz from the Farmer's Market was like a slingshot bounce, as the car rebounded to the east.

"I've been to his house."

"You haven't mentioned it."

"Just like you won't tell me where you live."

"I guess we all have our secrets."

"But why?"

"Tell me about Stinson."

Bobby could have played a game on Wilde. He could have withheld his information until Wilde coughed up his. It wasn't worth it.

"He didn't have much to say and all I saw of his house was the kitchen."

"He invited you in for a cocktail? Very sophisticated."

"Yeah, just like in the *Thin Man*."

"I saw that movie. That Myrna Loy, hmm. Some spunky dame."

"If you like 'em spunky."

"I like 'em any way they come, long as they have two tits pointing in the same direction."

"No drinks, no cigars. He wasn't very cordial." Bobby hoped Wilde couldn't see his discomfort talking about women and his attempt to switch back to the subject at hand. "The one thing I noticed is that he was squeezing the handle of his briefcase so hard his knuckles were turning white."

"Soes the question is did he have something in there he didn't want you to see, something to hide, or was he just nervous? Pissed off?"

"It's hard to say. I guess I'm not very good at reading people."

"If you wanna be a private dick, kid, you better get good at it.

* * *

Bobby and Wilde cruised slowly by Stinson's house. Before he hit Vermont, he made a three-point turn in the street. Too much military traffic to and from the Greek Theatre on Vermont and if he was seen going back and forth, they might think he and Wilde were Nazi spies. He drove back the other way, beneath the palms that lined the street and by one Spanish colonial house after another—L.A. chic.

"It's the middle of the day. I doubt anyone's home."

They parked two doors down, walked nonchalantly—as nonchalantly as possible for Bobby considering his knees wanted to clack together with every step—to Stinson's driveway. They furtively ducked down the driveway to the back door.

"Does he have a wife or kids?" Wilde whispered, pulling out his set of *dentist tools*.

"I don't know."

"Now would be a hell of a time to find out."

"I don't think so. I didn't see anyone when I was here or any of the times I drove by."

"Lead pipe cinch," Wilde said, as the lock clicked. He paused on the threshold, listening. Gently pushed the door open. "Sounds empty."

"How can a house sound empty?"

"You hear anything? Not even one of those silly radio soap operas. Let's move out."

They entered the service porch, soundlessly closing the door behind them. Bobby was about to keep going, when Wilde's arm shot across his solar plexus. The thick forearm was like an immoveable object. Bobby stopped dead. They listened.

"Alright, I think it's okay," Wilde finally said. They stepped into the kitchen. "Look familiar? This is where you had your tête-à-tête?"

"Yes, aperitifs and canapés." Bobby eyed the drawers and cabinets. "So, what are we looking for?"

"You're the detective, but I guess we'll know it when we find it, like another key that matches. His briefcase maybe."

Stinson's house didn't yield anything new or intriguing. In fact, his house was as barren as his personality, definitely no woman's touch. No art, no knickknacks or photos. Just utilitarian furniture. About as inviting as a military barracks. Bobby collapsed, dejected, onto the chair of a small kitchen table that sat under a window. Silky sun streamed in through the gauzy curtains. From this angle the world seemed at peace. In the distance a baby cried. Jimmy Dorsey's "Tangerine" drifted in from a radio or phonograph up the street.

"Now what?" Bobby said.

"He must have the briefcase with him."

"What're we supposed to do, stick him up?"

"Not a half bad idea, kid."

"Maybe he just has his stash of nudie pictures in it."

"I think we should follow him. Maybe he'll go in somewhere, a store, restaurant, and we can snatch the case from his car."

"It's the middle of the day. He's probably still at work."

"What's up, kid?"

"What do you mean?"

"I get the feeling you don't want to be here, don't want to follow him."

"Hey, I've done pretty good on my own."

"Spill."

Bobby clenched his fists. "I met him here before."

"So you've said."

"He, he won't be bluffed. I told him I had a gun. He didn't believe me. He—"

"Maybe it was your boyish complexion he didn't believe, *sweet cheeks*. Don't worry about him. He won't be so tough when—"

Soft metal-on-metal scraping played through the room.

"What's that?" Bobby whispered.

"The maid," Wilde said, even more softly, pointing to a woman in a black-and-white uniform outside the kitchen window. He grabbed Bobby's coat sleeve, tugged him toward the front of the house. They heard the maid setting her things down in the kitchen as they crept to the front door. As quietly as possible, Wilde turned the lock, opened the door, and closed it behind them.

Bobby started running toward the car. Wilde grabbed him. "Make it look normal. We're just two guys out for a stroll."

"Fuller Brush salesmen."

"Yeah, I'm training you."

"Where's our sample case? What's she gonna do when she finds the front door unlocked?" Bobby's heart raced.

"She'll think your pal Stinson left it unlocked."

"I hope so."

"Turn down Vermont, then right on Franklin to Western. Head south."

"Toward the pool hall?"

"Sure, kid."

Bobby drove all the way down to Western and Pico without either of them saying a word. His bones ached with exhaustion. Right now he hated his life, hated the choices he'd made. Wished more than ever he could be landing on a beach in the Pacific with the marines. At least those boys knew what they were doing; they had a purpose, to make the world safe for democracy, as Woodrow Wilson had said during the First War.

"Just pull over and park anywhere near Brownie's."

Bobby followed orders. He would have made a good soldier. They got out of the car; Bobby started to lock it.

"You don't need to lock it. No one's gonna steal it."

Bobby wasn't so sure; being the good soldier, he followed orders. Headed toward the pool hall entrance that cut across the corner of Pico and Western.

"This way, kid." Wilde took him to the western side of the building. A narrow door led to a tight, steep stairway. Bobby followed Wilde up the stairs and down a hall of naked, dangling lightbulbs and threadbare carpet of dubious color. Halfway down the hall, he slipped a key into a door.

"Home, kid."

Bobby looked around the tiny one-room apartment with a kitchenette in the corner and a door that he supposed led to a bathroom. It made his apartment at Mrs. Hazelton's seem like Buckingham Palace by comparison. Wilde went to the small fridge, pulled out two cone-top cans of Schlitz beer.

"Now we're cookin' with gas," he said, handing Bobby a beer.

"You didn't want me to see your place? You were embarrassed, that's why all the secrecy?"

"It ain't exactly the Taj Mahal."

"Right now it's better than what I have. I mean my digs are reet, but they're not mine. And if I don't solve this case, I'll be out on my ass."

"At least it doesn't snow here in sunny southern California. But you'll have to excuse the mess. Maid's day off."

"Ah yes," Bobby said, putting on his best imitation of a movie butler. "You're giving her too much time off. There's a hundred people who would die to work in such a lovely abode. Maybe we can ask Mr. Stinson's maid if she'd like a change of scenery."

"I think that one sip of beer you had is going to your head."

And it was. Bobby still wasn't used to drinking and when he did it didn't take much to make him silly. He knew he shouldn't drink too much or he'd give away his secret.

Wilde picked up a shoe, catapulted it at a roach scurrying across the floor. Winged him, but the bastard got away.

"What are your secrets, kid?" Wilde said, finishing up his second Schlitz.

"Secrets?" Bobby's heart pumped; his face turned red hot. "I don't have any."

"Everyone's got secrets."

"What are yours?"

"I don't have any either. Guess that puts us in the same boat."

But Bobby knew that Wilde was right. Everyone has secrets,

large and small. Did anyone have as big a secret as he did? He felt the urge to confide in someone again. There was always Marion Jones. But she was too strident, pushing too many things on Bobby. He didn't really want to be part of her circle. He just wanted to be accepted as Bobby, as opposed to Roberta or Bobbie. To not be thought of as a sideshow freak.

What would happen if Bobby came clean to Wilde? He was too much of a coward to find out. He liked Wilde. He wasn't smooth and sophisticated like Cary Grant, wasn't quite as dashing as Errol Flynn. But he was certainly a man's man like Clark Gable or Gary Cooper. Bogey. And he seemed to have integrity behind that gruff exterior. His opinion of Wilde was changing. In short, he was the kind of man Bobby aspired to be, though in better digs and with a different career path. He was someone Bobby could look up to and model his male self after, besides the movie stars he had been doing that with for years. Because he certainly couldn't and wouldn't want to model himself after his own father.

When Bobby was a little girl—how odd that sounded, to be sitting here in this dump, drinking beer, looking and acting like one of the fellas thinking about this—Franklin Saxon loved her more than anything. His little girl. His princess. She could have anything she wanted. Anything except what she wanted most, to be a boy. To play with boy toys, like her brother's lead soldiers, and dress like a boy and climb trees and go fishing. As she got older, had more of a will of her own and started doing those things, her father grew more distant, until the point where he not only ignored her and favored her younger brothers, but where it seemed as if he hated her completely. Why? She was a good kid, though certainly not what her father expected. He couldn't deal with it on any level. Bobby was an embarrassment in front of the family, friends. Neighbors. How do you explain someone like that? Franklin Saxon sure as hell didn't know. Bobby wasn't even sure he knew.

Franklin Saxon was a decent working stiff, who busted his ass, provided for his family. But he didn't understand his daughter—his third *son*—and made no attempt to. On the one hand, Bobby understood. On the other—

"'Nother beer?"

Bobby shook his head. He wanted to come clean to Wilde. Wanted Sam Wilde to accept him for who he was. Instead, he folded his arms and pulled his legs up to his chest, caught himself doing this girly thing and stretched out. Closed his eyes and waited until it was time for them to go.

"So many strings and nothing to tie them together," Bobby said, as they sat in his car across from the Bradbury Building. They had reviewed the case on the drive down.

"Hey, that's his car." Bobby pointed to the Packard pulling into traffic. "He's leaving early."

Bobby pulled a U-turn—horns honking at him—followed Stinson at a distance.

"He must have an appointment somewhere," Wilde said.

"Jesus, please. Make it something to pull all this together."

Stinson drove north to Beverly Boulevard, then west until he hit Chasen's, a famous watering hole and restaurant for Hollywood's elite. Director Alfred Hitchcock even had his own booth. Stinson gave his car to a valet. Bobby drove slowly so they could see where the valet parked the Packard.

He stopped at the corner. Wilde opened the passenger door, slammed it, stuck his head in the window.

"Circle the block, slowly. Till I meet you back here."

Wilde was off. Bobby moved out, trying to keep an eye on him. On the first circle, He saw Barbara Stanwyck and Robert Taylor heading inside the restaurant. After two circles, Wilde was back at the curb and Robert Taylor was standing, joking with the valet.

"Take off. Pronto!"

Bobby rammed the gas pedal to the floor. The Olds squealed,

burning rubber.

"No briefcase. I even popped the trunk." He held up his set of *dentist tools*.

"Criminy!"

"Drive, kid."

"What's the point? Everything's a dead end. Hell, I'll be lucky if I can solve this case by the year 2020."

"If you don't solve it before then you won't need to worry about it."

"Why not?"

"You'll be dead. How old would you be in 2020, a hundred? Good luck." Wilde lit up a Camel. Shook another out, offered it to Bobby. He normally would have preferred one of his Viceroys. Instead, he took the unfiltered cig between his lips. Wilde flicked a lighter and Bobby sucked in.

The sun slid behind the Pacific and a curtain of dark descended on Los Angeles. Wilde told Bobby to head back to the Bradbury. Bobby did as ordered, not wanting to think about anything more immediate than the traffic. How long had it been since he'd found out anything significant? Sure, they had the keys that matched up. That wasn't that long ago, though it felt like a decade. He barely remembered the thrill of playing with Booker's band the first time and at that time he'd had an apartment and a possible permanent gig with the band. His future looked bright. Now he was unsure of the future, unsure of himself. Unsure of the people he knew, from Booker to the man who sat across the carseat from him. His confidence drained from him like water from a leaky radiator.

About half the lights in the various Bradbury offices were still on. People occupied the building, even at this hour. Bobby knew what was coming. He shouldn't have felt nervous—it was getting to be old hat. What he really wanted to do right now was go home. Back to the Dunbar. Open the windows, crawl under the covers of his bed and listen to the music wafting over from the Alabam. Lose himself inside the music. Lose himself forever.

"What time does your pal at the newsstand go home?"

"Pop? I don't know."

"Well, we don't want him to see you."

That only made Bobby's heart pound harder.

They parked on the street, tried the rear door to the building. Locked tight.

"I guess we have to use the front door. You stay to my side, in case your pal is there. Don't let him see you."

Sneaking into the building alongside Wilde, Bobby felt they must have looked like Mutt and Jeff. Pop sat on his stool, waiting for the next customer for the evening paper. Maybe he slept here all night? Bobby and Wilde sidled up to the elevator. It disgorged several people just as they got there, including Stinson's secretary. Bobby pulled his hat down low and used Wilde's mass to hide behind. It must have been later than he thought as there was no operator. When the elevator was clear, they slipped in, unnoticed by Pop or the secretary.

"Keep an eye out," Wilde said.

Bobby stood in the hall outside the IBM offices, glancing from one end to the other. He hoped no one would emerge from any of the other offices while Wilde performed his dental surgery on the lock.

"What if someone's still here? Just 'cause Stinson left—"

"Didn't you tell me this seemed more like a small distribution office? Don't worry. But that reminds me, maybe we should be looking for a bigger operation."

"I think their main offices are back East."

"Figures. The West Coast don't count for squat with those corporate boys, 'ceptin' for Hollywood and the airplane industry." Wilde popped the lock. They scurried inside, like roaches trying to hide from the light. "There's no one here. If we do this right no one will even know we've been here. Start looking."

Bobby felt control of this case slipping from him to Wilde. He had mixed feelings about that. He went to Stinson's private office, while Wilde devoured the outer office. Bobby heard drawers opening, closing. Wilde shuffling from the receptionist's desk to the credenza.

Bobby rifled Stinson's desk drawers, all unlocked except the largest one on the bottom right. He went through the papers on the desk, making sure to put them back exactly as they were. He even looked under the rug. Nothing.

"Nothin'," Wilde said, entering the sanctum sanctorum.

"Nothing here either, except one locked drawer in the desk." Bobby pulled out Thomas' rabbit's foot key and the other keys they had no known locks for. None worked. "Damn!"

Wilde grinned. "Let me have at it."

Out came the lock picks. Wilde inserted one, easily springing the drawer lock. Slid it open.

"Aces!" He pulled out Stinson's briefcase.

Bobby drummed his fingers in anticipation. He tried to flip the thumb catches on the briefcase. Locked. He tried the matching keys. No dice. Wilde came at them with his magic picks. The first lock popped open.

"A breeze," Wilde said.

He went to work on the second lock.

"Damn! The goddamn pick broke off in the lock."

"Shit."

Wilde picked up the case, ready to throw it. Bobby took it from him, set it back on the desk. Half of it opened. He stuck a wooden ruler from Stinson's desk in the crack to try to pry it. "If I do this, it'll break for sure. Can you get the broken piece out?"

Wilde tried. He shook the case. Stuck another pick in to try to jiggle the first piece free. "No dice. Let's just crack it open."

"Stinson'll know we've been here," Bobby said.

"He'll know someone has."

"Either way, he might take it on the lam."

"All right. We'll be delicate." Wilde played with the case some more. He jiggled the stuck lock. "Fuck it." He tore the case open, snapping the lock, leaving the broken pick in.

"Criminy."

"Forget it. Let's see what's what."

The case had the usual things one would expect. Bobby sifted through the papers. He reached into a leather pocket on the top side. Pulled out a stack of pictures.

"Look at these."

Wilde whistled.

"They're the same concentration camp pictures that Thomas had."

"Why do they both have them?"

"You think Thomas was blackmailing Stinson? If he was, why?"

"Now we know for sure they're connected one way or another."

They flipped through the photos. It was, indeed, the same set. "And look at this." Bobby pulled a key from Stinson's briefcase. Pulled two matching keys from his pocket. Held them up to Stinson's.

"Looks like a match."

"Close enough. And we'll have to go on faith here 'cause we can't take Stinson's key to the locksmith."

A piece of paper dangled from a paperclip attached to Stinson's key.

"What's the paper say?" Wilde said.

"It's an address. 211 Pine."

"Now we know where to find the hole our keys'll fit."

"That number sounds familiar. Remember, *Hans 211*, from the list in Thomas' briefcase."

"I told you things were going to break."

"Let's put everything back."

They tidied up as best they could.

"Can you get that damn pick out of the briefcase?"

Wilde spent ten minutes but finally managed to tweak it out.

"I can get it out, but the damn thing won't lock now."

"Close it as best you can and let's get out of here and find a map."

They turned off the lights, headed out.

CHAPTER THIRTY-ONE

The early evening sun illuminated the Los Angeles map Wilde had retrieved from Thomas' briefcase. Bobby's hands shook as he unfolded it. Wilde took one end.

"Stop shaking, kid, or we'll tear the damn thing in half."

They looked up Pine.

"There's two Pines," Wilde said. "Pine Street and Pine Avenue."

"Let's hit the closest first. If that's not it, we keep going."

"I wouldn't get my hopes up too high, kid. It looks like it might be a residential neighborhood."

"Well, why not? Maybe it's a house, someone Stinson knows or is in business with."

"Yeah, but we're looking for the place they hid the bodies and whatever other secrets they have."

"Wouldn't be the first time someone buried bodies in their back yard."

Bobby followed the map to a neighborhood west of downtown.

"Dietrich's apartment's not too far from here," he said, unable to hide his excitement at the possible connection.

"Might mean something."

He turned onto Pine Avenue, drove slowly up the street, watching the houses crawl by. He counted address numbers. "It's got to be the next one."

Bobby slowed the car to a snail's creep. As the house was on the west side of the street, Bobby had the better view from the driver's window. Wilde leaned across the front seat, almost resting his chin on Bobby's shoulder to get a look.

Bobby pressed the brake; the car stopped. Both men looked out the window to see a couple boys around nine tossing knives into the grass, playing mumblety-peg, and a girl of eight or so gliding on a swing set in the front yard.

"I don't think this is gonna be it," Wilde said. A horn honked. He turned around. "Fuck that SOB."

He looked ready to spring from the car. Bobby's hand on his elbow calmed him. The driver swerved around them, sped off.

"Pull over."

"Huh?"

Wilde got out of the car. The girl looked up, no fear in her eyes. The boys smiled at him. "Hey kids."

"Do I know you?" the girl said.

"I'm looking for a friend of mine's house. Mr. Stinson. Does he live here?"

One of the boys shook his head. "No," the girl said.

"Do you know anyone by that name?"

They both shook their heads.

"What about a Mr. Thomas or Mr. Dietrich?"

More shaking.

"Thanks anyway." Wilde reached in his pocket, retrieved a Tootsie Roll, handed it to the girl. "I'm sorry. I only have one but maybe you guys can share."

The kids said nothing; Wilde got in the car. As Bobby gassed it, he could see the girl breaking the candy in three.

"Head on, kid. 211 Pine *Street* here we come. Why couldn't that Stinson SOB have added a little more direction, like street or boulevard?"

"It was very inconsiderate of him to not spell it out or, better yet, have it marked on a map," Bobby said.

The address sat on a corner lot in West Hollywood. Another house. This one dark. No kids. No lights. No cars. Bobby and Wilde parked right in front. Walked to the door. Knocked.

Rang the bell.

"No one's home," Bobby whispered.

"Get out the keys."

"What if the neighbors—"

"Screw the neighbors. We gotta push this thing forward."

"It always does go faster in the movies."

"Yeah, but the movies ain't real life. Still, we need to make some waves."

Bobby slipped one of the matching keys into the front door lock. It wouldn't turn the tumblers. They slipped down the driveway.

"Times like this I wish I had a gun," Bobby whispered.

Wilde lifted the tail of his shirt to show a pistol tucked into his waistband.

"You got a spare?"

"I can get one."

Bobby tried the keys in the back door. No go. Wilde pulled his *dental tools* out, slipped one in the lock. It opened easily.

"Glad it didn't break off," Bobby said, gulping air, as they entered the service porch, silently closing the back door behind them. He fired up the small flashlight. They walked in tandem through the house, Mutt and Jeff again, shining the flash on walls and counters, poking through cabinets. Nothing looked unusual or out of place. The family must have been out for the evening.

Bobby held the flash on a small writing desk in the bedroom as Wilde flipped through papers.

"What's that?" Bobby said.

"Huh? Oh Jesus, they're home." Wilde dropped the papers, not bothering to put them back the way they'd been. "Let's lam."

"We can't go out the way we came, they're out there."

They forced open a window.

"Who's there?" a man's voice shouted from the front of the house.

"What's going on?" A woman.

Footsteps heading their way.

Wilde flew out the window, Bobby right behind—neither caring about the noise they made. They ran down the driveway for the Olds, escaping down the road as the man tore out of the front door. He ran down the street until his legs couldn't compete with the car anymore.

"Do you think he got my license?"

"I don't know, kid." But Wilde didn't seem scared. He seemed elated, fired up. "Whew!"

"You enjoyed that."

"Most fun I've had in ages. Maybe I should be a break-and-enter guy for real. Gets the juices flowing."

"That it does," Bobby said, trying to catch his breath. "But we still don't know anything."

CHAPTER THIRTY-TWO

Bobby plinked the Alabam's piano with one finger. That tune the fellow was playing came back to him. He fingered it on the keyboard. Sang a few words:

The blues don't care who's got 'em,
The blues don't care who cries,
And the night's don't care who's lonely,
Or whose tears are in whose eyes.

"Nice song," Gaby said, sweeping the floor, while Lawrence cleaned and tidied the bar for the fast-approaching night.

"That guy who wrote it, Vic Abrams. He come 'round here a lot?" Bobby leaned back on the piano bench, stretching hard.

"Sometimes, when he's in town. Mostly a New York guy, I think."

Bobby went back to the keys. The piano could relax him like nothing else. And after the day's adventure with Wilde and the case cracking a bit he needed to unwind, while he thought about their next move. Lucky Strike smoke swirled about him, strangling him like a noose; he couldn't stifle his cough. Booker must be here.

"Where's your shroud, man?"

"Booker."

"You look like death warmed over." Booker chuckled. "Any news on the case?"

"I'm making progress, but for every step forward there's another wall to go around or over."

"Long as you got the means to get over it you're doin' okay."

Bobby wanted to ask if Booker had heard from Leach about the Apollo reopening. Thought better of it.

"And speaking of death, tomorrow I'm going to a funeral. Dietrich," he said, "the guy that started all this."

"You need something in the meantime to lift your spirits? Go on next door to the Dunbar, take a shower, dress to the nines, call your girl—"

"—And take her where?"

"The Cocoanut Grove, man."

"You're out of your mind. I don't have two nickels to rub together."

"Just check in with the maître d' when you get there. Don't worry about the rest. I got favors to call in."

"Booker?"

"Don't say anything. Just get on out of here."

Bobby tried calling Margaret before and after his shower. She wasn't home and he couldn't reach her at the May Company. He put the Olds through its paces driving there. He'd wanted to talk to her anyway. He liked her—he wanted to keep liking her. But he felt she was hiding something, knew more than she was letting on. Maybe a night on the town, letting their hair down, would get her to open up.

On the ride to the May Company, he also thought what it might be like to go on a date with David Chambers to the Grove, as Roberta, of course. Be wined and dined. Dance. Then who knows what? *Silly girl, is that really what you want?*

He parked, jogged from the car to the Ladies' Gloves and Hats department. Margaret didn't see him enter, but Mrs. Ford watched him like a Mitchell BNC camera tracking Joan Crawford walking across a department store set.

Margaret looked up. "Bobby, I can't talk now."

"I've got tickets to the Grove. Come with me tonight." He put his hand on her forearm, pulling her out of the glove department.

"Don't bother coming back, Miss Lane," Mrs. Ford said. Under her breath she added, "One less kike."

Bobby charged Mrs. Ford. Got up in her face. "What did you say?"

Startled, her eyes wide, Mrs. Ford looked around for help.

"C'mon, you can say it. Everyone heard you anyway."

"If everyone heard then I guess I don't have to repeat myself."

Bobby went nose to nose with her. In her heels she was two inches taller than him. "I'm not going till you say it."

"You don't frighten me. You're probably one too."

"Isn't this the kind of BS that our boys in Europe are dying for?"

"—Maybe we're fighting on the wrong side. Now leave or I'll call for the manager, Mr. Beamish."

Lanky, too tall on spindly legs, blonde hair like Leslie Howard— maybe a little too old for the war—Beamish was as anemic-looking as his name. He had been watching the whole time. Didn't seem to want to get involved. Bobby didn't care, he leaned into Mrs. Ford. She backed off.

"Kike. Okay, I said it. Are you glad? Tough man. Tough *little* man."

He slapped her on the cheek. Stunned looks all around.

A woman in a gabardine suit walked up to Mrs. Ford. "If that's how you think of people maybe you don't need my business. Aren't we fighting Hitler over things like that?" Another customer nodded her agreement, as did Mr. Beamish.

Margaret's expression turned to happy surprise.

"I'm taking the rest of the day off." She grabbed her hat and purse from under the counter.

"Don't bother coming back," Mrs. Ford said.

"Don't worry, I'll be back. You can't get rid of me that easily, and you, Mrs. Ford, don't have the authority to fire me."

Mrs. Ford's eyes searched Mr. Beamish's face for support. His eyes said nothing.

Margaret and Bobby headed for the exit.

"May I have a word with you, Mrs. Ford?" Mr. Beamish said. Bobby noticed a slight smile on Margaret's face.

The Cocoanut Grove nestled in the Ambassador Hotel, which dominated its share of Wilshire Boulevard, not far from Dietrich's apartment at the Bryson. Bobby drove up in his Studebaker, which looked out of place among the Caddies, Duesenbergs, Packards, and other luxury cars.

"My God, that's Louis B. Mayer," Margaret said as the valet opened the door for her. Bobby walked around the car. She put her arm in his and they ambled up the walk alongside Mayer and his party.

"They say he's the highest paid man in America. Makes more than the president even," Margaret whispered.

"I heard he's the first American to make more than a million dollars salary."

The inside of the club looked like a tropical paradise—or at least Hollywood's version of one, with papier-mâché palm trees and twinkling hundred-watt stars.

"This is a fabulous table," Margaret said after they were seated.

"You look fabulous." Bobby smiled warmly. They had stopped at her house so she could clean up and change into a champagne-colored, chiffon evening gown. Margaret's father had been concerned about her going out with him. Normal fatherly concern? Or something else? Bobby had worried that Booker was more talk than action, but it couldn't have been easier for them to get in and now look at this table. Margaret was right, it was fabulous. Close to the action. Close to Freddy Martin's bandstand.

"You must have connections in the right places."

"Booker got us in."

"I like Freddy Martin's band."

"Well, you're going to see them tonight."

They ordered exotic Mai Tais. A lot of things swirled through

Bobby's mind: here he was on a date with a girl. Would he be able to pull it off? He was hiding a lot of things about himself—one huge thing in particular. Was it right to keep it hidden? What if he got caught?

On the other hand, what was Margaret hiding? "I'm glad you invited me."

"I'm glad you came. I didn't know if you would."

"You put yourself together quite nicely when you want to."

"Clothes make the man." Bobby had a private chuckle about that one. "That Mrs. Ford is something else. She clearly doesn't like Jews."

"Yes. Or coloreds. Or—" Margaret squirmed. "Mrs. Ford is an anti-Semitic bitch, just like the man who makes cars with that name—"

"Maybe it's something about the name Ford."

"Mostly I think she doesn't like herself."

"That's the way it is with a lot people. They take out their dislikes about themselves on other people. It's a lousy world. Just look at Europe today."

Margaret said nothing.

The waiter took their orders. Margaret ordered lobster Thermidor, Bobby the beef Wellington.

He stood, put out his hand. She took it and he led her to the dance floor. In her heels, Margaret came up to just about the right height for him.

Freddy's band launched into Benny Goodman's "Sing, Sing, Sing," a jumpin' swing tune in four-four time. Bobby grabbed Margaret for some spicy jitterbugging. He prided himself on being a good dancer, was glad to see that Margaret equaled him in that department. People cleared the space around them as they Lindy hopped in a circle of light, tearing up the floor.

Freddy nodded. All of a sudden the lights went down. A follow spot hit Bobby and Margaret. They were the center of attention.

When the number ended, people applauded them as much as they applauded the band.

"The band's in good form tonight," Bobby said.

"So are you."

"You cut a mean rug yourself."

Freddy and his band launched into "The Way You Look Tonight," a slow song. Bobby took Margaret in his arms, held her close. The dance floor filled up again.

They swayed across the floor, Bobby in the lead.

"I can't figure you out, Bobby Saxon. Musician. Detective. Cutter of rugs. What are you really?"

"Sometimes I have a hard time figuring that out myself, especially lately."

Bobby looked into her eyes, staring a little more intensely than he meant to.

"Why are you looking at me like that?" Margaret squirmed in his arms.

"I thought you might be upset about Dietrich."

"Did you ask him out or me?"

"I didn't mean anything by it. Still, what's wrong with talking about him? It is sort of what we have in common."

"Maybe it's all we have in common." Margaret stormed off the dance floor, yanked her chair out and sat just as the waiter brought their dinners, which she didn't touch.

"Aren't you going to eat?"

Several minutes passed.

"It'll get cold."

"I'm upset. A friend was murdered. The funeral's tomorrow."

"Seems a long time after the death."

"That's because of the coroner's investigation." She pushed her uneaten food away. "Surely you don't suspect me of having something to do with his death?"

"Of course not. I'm just making small talk." Bobby looked at her across the table.

"Some *small* talk. Do you want to interrogate me now?" She fumbled with her water glass.

"Can't a man just look at a woman?"

"Not like that. You're on the job, even now."

"I'm just trying to have a good time here. Do you want to dance again?"

"I'd rather not."

Bobby wasn't sure what he'd said. He wasn't used to dating, men or women. He didn't think he'd done anything. He didn't think he had been looking at her like a suspect. Was it really the way he was acting or was she feeling guilty and trying to put it on him? Of course, if that was the case why'd she go out with him in the first place? Maybe she was trying to see what he knew, as he was doing the same with her.

"I'll take you home if you'd like."

"I just want to go to the ladies' room."

She picked up her purse and wrap, walked off. Bobby waited. And waited. She didn't return. He was about to go after her when Freddy's band launched into a hot two-piano-based number he called "La Tempesta." The dueling pianists really tore up their eighty-eights like there was no tomorrow. Bobby had to get a chart on this one.

On his way home he drove by her duplex, slowed. A silhouette of a woman stood framed in a halo of light in a front window. He hit the gas, burning rubber down the road.

Bobby and Wilde joined the gathering of twenty or so at the Green Lawn Cemetery. He'd had to pick up Wilde and they'd missed the church service. They stood off by themselves under a white birch tree, while Margaret was seated next to Dietrich's casket on the far side of the grave. She barely acknowledged him. *Criminy, what the hell have I done? Women! Can't live with 'em—can't live as one.*

A large, shiny black Caddy pulled up along the road near Dietrich's final resting place. Bobby watched. Stinson got out, closed the door behind him. Bobby thought he saw someone else in the car; the glare from the sun made it hard to tell for sure. The other person, if there was one, stayed in the car.

Sergeant Nicolai approached Bobby and Wilde.

"You'd think he'd want to be buried in Germany," Wilde said softly.

"Maybe it's cheaper this way." Nicolai reached for a cigarette. Put it back in the pack. "You learn anything new?"

Bobby filled him in on the warehouse and the Mirror Maze people. I haven't learned much either. Nothing on that license you gave me, but it's still early. Those boys in Sac'to got a lot on their hands. But I did get the lab results on that bottle you gave me. Nothing but good ol' film developer. And I'm getting pressure to move on. They know I haven't let go yet, even though they've told me to."

"I still wonder why they just don't care about this case."

"I hate to break it to you, kid, but he is a Negro and nobody cares, they think they've got their man. Besides, this case is already cold as a dead fish and with no new leads and plenty of cases—" Nicolai spit. "But you don't have any new cases."

"You want me to keep working it?"

"Somebody's got to see justice is done, Capra-corny as that sounds."

"I thought cops were supposed to hate private dicks," Bobby said.

"They do, but are you a private dick? Do you have a license?"

"Nope."

"Then I guess I don't have to hate you. Just don't go gettin' a license."

"You seem to have changed your tune, Sergeant."

"Guess I'm getting old. Don't like being pushed around, not even by the brass."

The ceremony over, the crowd dispersed. Bobby kept looking at that big, shiny car that Stinson had gotten out of. He and Wilde *accidentally* came up on Margaret.

"I missed you last night. I thought you were just going to the ladies' room."

"I did too. I guess I'm just upset about all of this."

"I should have known when you grabbed your wrap. Not a very good detective."

Margaret showed the slightest hint of smile.

"Or a very good date," Bobby continued.

"You have your moments."

"Not enough, I guess."

"That's how musicians are. Or are you just a private eye dressed up in musician's clothing?"

"Sometimes we're not all we appear to be on the surface." He gave her a wry smile. "Give me another chance. I'd like to get to know you better."

"Me or Hans?"

"You. But I won't deny it. I'd like to get to know more about Hans. Don't you want to find his killer?"

"I thought *I* was his killer."

"You're reading too much into a look that meant nothing."

"I have to go."

"Why are you so angry with me?"

She hurried off without responding. Bobby didn't go after her. He knew he'd have to confront her sooner or later, even if he might not like what he learned. His eyes followed as she walked toward the row of cars.

Stinson was heading back to the car. Bobby chased after him. Wilde and Sergeant Nicolai followed.

"Mr. Stinson."

Stinson turned. "You again?"

"What're you doing here?"

"I might ask you the same question."

"Well then let me ask," Nicolai said, producing his badge from his suit pocket.

"Is this to be an interrogation? Why don't you arrest this young man? He's been harassing me. Thinks I have something to do with Hans' death."

"Murder," Bobby said.

"Murder, then. He was a friend. Business associate. That's all. I came to pay my respects. Is that all right with you three stooges?"

"What kind of business?" Nicolai said.

"What is this, the Gestapo?"

"If this was the Gestapo, you'd be in a concentration camp by now."

"Hans is in the import-export business—was in it. I sell business machines. Typewriters, tabulators, that type of thing. We did some business in the past." Stinson left abruptly.

"*Auf wiedersehen,*" Nicolai said. He turned to Bobby. "That guy's a real peach."

Bobby nodded. "Stinson drives a Packard. So who's car is that?"

Nicolai pulled a small pad and pencil from his pocket. Jotted something down as Stinson got in the Caddy and drove off. Bobby spit—he couldn't quite pull it off like Nicolai had. Decided it wouldn't be part of his being a man. Besides, it was disgusting.

CHAPTER THIRTY-THREE

Bobby and Wilde followed Nicolai to the Pig 'N' Whistle next to the Egyptian Theatre on Hollywood Boulevard. Nicolai parked in a red zone. Bobby parked up the block.

They settled into a dark booth under a paneled, heavy-beamed ceiling. Across from them sat Tarzan Johnny Weissmuller and his ex-wife Lupe Velez. Hmm...

After ordering, Bobby said, "I'm beginning to understand why the cops beat some people up."

"We don't do it for fun—leastways I don't." Nicolai sipped his beer. "Sounds like this Dietrich was up to no good or at the very least mixed up with the wrong element."

"Stinson. IBM?"

Nicolai nodded. "Maybe you should quit before they make you quit, if you know what I mean. Let the police do our job."

"You told me they're all laying off. Nobody gives a damn but me."

"I ain't quitting."

Nicolai looked Wilde in the eye. "You should join the force. We need men like you."

"So, Sarge, whaddaya think?" Bobby ran his fingers around the condensation on his Bubble Up glass, wishing he could join the police department.

"I think Stinson's good for it."

Was he? Or was Nicolai trying to steer him that way? Bobby still didn't trust anyone completely. And how the hell would

Nicolai know—he just knew what Bobby had told him.

"What about your gangster pal, Leach?" Nicolai said.

"I thought he was your gangster p—"

That pulled the conversation up short.

"Look kid, I make a little money on the side. Doesn't mean I'm a crook-crook. Not everyone's pure as the driven snow." He looked sharply at Bobby. Bobby probably did come across that way to people, young. Naive.

"So what if it is Stinson?" Bobby said.

"Okay, IBM is the bad guy, Stinson. Right now it's all supposition on our part. I see you didn't think I'd know such a big word. Sup-po-si-tion. Four syllables. We're not all dumb cops, you know."

"I never thought you were dumb, Sergeant."

"The problem with your IBM-Stinson—"

"—supposition—" Bobby watched Nicolai—wasn't it his supposition? Wasn't he the one who had just said Stinson was good for it? Was he playing devil's advocate or just trying to confuse things?

"—is that you have no motive," Nicolai went on. "I've checked on this IBM since talking with you. They're on the up and up. Straight and narrow top o' the line company. So unless you got motive they were just business partners and Mr. Stinson came to his friend's funeral to see him off."

"There's motive. We just can't put our finger on it—yet," Wilde said.

"You got nothing." Nicolai put down a fin, said his goodbyes.

Bobby remembered something. "Hey Sarge, can you run a license plate for me? Someone beat the daylights out of me outside of Musso and Frank."

"Gimme the number."

Bobby rummaged around in his pockets till he found the piece of paper with the incomplete license number on it. Gave it to Nicolai.

"I'll see what I can do. Hard with a partial like this."

Wilde waited for Nicolai to leave, turned to Bobby, "He wrote it down, you know."

"Wrote what down?"

"That big black Caddy's license."

"Guess he wanted it for the record."

Wilde scratched at his scars. "So, what do you think, Bobby?"

"I think something's going on. I don't know what it is, but I want to find out."

"I got you covered, man."

They hoisted their glasses.

Bobby's fingers danced over the Alabam's ivories. Gaby darted around, setting up the tables for the coming night's festivities. Lawrence set up the bar.

Bobby noodled around with "Ac-Cent-Tchu-Ate the Positive," but his fingers eventually began to pick out "La Tempesta," the tune he'd heard Freddy Martin's band play at the Grove. He sipped his Bubble Up. Went back to the tune.

The front door opened. A blast of white light shot through the 'Bam. Bobby looked over, expecting to see Booker. The shape said: woman.

Margaret.

She joined Bobby at the piano.

"I thought I might find you here. Nice piece."

Bobby wanted to say she would have heard it in its full two-piano glory if she hadn't left the Grove early the other night. Thought better of it. "You found me."

Lawrence asked if she wanted a drink, winked at Bobby.

"Bloody Mary, please."

Bobby walked her to a table in the far corner. Lawrence brought her drink over, then left them alone. Bobby didn't know what she had come for; he knew what he had to do.

"It's like a different world down here."

"Say it a little louder why don't you."

Margaret ignored his comment. "When I went back to work it was like nothing ever happened. Mrs. Ford just smiled and Mr. Beamish, well he just beamed."

"I'm glad for you."

"Is there a chill in here? I didn't realize this place was air conditioned. You don't have to be so snippy. Because of you, I could have lost my job."

"Not because your boss is an anti-Semitic harridan. Besides, you could always get a job in a war plant."

"Rosie the Riveter?" She laughed.

That seemed to calm the waters for a moment.

"I came down here to apologize for my behavior at the Grove. But you *were* interrogating me."

"I just want to help you find out who killed your friend."

"You don't care about Hans. You're just doing this so you can get a seat with the band."

"Not anymore. I want to find out what happened and why. I want to get James out of jail. I need your help, but you keep putting up walls. You don't trust me."

"Why should I? You think I'm a suspect—I'm involved."

"You have to admit there's a Jewish connection."

"I do? What Jewish connection?"

"The concentration camp pictures. I think they're the key to everything. Maybe some Jewish people killed Dietrich because of his connections to Germany, the Nazis?"

"Oh yes, it was me," Margaret scoffed. "I stabbed him or shot him, which was it, I forget? Then I hung him up there on the rafters, all by my little ol' self."

"Well, maybe you had help." Bobby instantly regretted his words.

"Maybe I did. But I don't need yours." Margaret jerked her chair back with a loud screech on the floor. She huffed off. Bobby jumped up, jogged in front of her, blocking her path to the exit. Both Lawrence and Gaby's heads turned.

"Are you going to accost me right here, in front of your

friends?"

"Why are you so angry if you have nothing to hide?"

"Why are you treating me like a suspect? You're not even a cop."

"Why are you so upset?"

"Because I'm scared," Margaret blurted. She stopped moving toward the exit. Her whole body seemed to sag. Bobby guided her back to the table. They sat, went back to their drinks and conversation.

"What are you afraid of?"

"These days, my shadow."

"But you weren't afraid to come down to this part of town to see me."

Bobby looked her in the eyes. He wanted to change the subject, get back on track. "Why wasn't Dietrich's body sent back to Germany for burial?"

"Germany? He hated what's become of Germany."

"But when he was arguing with James, he was the perfect Nazi."

"He was putting on an act. He wanted certain people to think he was a Nazi."

"Who?"

"Stinson? I don't know. He wouldn't tell me. To protect me."

"Then why?" Bobby said.

"Because Hans knew they were doing something, something bad. He wanted to stop it. And no, I don't know what it was."

"What was your relationship with *Hans*?"

"We were friends." The fight seemed to drain out of her. She looked tired. And wary.

"That's all?"

Margaret scrunched her eyes closed, as if by doing so she could shut out the world, the war, everything that made her cry. Bobby used to do the same thing when he was a *girl*, trying to shut out the yelling of his parents and their refusal to accept *him*. It didn't work for him then and he knew it wouldn't work for Margaret now. Scarlett O'Hara may have said "I'll think about that tomorrow" in *Gone With the Wind*, but tomorrow would always come and you couldn't keep your eyes closed forever.

Margaret sank down into the chair's cushion. Bobby slid his chair toward her. Took her hand. "I'm sorry if I was too tough on you."

"No. I should be able to take it."

"Take a load off. Tell me what's going on."

Bobby signaled for Lawrence to bring them another round. They waited till he'd come and gone before continuing. The respite let them catch their breaths.

"I don't know much, really." Margaret downed half of her second Bloody Mary in one sip. Fortification. "I wasn't Hans' girlfriend, though we played it that way sometimes for appearances' sake. We had a common goal."

"What?"

"It's so complicated but here goes: Hans was interested in helping Jewish refugees from Germany. Our synagogue was doing fundraising to help sponsor Jewish families and bring them to the US. Hans came to us wanting to help." Margaret hesitated. When she spoke again it was haltingly. "And my dad is the third man in the photo. He and Dietrich met at a fundraising event several years ago."

"Why didn't you tell me?" Bobby felt hurt but knew he shouldn't be.

"I didn't want to get my dad in trouble."

"And Thomas?"

"Mr. Thomas' wife was Jewish. He met her on a buying trip to Germany before the war. She went back to try to get her family out."

"Wasn't that dangerous?"

"Yes. He didn't want her to go but she went back anyway; the Germans assured the Thomases that she'd be allowed back into this country after they *talked* to her. When she got there, they said she was a German citizen and wouldn't let her leave."

"What happened to her?"

"They slapped her in a camp. And most of her family was either dead or already in the camps. It's a nightmare." She pulled a handkerchief from her purse, dabbed her eyes.

"So Thomas and Dietrich were trying to get her back to the States?"

"Well, they did try but they saw very quickly that it was hopeless. But they didn't want to do nothing. So they decided to help get any Jews out they could. And some of those came here on a sort of underground railway of trains and boats and any other way they could. You know that empty room you saw at Mr. Thomas' house?"

"Yes."

"It was filled with mattresses."

"I saw them, down the hillside," Bobby said.

"They kept some of the refugees in that room until they could find homes for them. It was a sort of a—"

"—transshipment point?"

"Yeah. Yes, that's what you can call it."

"So they'd stay at Thomas' until there was a more permanent place for them," Bobby said.

"He tried to move them out as quickly as possible. But the army put an anti-aircraft battery on a hill near his house. Lots of military trucks going by. I think he got scared and decided to close that end of the operation. They sent the Jews who were there at the time to the next *station* in the underground railroad and got rid of the—"

"—evidence. The mattresses. And how are you involved?"

"I was the go-between for Hans and our underground rescue group. He didn't want anyone to know about his involvement with the group. He thought there might be German spies watching him and he didn't want them to find out about our group and what we were doing, so we pretended to be dating. That way I could give him information when we went out to dinner or a show."

"And what about Leland Russell?"

"He was part of our group, too."

"So who killed Thomas?"

"Wait. I'm not done yet," Margaret said. "After they cleaned out Mr. Thomas' place they didn't want to just quit. I guess they wanted to fight the war in their own way. Their own front, so to speak. They had been so friendly with the Germans before the war, most of their importing and exporting was done with Germany. Now they felt betrayed. So Hans and Mr. Thomas went looking for another dragon to slay."

"But neither of them was Jewish?"

"No. But they weren't Nazis either—"

"So why did Dietrich sound like one on the boat?"

"That was his cover. Being sympathetic. He thought he could find out about fifth columnists here. Turn them over to the FBI."

"He thought Stinson was involved in helping the Nazis somehow—that's why he pretended to be one?"

"Yes, I think so."

"But he and Thomas were working on their own?"

"At that point, yes. Before that they were working with Jewish groups. Anyway, they were working on something but I didn't know exactly what. I worked with them when they were doing the underground railroad but not after that."

"What about the photographic equipment in Thomas' bathroom, the concentration camp photos?" That equipment kept coming back to Bobby. He didn't think Thomas was just developing pictures of the local countryside.

"I don't know. I really don't know." Margaret's fingers wrapped tightly around her Bloody Mary glass.

"But that could have been what they were working on before they both got killed."

"So why did they have those pictures? They already knew all about the concentration camps."

"Maybe they wanted to show the pictures around," Bobby

said. "Maybe find somebody who knew someone who could show them to Roosevelt or some of his cabinet. Get him to change his mind about bombing the railroad tracks to the camps."

"You don't think Roosevelt knows already?"

"But those pictures. They must mean something."

"They do. But nobody cares," Margaret said.

"What about Stinson? IBM?"

"I know they did business with him before the war. Maybe he was trying to help them? All I know is that whatever they were messing with got them killed."

"And James Christmas thrown in jail for something he didn't do. So why're you scared?"

"I was afraid that whoever went after Dietrich and Thomas might also come after me and my dad for helping with the refugees."

"I'll protect you."

"Nobody can protect anybody twenty-four hours a day." She fidgeted with her handkerchief. "All I can tell you, Bobby, is you're messing with fire."

"You almost sound like you care."

"I do." She took his hand in hers. Squeezed tight.

He liked the feeling. Wanted to kiss her but chickened out.

Bobby smiled. He tried not to, couldn't help himself. "Now that we're on the same team, let's go muster the troops."

"Three margaritas," Wilde said. The waitress scurried off, her flounce skirts rustling in a self-made breeze. After the dinner hour and during the war, the restaurant had a few patrons but was far from full.

"We're spending money we don't have like the King of England."

"It's easier to spend when you don't have it."

Bobby wasn't sure that made sense. He also wasn't sure he wanted a margarita, whatever that was.

Bobby, Wilde, and Margaret looked at each other across the table at El Coyote, a Mexican café at First and La Brea that Margaret had suggested. Nobody said a word, each lost in their own thoughts. Bobby's head tilted down toward his menu, though his eyes glanced up now and then to catch a glimpse of Margaret or Wilde. What were they thinking? Would she go for a man like Wilde? He felt that he couldn't compete with a real man.

"So you've tried three Pine addresses, but none seems to be the right one," Margaret said. Bobby had filled her in on the ride over.

"Those are the only two Pines on the map, but one of them had a north and south address," Bobby said.

"We've got keys that probably go to the Pine address, the correct Pine address. If we can find it."

"Let me see that map."

Bobby handed it to Margaret. She unfolded it across the table. "This is a map of L.A."

"Yeah."

"Isn't there a Pine something-or-other in Santa Monica?"

Bobby slapped his forehead.

"A couple-a great spies you guys are."

"Not spies. Detectives," Bobby said, barely audible.

The waitress brought their drinks, took their food orders. Flounced off.

Wilde picked up his margarita. "A margarita for Margaret."

"To Pine in Santa Monica," Margaret said.

They clinked glasses. Two men in suits and hats entered. They were seated across the room, across a sea of interior white stucco, bullfight pictures, and brightly colored pottery.

"That guy looks drunk already," Bobby said, sipping his drink. He squinted at them.

"Wait'll he has a couple margaritas. He'll be so tight he won't know his mother's name."

"Wait'll I have a couple," Bobby said. He liked the taste of the tequila drink, especially the tartness of the lime juice and the salt on the rim of the glass. "I'm already feeling this one."

He stared at the two men some more. Something about them seemed familiar. They were too far across the room and he was just a little too *happy* to pinpoint what it was.

"So you found this Pine address in Stinson's briefcase?" Margaret sipped her drink.

Bobby nodded.

"When you broke into his office."

"Maybe we're not such bad detectives, after all." Wilde hoisted his glass, finished his drink in one gulp. "We should get the kid drunk."

"I'm not sure that's a good idea," Margaret said.

"He needs to loosen up. Needs to man up."

"Drinking isn't necessarily manning up," Margaret said, twirling her glass in her hands. Bobby liked her for what she said; it gave him hope that she wasn't enamored of Wilde.

"In whose book?" Wilde said, a little more gruffly than he might have had he not downed his whole drink at once.

"You know what else we found in Stinson's briefcase?" Bobby said.

"What?"

"The concentration camp pictures. The same ones that Thomas had."

Margaret's face went blank.

"That means your boyfriend was a Nazi," Wilde said.

"That's not true Dietrich and Thomas weren't Nazi's. They were helping Jews. Tell him Bobby—tell him what I told you."

"She's right, Sam. You're barking up the wrong tree. From what Margaret told me Dietrich and Thomas were working on something together. Something big. And they got killed because of it."

Wilde shrugged.

"Either way, we still don't know what the pictures mean," Bobby said. "What they have to do with anything."

"Can I see them again?"

"They're in the car. And I don't think you want to look at them over dinner."

"I've already lost my appetite." She darted her eyes at Wilde.

"Keys," Wilde said, standing. Margaret eyed him. Bobby knew it wasn't because he was going to get the pictures. She was angry that he'd cast aspersions on Dietrich. Bobby tossed him the keys.

"Why do you hang out with him?" Margaret said as soon as Wilde had cleared the front door.

"He's a good sounding board, believe it or not."

From the look in her eyes, Margaret was thinking *or not*.

"And if push ever comes to shove, I think it'd be good to have him around to shove back."

"Well, you might have a point there."

Wilde returned, spreading the photos on the table. They sifted through them one at a time, careful to block their view from other patrons and the waitress.

"I don't see anything I didn't see before," Bobby said.

"They're ugly. Very ugly." Margaret bit her lips, hard.

Bobby watched her eyes. He always marveled at people who said they could tell what someone was thinking by their eyes. Brighter people than him, no doubt.

"Given half the chance, man will always behave as badly as he can get away with." Wilde signaled the waitress for another round of margaritas.

"I thought persecution by Torquemada was bad."

"These Nazis make Torquemada look like a piker."

"Aren't they Christians?" Bobby asked.

"No," Margaret said. "They're Nazis, the national socialist party. I don't think they believe in anything. If they did they wouldn't be doing this." She sloughed the pictures away from her.

"What did your pal Dietrich believe in?" Wilde said.

"What are you implying?"

The waitress brought their enchilada dinners. Margaret pushed hers away. Bobby wanted to say something, Wilde beat him to it.

"Not hungry?" Wilde said.

"Not anymore."

"Neither am I." Bobby pulled out his pack of Viceroys. "I'm ready to head over to Santa Monica."

"Me too."

"Not so fast." Wilde slopped hot sauce on his enchilada. Before he was through he'd eaten all three of their dinners.

After picking up a map of Santa Monica at a gas station, the Olds Six shot down La Brea. Bobby made a hard right onto Olympic Boulevard, heading toward the Ocean. Formerly 10th Street, it was renamed for the 1932 summer Olympics in L.A. and was the fastest east-west thoroughfare.

"Did you have enough to eat?" Margaret said, turning back to Wilde, who had the rumble seat to himself.

"Man does not detect by margaritas alone. You have to stoke the furnace."

"I think you took care of that."

"Criminy!"

"What's wrong, Bobby?"

"That guy's headlights are blinding me." Bobby shielded his eyes from the rearview mirror with his hand.

"Maybe he'll turn off somewhere."

"I hope so, 'cause it's a long way to the beach from here, if that's where he's heading."

"Let him pass you."

Bobby slowed the Six to thirty miles an hour. With so little traffic on the road now that seemed criminal. The bright lights hung back. Eventually they couldn't stand the slow pace and passed Bobby on the right.

The big car stayed ahead of the Olds, but always in Bobby's line of sight. They both hit the stoplight at Sepulveda at the same time. Bobby tried to peer into the other car, couldn't see who was inside. The big car inched forward. Bobby moved alongside him. The big car nosed out into the intersection. Bobby didn't want to do that.

"I think they're following us."

Margaret ruffled the map. "Turn down Bundy to Ocean Park."

On Bundy they got behind a long line of deuce-and-a-half military trucks.

"They must be heading for Clover Field," Wilde shouted from the rumble seat, referring to the former movie studio site. Just about everything in L.A. was a one-time studio and this one now served as the home of Douglas Aircraft.

"Where's the field?" Bobby said. "You used to be able to see it day or night."

"Now that it's a vital war industry, it was a sitting duck for a Nip attack from the air, so Douglas had a team from Warner Brothers come out and camouflage it," Wilde barked. "Did a pretty good job."

"I'll say." Bobby couldn't see the hangers or airport lights. Just what looked like more houses. "Pretty amazing."

"I heard about that," Margaret said. "They strung chicken wire across a bunch-a tall poles, covered everything with canopies and fake houses. Even phony trees and clotheslines."

"The Japs'll never see the field from the air. They painted the runways green to look like grass. I hear even our pilots have a hard time finding it," Wilde yelled from the rumble seat.

The truck convoy continued south on Bundy, while Bobby turned west onto Ocean Park. It only took a block or so for him to realize that the bright headlights continued to glare back at him from his rearview mirror.

"I think they're back, the headlights. Behind us again."

Margaret looked over her shoulder. "Maybe it's a different car."

"Always the optimist."

"Just keep heading down Ocean till you get to 14th Street,

then turn right."

Bobby followed 14th to Pine, then made a left, the only way he could go.

"See, no headlights," Margaret said.

Bobby looked in the rearview mirror. Dark. He breathed deep.

They drove the five-block length of Pine. All three scanned the street signs and house numbers for 211. The numbers didn't go down that low.

"Damn!" Wilde said from the back.

"Three strikes and you're out," Bobby said.

"Maybe this isn't a strike." Margaret smiled. "It's just another challenge."

"This might not be a strike, but those headlights are."

The large headlights stared angrily at Bobby in the rearview mirror. Wilde and Margaret turned around.

The lights loomed larger as the big car bore down on the Olds.

"Get the hell outta here, kid."

Bobby jammed on the gas. The Six burned rubber, careening around the corner from Pine onto Seventh.

"Four strikes and you're definitely out," Bobby muttered.

CHAPTER THIRTY-FOUR

The Olds tore up Seventh until it hit Ocean Park—a T intersection. Bobby didn't know which way to go. He jerked the car left, pitching wildly back down Ocean Park the way they'd come. He crammed down the accelerator, picking up speed. The headlights were steady in the rearview.

Wilde jerked the pistol from his belt. Banged the slide back with a loud clack.

"You can't shoot now," Margaret shouted. "There's other cars, people."

"If it's kill or be killed—"

The Olds flew up Ocean Park. Brakes squealing, Bobby made a hard right onto 28th Street, heading for Clover Field.

"What the hell are you doing? You wanna get shot by the soldiers at the base?" Wilde shouted.

"I want them to protect us."

"Yeah, they'll protect us, after they shoot us. We're at war, you know, you can't just go crashing onto the base."

"Well, I guess we're dead either way then." Bobby could barely believe what he was saying, though he did think it sounded a little Bogartesque. The big headlights chased them down 28th.

"Where the hell is the base? This just looks like more houses."

Bobby smashed through a forward sentry post, whipping east onto Donald Douglas Loop North.

"Halt!" The sentry's shout trailed off into a chasm of dead air. Before he could aim his M1 Garand rifle, the big tail car barreled through.

Wilde whooped. "I think you found the base."

Bobby followed Donald Douglas Loop North until it became Donald Douglas Loop South. The big headlights in the rearview mirror were joined by narrow-eyed Jeep lights not far behind. He lurched onto Airport Avenue, heading west again.

"You're making me dizzy," Wilde shouted, giddy with the thrill of the chase.

The Olds made a two-wheeled turn onto Walgrove, alone at least for the moment. Bobby then turned left onto Morningside Way; left again onto Psomas Way, a street filled with tumble-weeds and tall, stringy grass, but no houses.

"No lights behind us," Margaret said, looking over her shoulder. Bobby could hear the hopefulness in her voice. He pulled over, cut his engine and lights, laying low behind the tall grass. They listened for other cars. It didn't take long. First the low rumble of the big car, then the sound of the four-cylinder Jeeps giving chase.

They waited for the minutes to tick by as if they were waiting for a bomb to go off. After five minutes of no lights, no bomb, Wilde said, "Kick on the engine, but leave your lights off."

Bobby glanced in the rearview at Wilde. Too dark to see the expression on his face, Bobby could only imagine it.

"You're crazy."

"Aren't we better off just sitting it out here?" Margaret whispered.

"They'll be here sooner or later," Wilde said. "If we lam now we just might be able to sneak on outta here. Go slow, lights off. Try not to grind the gears."

Bobby shot him a pissed off look in the rearview. He pushed the choke in, pressed the clutch, put the car in gear. The engine sputtered and died. "Criminy."

"Jesus!" echoed from the rumble seat.

Bobby went through the sequence again. A strong narrow beam of brighter than white light arced across the top of the grass. One of the Jeeps' searchlights. Bobby ducked, instinctively.

"Give them a second, then ease on outta here, kid." Bobby gave them thirty seconds—*one-one thousand, two-one thousand*—to move past Psomas Way. He put the car in gear. It slipped between the overgrown grass on either side of the street.

A tumbleweed cartwheeled across the road. Bobby slammed on the brakes with a loud squeal.

"Criminy!"

"We'll be lucky if they didn't hear that."

"Even if they did maybe they can't figure out what direction it came from."

Bobby followed Psomas back to Morningside. He wanted to turn left and head back toward L.A. Headlights coming from that direction forced him to go the other way, toward the ocean. Plus to go left would have taken him closer to the base and the soldiers in Jeeps.

Bobby turned up Penmar to Rose. More headlights to the east. He turned west again. The spit of the ocean slapped him in the face.

"Hit it," Wilde shouted. Bobby saw him looking over his shoulder in the rumble. He hoped Wilde would keep his gun in his pocket.

Bobby accelerated slowly, not wanting to make any sudden moves and call attention to the Six.

The headlights also accelerated, keeping a steady pace. He looked in the rearview. Was it a Jeep? The little military vehicle had a distinctive silhouette, especially when it had a .50 caliber Browning mounted on it. But the glare in the mirrored glass wouldn't let Bobby see what kind of car it was.

He jammed down Rose, past a Gilmore filling station, heading north on Lincoln, one of Santa Monica's main drags.

"Where the hell am I going?"

"Wherever it is, it's away from that damn Jeep following us."

So it was a Jeep. "Shit!"

Bobby shifted gears; the Olds went flat out. The chase car,

with its four cylinders, couldn't keep up. But they were still back there. The big car turned off, probably not wanting to tangle with the soldiers.

He two-wheeled onto Colorado, screaming toward the ocean. The Jeep stuck close enough to keep him in their sites, but far enough back that they couldn't throw spitballs. But that distance would be no problem for a Browning.

Bobby flew past Ocean Avenue onto the Santa Monica Pier, smashing through a wooden sawhorse barrier at the pier's entrance. Between the fog and military blackout regulations near the base, he could barely see any of the buildings on the pier. He felt the *thump-thump-thump* of the wooden boards under the Six's wheels.

"This is better than any ride down at the Pike," Wilde yelled.

"Bobby, we have to stop. Give up before they shoot us!" Margaret said.

The Olds roared ahead.

"Bobby, stop! You're heading—" Margaret's voice trailed off.

"What?" Bobby shouted over the roar of the engine and the waves. He flashed on the rearview. The Jeep was closing fast. Before Bobby could think what to do next, the Olds shattered the pier's wooden railings. Tiny wooden spears and saltwater splinters pricked Bobby's face as the Six took to the air. *Oh my beautiful car*, was the last thing he thought before time seemed to stop. The Six hung weightless in mid-air for a moment, then in slow motion descended toward the pitch-black water. He heard the waves crashing against the pilings below, the screeching of the Jeep's brakes above, and Wilde bellowing, "Davy Jones, here I come!"

Bobby lay stretched out on the sand. He shivered, snapped open his eyes. "I thought I'd be staring into the face of some cop or MP."

He looked at Margaret's face and his wet, aching body,

seemed to grow warm. Her stringy wet hair and white bandages on both arms made an impression on him.

"Are you okay?" he said.

"Just some scrapes and cuts. Nothing serious."

"I'm glad you're all right."

Margaret smiled. The welcoming smile was quickly replaced by the scowling face of one pissed-off-looking military policeman. A man in a white coat nudged the MP out of the way, put a blood pressure cuff on Bobby's arm. Pumped it up.

"How is he, doc?" the MP said, with absolutely no concern for Bobby's condition.

"He'll live. I don't think he has any broken bones. Lucky guy. But we'll have to take him to the hospital to make sure."

"He ain't going to no hospital. He's coming with us." The MP's fingers clamped completely around Bobby's forearm. Bobby was glad the ambulance technician had taken off the blood pressure cuff. The huge MP's grip would have made it pop through the stratosphere like one of those hammer and bell High Striker strength tests at the Pike.

"He's mine," said a man in a dark blue Santa Monica Police uniform with sergeant's stripes.

"He was trying to get onto the base, he's ours," the MP said.

"This isn't the base."

"This is war. We have jurisdiction."

"Did he actually get on the base?"

The MP hesitated. "No. But he drove through a perimeter sentry post."

"Then he's mine. Back off."

The MP loosened his grip. Bobby's hand had begun to tingle. He could already feel it start to wake up.

The Santa Monica police sergeant looked at Bobby. "You were the driver, weren't you?"

"Is Wilde okay?" Bobby didn't know what else to say, just that he didn't want to answer the cop's question.

"Your co-conspirators are okay. Some bumps and bruises.

You'll all live. Now answer my question."

"Yeah, yeah, I drove."

An icy, briny wind lashed in off the ocean. Bobby was chilled to the bone. He tried not to show it. What would Autry do in this situation? He, and the stars of the other B Westerns often found themselves innocently in jail. Bobby knew he would too. Whether it was the Santa Monica jail or the military police stockade, he was going to be behind bars.

The room they threw him into wasn't much bigger than his bathroom at Mrs. Hazelton's apartment house. He sat on a utilitarian ladder-backed chair that wobbled to one side. At least there wasn't a desk lamp to give him the third degree. Maybe this wouldn't be as bad as he thought.

The door opened, the Santa Monica sergeant, the MP, two other men in suits, one pinstriped, the other a solid dark gray, and a stenographer crowded into the room. It reminded Bobby of the stateroom scene in the Marx Brothers' *A Night at the Opera*. He couldn't help cracking a smile.

"You think this is funny," the MP growled. He whacked Bobby's hand with a billy club.

"Damn! I play the piano." Bobby rubbed his knuckles.

"What are you, some kind of fag?" The MP, who reminded Bobby of Charles Atlas, grinned. "Guess you won't be playing for a while."

Bobby lurched up. The Santa Monica sergeant hammered his hand into Bobby's shoulder and pushed him back into his chair.

"Far as I can tell, you're a spy. A traitor. You know what they do to traitors in time of war? They hang 'em," the MP said.

"You don't know what you're talking about." Bobby rubbed his bruised knuckles.

"Why don't you tell us," the taller man in the pinstriped suit said.

"Do I get to know who I'm talking to?"

"Just tell us what happened."

"Where's my lawyer?"

Now all their faces turned to scowls.

"You're in enough trouble, son. Make it easy on yourself."

"We were going for a ride," Bobby said.

"Joy ride?"

"You can call it that."

"There's a war on. Blackouts."

"I didn't say it was the smartest thing."

"What were you doing at the base?"

"I wasn't at the base. We took a wrong turn."

"Your buddy, Wilde, had a gun."

"Just for protection."

"So you know he had it."

"He always carries it." Bobby wasn't sure if he should have said this. Right now he wasn't sure of anything. "Whatdda you think, we were going to take over the base, where you guys have Browning machine guns and rifles and Tommy guns, with one crummy little pistol? We're not that stupid."

"Pretty stupid, though."

"Maybe so," Bobby said. The last thing he wanted was to go to jail. Treason charges would be bad enough. Being found to be a woman in a men's jail would be a thousand times worse.

The two men in suits—Bobby didn't know if they were detectives, district attorneys, or G-men, Jay Edgar Hoover's FBI—the MP, and the Santa Monica sergeant huddled in the corner of the room. They talked in low voices. Bobby could make out some of what they said.

"I believe him," the Santa Monica sergeant said.

"He's a fucking spy." The MP twirled his baton through his fingers.

"Look at him. He's barely old enough to shave."

"That's the best kind. You don't think they're spies. They

look young or innocent or just like everyone else."

The sergeant looked to the men in suits. The MP did the same. Their faces were impassive. Stone. They were finally introduced as FBI agent Gene Pallette and Santa Monica police captain Sean Gibson.

"Well, we gotta do something with them," the MP said.

"His story jibes with the other two."

Bobby was relieved to hear that somehow Margaret and Wilde had come up with the same tale. He worried about what would happen when they fished the Six out of its deep six and found the briefcase with the photos. Then what?

"Book 'im for reckless driving," agent Pallette said. "We'll dig deeper and if there's anything else we'll slam 'im in a military prison where he'll never see the sun shine again." This last part was said deliberately loud.

Bobby looked up at the man. "Thank you. I did something stupid. Not traitorous."

"We'll find out. Either way, you didn't get on the base."

One by one, the men shuffled out of the room. The MP slapped Bobby's thigh with the billy club—a goodbye tap. Bobby jerked in his seat. Only the Santa Monica sergeant remained.

"You're lucky I've got you instead of the MPs."

"What happens next?"

"You'll be booked. Arraigned."

"You're only booking me on reckless driving?"

"For now. You're one lucky son of a bitch. Guess it's your baby face."

Bobby rubbed his fingers across his chin. "I never liked this baby face of mine. Until now."

CHAPTER THIRTY-FIVE

"Sergeant, you've been square with me. Thanks."

The Santa Monica police sergeant nodded.

"What's your name?"

"Billy Duff." Duff pulled a panatela from his pocket. Lit up. "You want one?"

The pungent smell turned Bobby off, but he wasn't about to turn down the sergeant who may have just saved his ass. "Sure."

He took the cheap cigar from Duff. Lit up. Choked back a cough.

"They're cheap shit. All I can afford on a sergeant's pay."

"What happens next, Sergeant?"

"You'll be taken to Central Jail, downtown L.A. We don't do our own booking here this time-a night these days. Short-staffed, the war. The sheriffs'll book you and then you'll be arraigned. It'll go quick."

"Will I get jail time?"

"I doubt it. This ain't no major John Dillinger you pulled."

"What about my friends? How are they? Where are they?"

"The girl's already been let go. She wanted to come see you, but the G-man made her go home. Your buddy Wilde's another story. He shouldda tossed the gun when you went into the drink."

"What'll happen to him?"

"If his record with the China marines is as right as he says, he'll probably skate too. He didn't brandish the weapon. Maybe a slap on the wrist. All in all the three-a you are pretty lucky."

"Can you get word to a sheriff's deputy for me? Sergeant Nicolai."

"Ed, he's a good man. You a friend of his?"

"I'd say yes; I'm not sure what he'd say." Bobby didn't wait for Duff to respond. He didn't want him to have to say no. "I'll pay for the damage to the pier."

"Oh, that you will, kiddo. The judge'll see to that."

Bobby figured he'd have to live to one hundred to pay off the pier damage. A uniformed officer knocked, then entered.

"He's ready to go," Duff said.

Bobby turned to him, "Why, Sergeant? You don't know me from Adam."

Duff signaled the officer to wait outside. He closed the door, sucked on his cigar. Let out a big balloon of dark, tangy smoke. He stared at the blank concrete wall, as if he could see through it, to somewhere far off.

"I got a kid, 'bout your age, fighting in the Pacific. Lance corporal in the marines. I hope he's got a good platoon sergeant lookin' out for his ass. Now get the hell outta here." Duff opened the door. The uniformed officer took Bobby in hand, walked him off. Bobby turned once, saw Duff staring through the walls again. This wall faced west, to the Pacific Ocean and the distant craggy mounds of earth where the marines were island hopping their way toward Japan. Bobby's eyes looked down. There was nothing more to say to Duff, though he was grateful and proud to have met the man. As the uniformed officer took him outside to his ride downtown he said a little prayer for Lance Corporal Duff.

Bobby had spent the night in the drunk tank. A scraggly old man stood over him. "Jesus, kid, what're you in for? Been here all night and not even a whisk of a beard. You steal candy from your kid brother?"

Bobby turned away from the man. The stench of the cell

overwhelmed him. One lone toilet stood in the corner. But there was no way he was going to use it, and not just because of how fowl it was. He held everything inside—everything. He could show no weakness here. And this wasn't the nice jail cell Gene Autry found himself in when he was mistakenly thought to be on the wrong side of the law. Bobby's chest cinched up tight. He kept to himself. The less interaction with these drunks the better.

Bobby thanked God that they hadn't frisked him. They thought about it. Then some drunk made a scene and a sergeant said, "That kid. He's too young to hold his dick to piss let alone hold a gun." They threw Bobby in the tank and moved off to take care of the drunk.

The breakfast the sheriff's deputies brought, if it could be called that, looked about as appetizing as whatever else filled the tank. Bobby chose not to eat; thought about James eating this crap every day. By ten a.m. he was on a bench in Judge Elliot Leander's courtroom. The process was very mechanical, the assistant D.A. stated the crime. Guilty or not guilty asked the judge, the defendant pleaded. Bail or no bail? Bobby got bail, but he didn't know how the hell he would pay it, even if it was only a hundred fifty bucks.

Before he could be led back to jail, a woman stepped forward with the bail money—Margaret. She paid the cashier and Bobby was a free man, at least for now.

"Thanks," he said, as they left the courtroom and entered the corridor of the Hall of Justice.

They walked down the center of the hall. A group of men, shackled hands and feet, sat on several benches along one wall. Bobby tried not to look at them; couldn't help seeing them from the corner of his eye. And there was James, feet spread, hands at his sides, head bowed. He looked up just as Bobby and Margaret walked by. Their eyes met. Neither said anything for a long moment.

"James."

"What you here for, boy? Not for me, I know that."

Bobby knew it would do no good to tell James that he was, indeed, here for working his case. He started to speak; James cut him off.

"You smell like a pig sty, boy. Great White Hope-Great White Dope."

After languishing in jail, James didn't want to hear anything Bobby had to say. He and Margaret headed down the hall.

"Do I really smell like a pig sty?"

"If only you smelled that good." Margaret hurried out the door. "Who was that?"

"That's the guy I'm trying to help."

"You okay?" Bobby said, getting into Margaret's car.

"No broken bones. A few scrapes." Short and to the point. Following Bobby's directions, Margaret turned down Central, heading for the Dunbar. Every window of her car was open all the way.

"Is Wilde out of jail?"

"Yeah. They didn't even charge him."

"Not even for the gun?"

Margaret shook her head.

"Then why'd they throw the book at me?"

"You were driving. Besides, when they found out his story about the China marines was the real deal, it was all they could do to stop offering to buy him drinks. Wilde and the cops spent the night in Sammy's Bar telling war stories."

After that, silence engulfed the car. Bobby couldn't stand it anymore. "You're angry."

"Why should I be angry? I almost got killed but I escaped with a few scratches. They took my picture so now the cops know who I am."

"What do you care if the cops know who you are?"

"I, I don't, but—"

"And even if they do, your picture's only in one little Santa Monica police station."

"That's not funny."

Bobby turned to Margaret. "Did they recover the briefcase?"

"Wilde threw it out of the car before we went over the edge."

"You're kidding!"

"That's what he says."

"Turn down Washington."

"What?"

Bobby reached for the steering wheel. "We've got to get it back."

Margaret stared straight ahead.

"Turn. Please, Margaret. Turn."

She hung a right onto Washington, heading for the ocean.

"Thanks."

"I'm not sure why I should."

"Where did he throw it?"

"I don't know. He said everything was happening so fast. He thinks he tossed it when we were on the pier."

"How come you know so much?"

"He called me to pick him up at the bar, take him home."

"How come his cop buddies couldn't do that?"

"I think they were too drunk to drive him all the way back to Western."

"Why didn't you just tell him to call a cab?" A twinge of jealously punctuated the shield Bobby tried to live behind.

They passed Sepulveda, then Sawtelle. Bobby looked out the passenger window to the north.

"Jeez, the airfield's just a few blocks up," he said. "I can't even see the control tower in the daylight. They did a great job camouflaging it."

"I'd rather not think about the airfield. About last night or any of this."

"Criminy, we're all okay. And we're all free."

"And I'd like it to stay that way. I'm going to be late for

work. Really late. And Mrs. Ford doesn't like Jews. I'm already in Dutch with her."

"Good."

"Good?"

"What's she gonna do, fire you? With all the manpower shortages 'cause of the war? Don't worry about it."

"Sure, why not? The world's going to hell anyway."

"Yeah, well maybe we can cheat it out of one little piece of hell 'cause I have the feeling that whatever's going on has something to do with hell," Bobby said.

"What makes you think so?"

"Women's intuition." Bobby spoke before he had time to think. He regretted blurting it out. But he regretted even more that he would still think of himself as a woman in any way.

"Huh?"

"Just a figure of speech." He laughed. She did too and it seemed as if the remark had bounced off Margaret without causing any lasting damage to Bobby's reputation.

They came to Ocean Avenue and Colorado.

"Turn left. Left." Bobby's excitement rebounded off the dashboard.

"Don't have a heart attack." Margaret hesitated. A horn honked behind them. She turned left, onto the pier, driving past the Merry-Go-Round building. "Seems like I've been here before."

"Just don't drive too far down the pier. I hear there's no fence at the end of it anymore."

"Very funny."

She parked next to Jack's Fish and Chips. They walked up the pier.

"Where did he throw the case out of the car?"

"I'm not sure."

"Think."

"Listen, buster, you could have picked up the Wilde-man himself."

They walked across the wooden planks, each footfall a dull

thud on the dry, splintered wood. Margaret stopped every now and then to look for the briefcase in between the buildings.

They passed the shooting gallery. Margaret looked under a bench on the side of the pier.

"Two strikes," Bobby said.

"What?"

"Three strikes and we're out. We've had two." Bobby lit up. "Do you think he could have thrown it the other way? Maybe it's on the beach?"

Bobby ran to the stairs that led down to the sand. He jumped them two at a time till he hit the beach. A child's cries carried on the wind.

He stopped, stood at the bottom of the stairs, turning three hundred sixty degrees. Not many people filled the sand today. Cold wind off the ocean slapped him on the cheeks. Bobby sighted down the pier's pilings, toward the water. A young boy of six or seven sat Indian-style at the high tide line, among a row of seaweed and debris the ocean had deposited there. Luckily for him high tide had come and gone, though it would surely come again. A woman with medium-length permed brown hair stood over him, her hair and skirt billowing in the breeze.

The boy's cries pitted Bobby's skin as surely as the damp stinging salt. Though he was facing away from Bobby, Bobby could see him looking down at something resting on his lap. A briefcase?

He ran toward the boy as fast as he could in the sinking sand, Margaret on his heels. They stood over the child as he flipped through the concentration camp photos in the briefcase, each one eliciting a louder cry than the one before. Yet he kept moving through them. Stunned, his mother stood over him, not moving.

"I told you not to open it," she scolded. "It's not polite and you never know what you'll find." She tried taking the case away from him. He wouldn't let go.

"What is it?" Bobby said.

The boy's mother pointed to the pictures which, of course,

Bobby already knew all about. "Disgusting," she said. "How can one person do that to another?"

"I think people are capable of anything." Bobby leaned down, gently taking the pictures from the boy. The child let them slip from his hands to Bobby's.

His mother snatched the briefcase from her son, who stifled his tears and looked blankly out to sea, as if his childhood had been stolen from him. "I should take this to the police."

"We can do that," Margaret said.

"Who are you?"

"We just heard the boy's shrieks. We came by to see what they were about and if we could help." Margaret put a hand out for the briefcase. The woman held it tight.

"How do I know you'll really take it to the police?"

"What would we want with pictures like those? And you need to attend to your son." Margaret shivered. Bobby didn't think it was from the cold.

"I guess you're right." The woman took the pictures from Bobby, slid them into the briefcase, snapped it shut. Made a point of handing it to Margaret. "You'll take it to the police?"

"Right away. Our car's up on the pier."

"There might be a policeman on the pier," the young mother said.

"If there is we'll give it to him. Otherwise we'll take it to the Santa Monica police station. We know where it is."

"We sure do," Bobby muttered.

"All right. Thank you." The woman bent over her son.

Bobby and Margaret backtracked up the beach and up the stairs to the pier.

"How did you do that—get the boy to give up the pictures?"

"Sometimes a boy just needs a man." The irony wasn't lost on Bobby. "That was a close one," he said, opening the briefcase on the hood of Margaret's car. He checked the contents. "Looks like nothing's missing. Just a little sandy."

"Should we take it to the police?" Margaret's voice seemed

unsure.

"If we take it to the police, it'll just sit somewhere until someone maybe finds the time to do something with it. No, we, I have to follow it up. I made a promise to Booker."

"You just want a gig with the band." She glared at him. *Why?* Something was simmering under the surface with Margaret.

"I want to get James out of jail."

"He didn't seem to want anything to do with you at the courthouse."

"He's angry. Can you blame him? Sitting in jail for something he didn't do."

"Let your pal Sergeant Nicolai deal with it."

Bobby shut the briefcase, harder than he needed to. Without another word he got into Margaret's car.

Margaret was about to head inland.

"Drive north," Bobby said. "Up Pacific Coast Highway."

"What?"

"Malibu Sheriff's Station. Sergeant Nicolai."

The silence returned, but Margaret headed north.

"Can I help you?" the desk sergeant said.

Margaret explained that she wanted to see Sergeant Nicolai. The desk sergeant looked her up and down, sent her toward the back of the building. Nicolai didn't exactly greet her with open arms. Was more than curious why Bobby hadn't come in himself, when she explained what she was here for.

Bobby waited by the picnic table that he and Nicolai had talked at before. Margaret and the sergeant came out as a gust blew in off the ocean.

"Jeez," Nicolai said. "Now I know why you didn't come in the station. Where the hell you been, the drunk tank?" Before Bobby could respond, Nicolai went on. "I hear you been having some fun down at the pier."

"Sergeant Duff called you?"

"He's an old friend. He didn't say, but I know you were still working the Dietrich case." Nicolai kicked the sand. "Give up already. You don't have to get that spade out."

"I do."

"Oh yeah. So you can join the other spade's band."

Margaret squirmed.

"That's not the reason."

"I know, kid. I know. It's some altruistic thing you got going."

"It's not—"

"Never mind. So you making any progress?"

"I thought we were till my car sank into the ocean."

"Yeah, that's too bad." Nicolai turned to Margaret. "How well did you know Dietrich?"

"I still think it's tied in with these photos." Bobby interrupted before Margaret could respond, patted the closed briefcase. He pointedly looked at her. She blinked, tapped her fingers on the table. "Something we're just not seeing."

"You looked at 'em. I looked at 'em. I'm sure you had her look at 'em—"

"—And about a dozen other people. No one can figure it out."

"Maybe it's not the photos then."

"If it's not the photos, I might as well pack my bags and move back home with my parents." Bobby knew what that meant. And that was the last thing he wanted.

"Sometimes a photo is just a photo."

"But these are photos of the camps. They have to mean something."

"I been a cop long enough to know that sometimes there ain't nothing to anything. And sometimes it's the littlest thing."

Bobby started to speak, Nicolai held up his hand to stop him.

"Hold on. Tell me more about what you were doing last night. Let's not charge off half-cocked."

"We were following up the only real clue we have. A piece of paper with the address 211 Pine. We tried one address near downtown, another in West Hollywood. Then Santa Monica. Someone was following us, and then somehow I managed to get the MPs on my tail."

"Yeah, you gotta be careful these days."

"Hell, I don't even know if that address is a clue. Maybe it's just Stinson's girlfriend's address? What's the point anymore, what's the fucking point?" Bobby looked at Margaret. She turned away, staring out to the ocean, seeming fidgety. "Sorry. But I'm no detective. I couldn't find my way out of a paper bag with a flashlight."

"Takes a while, kid, but then you get a feel for it."

"I have to get to work," Margaret said.

"You need a car, kid? I got one I been tinkering with. She ain't your snazzy Olds Six, but she'll do. Belonged to a buddy of mine. He had me keep it for him when he went into the service. He won't be needing it anymore. Sicily." Nicolai's voice broke. "A black-and-red Studebaker out behind my dump. Keys are under the rear wheel."

"Thanks, Sarge." Bobby started to walk off with Margaret.

"I'll be in touch, kid," Nicolai said, heading back into the station. Halfway in the door, he turned around. "There's a Pine in Long Beach, y'know." He saluted and was gone.

CHAPTER THIRTY-SIX

"Long Beach, let's go."

"What am I now, your chauffeur?" Margaret pulled in behind Nicolai's "dump." The 1941 Studebaker Champion, with a bright red stripe girthing its body, was right there, taking a beating from the sand-pitted wind.

Bobby sat in Margaret's car for several minutes, briefcase on his lap. Neither said a word.

"Pine. In Long Beach. Now you're cookin' with gas." Bobby echoed Wilde's favorite saying, his voice dripping with excitement.

"There's got to be a million Pines, Bobby. Every city's got one. Sometimes two. Pine Street, Pine Avenue, Pine Lane."

"Don't you see? The Pike, the house of mirrors, where Wilde and I met those crazy people, Esmeralda and Jerry. Lois took him there. She dropped off letters. Packages. For Dietrich." He rummaged through the briefcase, pulled out a map with more wrinkles than the Hundred-Year-Old Woman at the Pike. Spread it across the dashboard. "There. Right there. See. Pine in Long Beach is only a few yards from the Pike. Right there." He stabbed his finger through the map. "Come with me down to Pine in Long Beach."

"Take Wilde. He'll do you more good than me."

"I'd rather take you." Bobby's voice was almost inaudible. "Besides, I thought you didn't like him."

"He's not a good influence. You can do better than him anyway."

"Right now he's the only friend I've got. Do you think he's still at home?"

"Probably sleeping off his binge after those cops took him drinking."

Bobby pushed the cigarette lighter in, shook a Viceroy from the pack. "Some people have all the luck."

Margaret gave a small laugh.

"I need your help, Margaret."

She looked away from Bobby, aloof.

"You saw James at the courthouse. Don't you want to get him out?"

"He killed Hans."

"I don't think so. He had no reason."

"Who does?"

"Will you keep the briefcase for me? Make sure nothing happens to it? I know I can trust you." Bobby opened the case, took out the keys and the one key on the rabbit's foot key ring and pocketed them. Placed the case on the seat between them. The lighter popped out. Bobby tamped his cigarette on the dash, lit it on the glowing red coil. He opened the passenger door, walked to the Studebaker without looking back. He heard Margaret's engine rev and her car drive off.

He tried to feel for the key to the Studebaker under the right rear wheel. Nothing there. He tried the driver's side rear tire. Sure enough. Bobby snatched the key, unlocked the car. He didn't know what he'd do for a car permanently, but this was great for now. A '41, not even that old. And now they weren't making civilian cars. Everything was geared toward the war effort, tanks, planes. Jeeps, like the one that chased him off the pier last night.

The cold engine took a while to start. It stalled twice before it purred and Bobby drove onto Pacific Coast Highway. He tried to concentrate on the case. He tried not to think of Margaret during the drive. He thought of nothing but her.

* * *

He wanted to run straight to Wilde's, get on down to Pine in Long Beach. Needed to go home and change and shower first, get the stink of the drunk tank off him. He pulled to the curb in front of the Dunbar. Two colored women looked at the grimy white man messing up their neighborhood. Said nothing.

Bobby scrambled to his room, stripped off his clothes. "Might as well burn these." Looked at himself in the bathroom mirror—naked. Breasts and genitals exposed. He fantasized about what Margaret looked like naked. Fantasized about what they might look like naked together, on the bed in the next room. He wanted Margaret. Feared she wanted a real man. He was too frightened, too nervous. He turned on the shower to scalding. Stepped in. Bobby let the hot water scorch his body, watching his skin turn red. Redder. He didn't think any amount of heat or soap would get the stench off him. When the water started to run cold, he turned it off, toweled off. Stood in front of the mirror once again. Bound his breasts. Combed his hair off his face. Put on a fresh shirt and pants, then sat on the edge of the bed, putting on his shoes and socks.

He stood in front of the mirror, tying the hand-painted Rayon tie around his neck and tipped his hat just so over his eyes. Now he looked ready to play the part of a real detective.

CHAPTER THIRTY-SEVEN

"Wild times," Wilde said when Bobby charged into his apartment. He seemed unworried about anything—the events of last night, including the dip in the ocean and the *soiree* with the police and FBI. Even if they hadn't dropped the gun charge Bobby didn't think Wilde would worry about it.

"Two-eleven Pine is in Long Beach," Bobby said.

"Long Beach?"

"Right down by the Pike. The Mirror Maze."

"Damn, you're right. There is a Pine down there." Wilde threw a shirt on over his undershirt. Didn't bother tucking it in.

"We still don't know it's the right Pine."

"I'd bet my—Criminy, I don't have much left to bet."

"Well, don't bet your life, kid. You might lose." Wilde grabbed a tie, decided against it, threw it on the bed. Stuck his hat on his head. "Did you find the briefcase?"

"Yeah, it was under the pier. Margaret's safekeeping it for me."

"Good thinkin' on my part to toss it. If the cops found it who knows what they'd think."

Bobby felt in his pocket for the key.

"Can I borrow your gun?"

"The cops have it, but I can get one."

Before heading out, Wilde made a stop—alone—in the pool hall downstairs. He came out with a .45 auto pistol and three full magazines. "This oughta do."

They pooled their money to fill the Studebaker's tank, and Bobby secretly thanked God that today was that car's ration day.

"Nice wheels," Wilde said.

"They're not mine. Let's try not to smash 'em up."

"You're great at that, kid, I'll say."

"Thanks."

Bobby was getting used to the long drive down Western. He relished it when they came to the end of civilization and the open fields and truck farms that filled the gap between Los Angeles and Long Beach. But soon enough civilization reared its ugly head again. Eventually Bobby hit Pine, started looking for 211.

"There it is," Wilde said, pointing to a brick warehouse with high arched windows and several loading bays facing the street. There wasn't a car or truck in sight.

"There's not even a sign with a name on it. It looks deserted," Bobby said.

"From the outside, at least. But you can't go by that. And the fact there's no sign bodes well for our cause, I'd say. Take it slow."

Bobby parked. Retrieved the ring of keys from his pocket. They walked to the door.

Wilde knocked. Rang the buzzer.

"It's business hours," Bobby said. "Someone should be here."

"Ssh."

They waited. A minute. Two. Five. No response.

Wilde tried again. Nothing. He nodded to Bobby.

Bobby pulled out the key on the rabbit's foot—the one that matched Lois' and Stinson's keys. Wiped sand from it and rubbed it for luck. "Do your stuff," he said to the key. Wilde just stared as Bobby slipped the key into the lock.

The tumblers fell into place.

The door popped open.

Bobby looked to Wilde. Even the hard ex-Marine had to grin now. He pulled the .45 from his waistband. Slipped inside. Bobby followed.

He couldn't stifle a cough.

"Ssh."

"I can't help it," Bobby whispered. "It's so dusty in here."

He locked the door from the inside.

They were in a reception area. Two desks. A calculating machine. Typewriters.

"IBM typewriters," Bobby sputtered.

"Now you're cookin' with gas."

"Maybe. Or maybe a lot of people use IBM typewriters. Let's start digging." Bobby opened an unlocked file cabinet drawer. Empty.

"Before we do that, let's reconnoiter. Make sure we're alone."

They walked through the reception area, opening doors to the *executive* offices, if that's what they were, with their dreary wood paneling and bad reproductions of Rembrandt, Titian, Da Vinci, and Gainsborough. Checked the bathrooms, men's and women's. Made their way to the stockroom. The building was three stories tall, but without a second or third floor. Just a cavernous room. But the whole big damn room was empty.

The huge room was a barren desert of wooden floors, brick walls and hanging lights, with dust trails of daylight streaming in through the tall windows and skylights.

They searched every inch, looking for anything and everything, including false floors or compartments. They searched the offices, desks, file cabinets.

"Cleaned out," Wilde said.

"But we know it's the right place, the key worked." Bobby's disappointment was still more than evident.

"Look here, kid." Wilde pointed to a spot in the dust where there had obviously been crates. "There's not as much dust here. That means something was here, recently."

"They're moving something, but what?"

Bobby excused himself to use the restroom. He closed the narrow door behind him, splashed water on his face. He knew he was in over his head, hoped the ceiling wouldn't fall in on him.

"We got several choices." Wilde spoke loudly so Bobby could hear him on the other side of the door. "We can stake the joint out, but we don't have the manpower to really watch it. We can go back to Jerry and Esmeralda, those loons at the Mirror Maze, see if they're involved, which seems likely since Lois was sent there. Well, maybe we only got two choices."

"Neither of them good. Why would it be empty? Maybe they're not coming back."

"Could be. Or maybe they only use it when they have to, sort of a transshipment point."

"They keep it empty, pay all the bills, and just use it sometimes?"

"Maybe whatever they're doing makes 'em enough money that it's worth it."

"Maybe, but who the hell are *they*?"

"We're getting closer, kid. I can feel it."

The Pike was the proverbial hop skip and jump from 211 Pine. They walked past the Cyclone and Davy Jones' Locker. Unfortunately, the Mirror Maze was locked up tighter than Fort Knox.

"Criminy! What do we do now, break in?"

"Too many people around and it's still too light out."

Bobby watched the sailors and their girls stroll past. He wished he were part of a couple, *an item.* How would he and Margaret look strolling along the boardwalk? He liked the image in his mind, wondered if Margaret would. He wondered, too, what would happen if Margaret knew the truth. Would she be upset that he hadn't been upfront with her?

They walked around the side of the Mirror Maze, peered in through a sliver of clear glass in a soaped-over window.

"Looks the same as the last time we were here," Bobby said.

"I wonder where the hell they are. Don't they want to be making money here?" Wilde watched a sailor and his girl go by. His eyes followed the girl. The sailor glared back at him, but not for long, seeing the look in Wilde's eyes. Bobby thought he should be looking at the girls too, just like any other guy.

"Maybe they're not involved?" Bobby said.

"You know they are. I came here with Lois. I wish we could just bust the G-D door down. Maybe we'll come back at night and do just that. Let's go."

They snaked through the sailors, the girls, the children, over to the Laff in the Dark booth. Barged to the front of the line.

"Hey." A sailor with stripes on his sleeve was ready for a fight.

"Take it easy, Chief," Wilde said. "We're not taking cuts. We just have a quick question."

"How'd you know my rank?"

Wilde nodded at the insignia on the chief petty officer's arm. "I was a gunny at one time myself."

The chief grinned wide. "We used to eat you leathernecks for breakfast."

"I hope you're not hungry now."

The chief slapped Wilde on the back. Wilde tipped his hat to him. Turned to the man in the booth. "The Mirror Maze's closed?" Wilde asked.

"Yeah, so, whadda ya want me to do about it?" the ticket seller said.

"What about the folks who work there, Jerry and Esmeralda? Know where they are?"

"I ain't their keeper."

"You got a clear view to their joint. Maybe they asked you to keep an eye on it?"

The carnie's face remained impassive stone. Wilde pulled out a fin. Waved it in front of the man.

"Maybe they did."

"So where are they and when they comin' back?"

"Can't say for sure to either question. I think they're down to the docks."

"What're they doing there?"

"How the hell should I know? T' answer your next question, probably not till late tonight."

Wilde slapped the five down. "Gimme two tickets outta that."

"I thought it was all for me."

"Two."

The carnie did. Wilde let him keep the change, gave the tickets to the chief.

"Thanks, gyrene."

Wilde nodded. He and Bobby hoofed it.

"Batting a thousand."

"Hell, I don't even feel like ridin' the Cyclone today," Wilde said.

They grabbed a couple greasy burgers from the Pike, ate them in Nicholai's car. Wilde dripped grease on the upholstery, Bobby wiped it with his handkerchief. The stink of the burgers reminded Bobby of how he felt inside. This whole case stunk and he wished he could just ride past it like Hopalong Cassidy riding into the sunset at the end of a movie. Soon these lousy burgers, the Pike, the whole case would only be visible in the rearview mirror, with just a slight lingering odor left in Bobby's nostrils.

"You haven't talked much about Lois lately."

"Don't have much to say. Just this: if those bastards had anything to do with her disappearance, I'm gonna tear their arms off."

They decided to sleep in the car, Bobby stretched out in the front, Wilde in the back seat, until the glaring sun woke them the next morning.

Bobby and Wilde cruised down Pine just as the sun rose high enough to make Bobby squint. The Studebaker Champion hit a little strip of parking next to the Pike. They walked down the midway, the Walk of a Thousand Lights. And though the lights were still on they were all but blanched out by the rising sun. Earlier in the war they would have been off all night. Bobby guessed someone high up thought a Japanese air attack was less likely these days.

The house of mirrors stood lonely and garish in the intense light of day.

"You really think we'll see anything?"

"It was your idea, kid. 'Sides, we'll do the three strikes rule. We been here once. This is our second at-bat. If we strike out today and the next time, we'll go to Plan B."

"And what is Plan B?"

"Hell if I know. This ain't a movie, kid. There's no script. We just make it up as we go along."

The carnies who ran the rides and slept by them were beginning to stir. Some were already checking their equipment to make sure it was in working order.

Bobby and Wilde walked around the Mirror Maze concession. They tried windows, all of which were soaped or painted over. They tried doors. Nothing opened.

"Nobody's getting this thing ready for the day."

"I guess there's not much to get ready in a house of mirrors," Wilde said. "Maybe Jerry and Esmeralda are sleeping in."

"I don't think so." Bobby pointed to the side door, creaking open. Jerry and Esmeralda stepped out, dressed like normal people. Bobby and Wilde hung back, behind a cotton candy kiosk. The two carnies headed up Pine, talking animatedly, arms swinging back and forth. Bobby and Wilde trailed at a distance. Bobby couldn't hear a word.

The carnies went in the front door of the warehouse, but Bobby hadn't needed a crystal ball to know where they were going.

He and Wilde watched the warehouse from behind a low wall across the street. Ten minutes later a large canvas-topped truck backed into the loading bay. There were no markings on it. Three guys, who looked like longshoremen, one in coveralls with a tattoo of a serpent on his arm, another in a leather jacket, and the driver wearing a flat mariner's cap, slid off the front seat. The huge loading dock door slid open. Jerry stepped out, greeting the driver with a slap on the back. "Hey, Watson."

"Everybody seems to be having a hell of a time," Wilde whispered. "What the hell are they delivering?"

"Or picking up? I can't tell if that truck's empty or full up."

"They're offloading. See how it lays heavy on its rear axle."

Sure enough, the beefy truckers used a pallet jack to clear out the truck. The pallets were piled high with wooden crates.

"I wish we had binoculars," Bobby said. "I can't read what's on the side of the crates."

Wilde grabbed Bobby's sleeve, tugged him into the street. They crossed to the warehouse side, dodged into the shadows of a building down the block. They inched up the sidewalk, trying to look as inconspicuous as possible to the cars driving up Pine. Not too many people were out walking, but a few. Wilde lit a cigarette.

"I don't like announcing us with smoke. But the regular folks on the street gotta see a couple-a regular guys, not two goons skulking in the shadows."

They waited until the truck was completely offloaded. The truckers and Jerry went inside. The bay door was still open.

"We can sneak inside," Bobby said.

"No way, kid. We'll go 'round back. They might still be in the front."

Wilde and Bobby backtracked down the block so they wouldn't have to pass the loading dock. They walked up the alley until they came to the back of the warehouse. Wilde scrambled up a trashcan so he could look in a window. It was still too high up.

"Give me a push," he whispered.

Bobby cupped his hands, slipped them under Wilde's shoe, pushed upwards with all his strength. Wilde grabbed onto the window ledge, balancing precariously on Bobby's cupped hands. He slid the unlocked window up, pulled himself over and in. He leaned out, signaling for Bobby to give him his hands.

Wilde clasped onto Bobby's wrists, pulled him up and into the window. Bobby helped as much as he could, but he knew

Wilde was doing most of the work.

They stood in the small restroom at the back of the warehouse space. Bobby hoped no one would need to take care of business, as Wilde cracked the door open. Bobby peeked around him.

Pallets were double stacked across the warehouse. More than had been off-loaded from this one truck—several deliveries' worth. The wooden crates on each pallet stacked up taller than Bobby. They couldn't see the front of the warehouse. Voices were barely audible from somewhere on the far side of the pallets.

"Shit. Someone's coming."

They scrambled for the window. Too late. The door opened.

"Watson," Tattoo yelled, grabbing Bobby, slugging him and pitching him to the ground. Bobby's head hit the toilet rim. He felt a warm trickle of blood slobber down his cheek. Some Bogart.

Wilde spun on his feet, coming about with a flying round-house to the trucker's head. The trucker wobbled. He might have fallen, but there was nowhere to fall in the tiny room. Wilde jabbed him with a left and Tattoo was down, on top of Bobby. The only place to fall.

"Let's get out of here, kid." Wilde propelled the window all the way up, so hard that the glass cracked. He yanked Bobby up. Pushed him toward the window.

Bobby's head swam. He was still reeling from the trucker's sucker punch. He tried to put one foot on the windowsill. It fell back to the floor. Wilde started pushing him through the window.

The bathroom door crashed open again. Watson filled the frame. Jerry leaned around him.

"What the f—?"

Head down, Wilde tackled the driver with the force of an angry locomotive—as much force as he could build up within the small confines of the room.

Watson hurtled backwards into Jerry, the two of them tumbling over each other, as Wilde's momentum propelled him out the door. He jumped over them, running headlong into the first row of pallets. That stopped him cold.

The dizziness gone and adrenalin pumping, Bobby shot out the door, jumping over the still-sprawled Jerry and the driver.

"Goddamn," Jerry yelped, groping for a hold to pull himself up.

"Let's lam," Wilde said, grabbing Bobby. They ran up the middle aisle toward the bright light streaming in from the open loading door.

And ran smack into the third trucker, Leather Jacket.

Wilde whipped out his borrowed pistol.

"Jesus!" someone shouted.

Leather Jacket body-slammed Wilde. Domino-like, Wilde ricocheted back into Bobby, the pistol barreling down the aisle. Watson, Jerry, and Tattoo tore down the middle corridor. Wilde lay crumpled on the floor. Bobby looked around. The three truckers blocked both possible exits. He looked to Wilde. Saw the defeated look on his friend's face. He felt like slithering down the crates to the floor and putting his head between his legs. He knew he had to stand tall. For himself and for his friend, who'd stood by him.

Jerry leaned in close. He and Bobby were about the same height. "I know you, dumb fuck. Don't I?"

Bobby didn't answer. Jerry popped him in the face with a closed fist. Bobby wanted to cry. He wouldn't give them the pleasure. He knew that Bogart or any of the B Western stars he admired would have done the same. Still, he sure as hell felt like crying. Watson grabbed Bobby. His two trucker buddies each took one of Wilde's arms. There wasn't much fight left in Wilde. Bobby kicked and flailed as Watson tried to yank him up the aisle. Bobby fell free, knocking into one of the pallets. A crate toppled over, missing his head by inches. It fell to the floor, the wood slats tearing apart. Some sort of machine tumbled out, crashing onto the concrete floor. Bobby eyed it—*what the hell is that?* It looked vaguely familiar. His eyes wandered to the stacks of crates and the stenciled writing on them. Watson yanked him to his feet, shoved him forward.

They tied Bobby and Wilde to a stack of pallets.

"Tough guy." Tattoo jammed a heavy-booted foot into Wilde's gut.

"Unhh!" Wilde groaned.

The boot then blasted into Wilde's face. *Crack.* Something broke. Wilde slumped off to the side.

Jerry held Tattoo off from his next kick. He, Esmeralda, who had come out to see what the ruckus was, and the three truckers stood over Bobby and Wilde.

"Who're you working for?"

Wilde couldn't talk. Bobby wouldn't.

Jerry stepped into Wilde's face, leaning all his weight down. Something cracked again. Jerry turned to Bobby. "You want to end up like your friend? Such a pretty face. His face, no great loss. But yours—"

Bobby didn't know what to do. His head was still spinning from the hits he took. He didn't have time to think of a story so what the hell, he'd tell them: "Dietrich."

"Dietrich? What's he got to do with this?"

"James's in jail for killing him, but he didn't do it."

"And who the hell is James?"

Between gasps for air, Bobby told Jerry an abbreviated version of the story.

"All this for a nigger? You're gonna die for a lousy nigger? What do you care who killed Dietrich?"

"Did you do it?" Bobby's breath came short, the words staccato. He could barely get them out.

"You're never gonna know who did it. 'Sides, what's it to you?"

"The band."

"The band? What are you, crazy?"

"I could have a spot in the band if I find out who killed Dietrich."

Everyone laughed at Bobby—everyone but Wilde, whose breath came in short, quick bursts. At least he was breathing.

Jerry turned to Watson. "Drag these carcasses to the truck. Tie 'em up. Then get 'em the hell outta here, far away. I don't wanna see 'em again. I don't want anyone to see 'em again."

Watson nodded to the two other truckers. He, Jerry, and Esmeralda went into the warehouse office. Bobby heard muffled voices. The other two truckers jerked Wilde up, the same as they would a sack of potatoes. They lugged him to the truck. Shoved him in. They returned for Bobby. Did a repeat performance.

They tied Wilde to the slats on the passenger side; Bobby to slats on the driver's side. They shoved dirt and gasoline-crudded rags in their mouths. Pulled the canvas flap down over the back of the truck.

It wasn't long before Watson joined Tattoo and Leather Jacket up front in the cab and Bobby felt the quivering of the road beneath him. He was glad the truckers all went back to their positions in the cab instead of leaving someone to guard him and Wilde. He guessed they figured neither was in any shape to do much and, besides, they were tied up.

Bobby worked the rag out his mouth with his tongue, lips and jaw. He spit it out and spit out the dirt it left behind. He looked across what might as well have been miles of empty space to Wilde. His friend looked all out, eyes vacant, mouth hanging open, the rag stuffed in it. Snorting more than breathing.

"You okay?" Bobby whispered. "I mean, I know you're not okay, but—"

Wilde lifted his head an inch or two, as if to say, *I'm alive*, if nothing else.

"Did you see what it said on the side of those crates?"

Wilde shook his head.

"IBM," Bobby said. "IBM."

Bobby jerked up, trying to get his hands, which were tied behind his back, up and over one of the truck's tie-downs. No go. He tried again. *Damn!* He didn't slice the rope on the slat but he sliced his hand pretty good. He thrust himself up again, started sawing his hands up and down, working the rope.

Hoping to God that he'd get the ropes sliced before the truckers stopped to check on them, or worse to deposit them somewhere where they wouldn't be found for a hundred years.

He looked up to Wilde again. "Underneath IBM it said *Hollerith*. I wonder what that means?"

Wilde didn't seem to notice Bobby talking. He went back to work on the ropes. This rope slicing worked in the movies; the hero always got away. Would it work in real life? Bobby sure as hell hoped so.

CHAPTER THIRTY-EIGHT

With every bump, Wilde groaned louder. It was obvious he was trying not to make any noise but couldn't help himself. Bobby kept working the rope up and down and crossways on the tie-downs. *Twang*, another cord busted.

Bobby sawed away. His hands tingled, then deadened with pain as the circulation choked off. Still, he couldn't stop sawing. He watched Wilde's eyes lose focus. His jaw hung slack. He couldn't imagine the pain his friend was in. He had to cut loose to help Wilde as much as anything else.

The truckers and Jerry had knocked the wind out of Bobby, but after that they'd sort of forgotten about him. They took out all their wrath on Wilde.

The rope bit into Bobby's wrists. He could feel warm blood trickling down his wrists as he slid them up and down the tie-down. The way they had him tied he couldn't stand and his arms and shoulders screamed in pain as he tried to slide up and down. He grunted. It wasn't as easy as it looked in the movies. Curse you, Gene Autry.

He needed a break. It felt like his arms were separating from his shoulders. Excruciating pain seared his joints. But he wouldn't rest. He had a mission—to get him and Wilde the hell out of there. And he would do it or die trying, as corny as that sounded.

Though his feet were also tied together, he forced himself up the slatted side of the truck to give himself better leverage. He began sawing at the rope on the tie-down again. It wasn't sharp like a blade, but it wasn't round either, coming to a sort of wedge in the front. Just enough of a point to damage the rope.

Impaled on the tie-down—through his own doing—Bobby continued sawing the rope on the cleat, up and down, up and down. Another strand of rope cord popped off.

He kept a steady pace, imagining a metronome in his head, ticking off time. He thrust up and down in time to the metronome. When that got boring he switched the metronome for a drummer—Gene Krupa. After all, if you're going to have an imaginary drummer count time, it might as well be the best.

He worried that he'd hurt his hands and not be able to play the piano or play as well. What did that matter when the alternative was being dead? He continued driving his hands and shoulders up and down to Krupa's beat.

Tired of Krupa, Bobby said out loud, "Beat me daddy, eight to the bar," thinking about the syncopated boogie-woogie beat song. Switched to that in his head.

A-plink, a-plank, a-plink plank, plink plank a-plunkin' on the keys,
A-riff, a-raff, a-riff raff, riff raff,
A-riffin' out with ease,
And when he plays with the bass and guitar,
They holler out, 'Beat me Daddy, eight to the bar.'

He plays a boogie, he plays eight to the bar,
A boogie-woogie, that is the way he likes to play on his piano,
And we all know,
That when he plays he puts them all in a trance,
The cats all holler 'Hooray,'
You'll hear them say, 'Beat me Daddy, eight to the bar.'

He tried keeping time with his foot, but it expended too much energy—energy he needed to put into obliterating the damn rope.

Up and down.

A-plink.

Up and down.

A-plank.

Another strand snapped. He could feel the rope weakening a bit. The binding wasn't nearly as tight on his wrists.

He didn't know how long he'd been sawing. He did know that every muscle in his body throbbed with pain.

Eventually he gave up on "Beat Me Daddy" and started counting time to every throbbing beat of pain.

One. Two. Three. Four.

One. Two. Three. Four.

Shit! Two. Three. Four.

Ow! Two. Three. Four.

Another strand of rope snapped. Two or three this time. Bobby pushed out from the truck wall. The rest of the rope ripped apart and he did a header onto the truck floor. He hoped the road noise would cover up his thump to the men in the cab.

Bobby slowly dragged his hands and arms along the truck bed, so they were under his chest. He pushed up, twisting himself, so he was sitting cross-legged on the floor. He stretched, rubbed his hands, trying to get the circulation going. Right now he wished he had one of those fancy-dancy Dick Tracy wrist-radios so he could call the cops. What a silly fantasy.

He wriggled over to Wilde, gently pulled the gag from his mouth. "You okay, Sam?"

Wilde's empty eyes just stared out ahead. Did they even see Bobby?

"Don't worry. I got the ropes undone," Bobby said, working to untie the ropes at his ankles. "I'll get us out of here. You're probably in shock. But we gotta beat it outta here."

Bobby yanked the last bit of rope off his legs. He pulled up his trousers. Rope burns tore at his flesh. Blood dripped. He rubbed his ankles to get the circulation going, stood up—or tried to. He was flat on his ass two seconds after trying to stand. He rubbed his legs some more. Stood again, grabbing onto the truck's slats to steady himself.

He bent down, untied Wilde's hands and feet. Rubbed the circulation back into them. He pulled Wilde up. He could barely stand. Bobby held tight to his friend, inching him toward the tail of the truck.

The gate was metal, as was the lower half of the cargo bay. But everything above a few feet was canvas. If it was just Bobby he would have tried going over the tailgate. But Wilde would never make it.

He held Wilde tight and close.

"When they stop for a traffic light, we scram," he whispered.

No response.

It wasn't long till they hit a stoplight. Bobby tied a rope fragment to the gate so he could lower it quietly and not let the truckers in the cab hear it bang down. He tried to open it.

"Damn!"

It wouldn't budge. *Must be locked.*

What am I gonna do now?

He leaned Wilde against the side of the truck, then climbed under the canvas and over the lip of the gate. He stood on the bumper—the truck lurched forward. Bobby grabbed onto a stake, barely able to hang on. Wilde lifted one leg over the gate; Bobby helped him pull the other over. They fell into the road. Bobby couldn't do a tuck and roll and Wilde fell right on top of him. They both rolled back another ten feet. Bobby heard something snap—something in Wilde. The big man groaned loudly.

Brakes squealed and horns honked as the cars behind them came to screeching halts. Bobby looked up. A Pontiac's bumper was three inches from his head. He looked the other way. The truck rolled on as if nothing had happened.

He'd pulled it off. Hooray!

A horn blast nearly blew him over.

"Get outta the damn road," the driver of the car behind

them shouted.

Bobby wanted to smack him in the face; no time for that now. He coaxed Wilde to the curb, sat him down, leaning him against a lamppost, his feet in the gutter. Bobby stood, feeling his heart pounding in his chest, wondering where the hell he got the strength, both physical and mental, to do all he'd done in the last half hour. He spied a phone booth halfway down the block. He didn't want to leave Wilde there alone, but he had no choice. He scrambled to the booth, digging in his pockets for some change.

He was a mess, torn clothes, blood everywhere. Dirt and cuts. Nobody on the street wanted anything to do with him. They all cleared a path.

Bobby fell into the phone booth, the door slamming behind him. He pulled himself up, sat on the little seat, put a quarter in the slot, though that was way too much for the call. He didn't care. He dialed. Less than five minutes later he was back at Wilde's side.

"Don't worry," he said. "The bastards in the truck never even noticed we were gone. They're a million miles away right now and by the time they realize we're not there, they won't have a clue where we fell off."

A woman and her child walked past, giving them a wide berth.

Bobby leaned back against the lamppost, nodding off. He was awakened by someone tugging at his arm.

"Booker."

"Jesus, man, I had no idea," Booker said.

"We have to get Sam to a hospital."

"Pronto," Booker said. He and Bobby loaded Wilde into Booker's silver Thunderbolt, a tight fit for the three of them. As they drove off, Bobby recognized the neighborhood. Western Avenue. The same street they'd driven to and from Long Beach several times. The truckers must have been heading up Western. Now he remembered. When he'd called Booker, he'd had to squint to see the street sign at the corner. They were back in civ-ilization. No fields or truck farms here. But he couldn't even remember what cross street he'd told Booker to find them at.

Booker headed north. At Santa Monica Boulevard he cut over to Vermont, headed north again. He pulled into the main drive in front of Queen of Angels Hospital, a massive building that domi-nated the entire area. Booker and Bobby helped Wilde through the front door. People moved aside. Was it because of Bobby's and Wilde's appearance? Or because of Booker? Coloreds weren't seen much around here, except as janitors and Booker certainly wasn't dressed for that. And his car said anything but janitor.

Bobby must have passed out. He woke up, squinting at the bright hospital room lights. His hands were covered in gauze and had a gooey substance on them. Same for his ankles.

"Wilde?"

"Your friend is in pretty bad shape. But he'll live," a nurse said.

"Will he be okay?"

"It's too early to tell what kind of permanent damage he has, if any. But you saved his life."

Bobby sat bolt upright in the hospital bed, swung his legs over the side.

"You've been through quite an ordeal *Mr.* Saxon," the nurse said.

Bobby felt his cheeks flush.

"Don't worry, your secret's safe with me."

Bobby's head was swimming. One minute lucid, the next in a fog. What did the nurse mean by his secret was safe with her? Did she know? Bobby froze. *Did Booker know?*

"I have no secrets, nurse Landers," Bobby said, reading from her name tag. "And I'm fine. Really."

"You can call me June. And you really should get an X-ray and let the doctor examine you, give you a complete physical."

He reached for his shredded coat. Nurse Landers took his arm, swathed a fresh coat of reddish-brown iodine on him.

Bobby reluctantly untensed his arm. But there was no way in heaven that he was going to let her or a doctor examine him.

Margaret came in holding a steaming cup of coffee in one hand, Thomas' briefcase in the other. The nurse left. Margaret walked to the bed.

"Bobby, how are you?"

"Where's Booker?"

"He had to get down to the Alabam. Said to look after you." Margaret blew the steam off her coffee to cool it. "I don't think he wanted to hang around here. Didn't feel comfortable."

"Who can blame him? Some people get beat up for being colored. Some for being Jews. And some just for being themselves," Bobby said.

"Which is it in your case?"

"I guess for sticking my nose where it doesn't belong." He smiled, at least he thought he did. "So when are we going dancing again?"

Margaret chuckled.

"I need to get out of here."

"Slow down."

"The nurse'll come back with a doctor. I don't need an examination."

"She already did one."

Bobby's eyes opened wide. "Where was I?"

"Out like a light."

"Were you there?"

"Don't be so bashful. But if it matters, I left the room when the nurse gave you the once over."

Bobby sighed. "How did you know where to find me?"

"Booker, you gave him my number and asked him to call me."

"I don't even remember." Bobby squinted, trying to focus better. "I have to get back on the case. You have the briefcase."

"I didn't want to let it out of my sight. And you should take some time off."

"I can't, I'm getting close."

"Too close. You could have been killed today," Margaret said.

Bobby held his scraped, tomato-red hands in front of his face. "My hands."

"Don't worry. You'll play again," Nurse Landers said, returning with a thermometer. "Still, we should take a look inside. You might have a concussion, probably need an X-ray."

"I'm fine." He turned to Margaret. "And I'm hungry. Let's get out of here."

"You're in no shape to go anywhere, Bobby."

"I'm in no shape to stay here, that's for sure. How do I look?"

"Like a truck ran you over."

"More like a steamroller."

"And a little sunburned. Definitely a little worse for wear."

Nurse Landers took Bobby's vitals, insisted he drink some orange juice. He insisted on going to Wilde's room. It wasn't easy and he wasn't steady on his feet, but he made it under his own steam. Wilde waved with one finger. He didn't look great, but he looked a hell of a lot better than he had a couple hours ago. Bandaged all over, jaw wired. He signaled that he wanted something. It was like a game of charades. "Food? Bathroom?" Bobby said. Wilde kept drawing a square in the air with his finger. "Picture? The pictures."

Margaret took the photos from the briefcase. She and Bobby stood over Wilde's bed, spreading the pictures out on the food tray. Bobby picked through them one at a time. Wilde gave them his full attention.

"I don't think those are a good thing for Mr. Wilde to be looking at in his condition," Nurse Landers said.

Wilde shooed her away with his hand, signaled for Bobby to move the pictures closer.

They went through the entire set of photos once. Twice. Five times. As Bobby was about to put them back in the case, Wilde grabbed for them as best he could. Several fell on the floor.

Bobby picked them up, put them back on the tray. Wilde stabbed his finger at the top picture. He slid it to the side. Stared briefly at the picture below. Stabbed again.

At what?

Wilde grabbed for the pad and pencil on his tray.

"Magnifying glass," he wrote.

"Do you have one?" Bobby asked Margaret. She shook her head, left the room immediately.

Bobby continued combing through pictures.

Margaret returned a few minutes later with a small magnifying glass. "The nurse wants this back. She said if we don't give it back, she'll keep Sam in here forever."

"Then we better give it back," Bobby said.

Wilde, with unsteady hands, took the magnifier from Bobby. He used both hands to steady the glass and look through the pictures.

He reached for his pad and pencil. It clacked to the floor. He used his finger to trace a pattern in the air.

"What's that?"

Wilde kept making the sign.

"H," Margaret said.

Wilde stabbed at several of the pictures. Bobby took the magnifier, held it tight to them. A small machine appeared in nearly every one. It had always been there, of course, but Bobby had paid it no attention. It had been unobtrusive, just part of the background.

"*H-o-l-l-e-r-i-t-h*?" Margaret said, leaning over Bobby's shoulder, reading through the magnifying glass. "What is it?"

"I'm not sure what exactly it is or does, but there were cases of them at that warehouse on Pine," Bobby said.

Margaret fanned through the concentration camp pictures. "There's one in almost every photo. At least the photos in camp offices."

"And guess who makes them?" Bobby grinned, handing Wilde his pad and pencil. "IBM and our friend Mr. Stinson."

Wilde scribbled furiously. *Stinson* → *Dietrich/Thomas/Lois* → *IBM.*

"What's he saying?" Margaret said.

"Stinson, Dietrich and the others are connected."

Wilde nodded until it just looked too painful and he stopped.

Bobby went on, "I get it. Dietrich and Thomas were in the import-export business. Stinson used them to ship the Holleriths. Now we have to find out to where and what the hell they do."

"To Germany," Margaret said.

"Exporting to Germany's been shut down for some time."

"Apparently that isn't stopping them."

Bobby put the magnifying glass on one of the pictures. He bent down close enough to see the IBM logo on the Hollerith machine. Just like the logo on the crates in the warehouse and on the door to Stinson's office.

CHAPTER THIRTY-NINE

Nicolai tooled his unmarked car down Western, taking Bobby to get the Studebaker Champion, still down at the Pike. Bobby had called Nicolai from a pay phone in the hospital waiting room. They decided that Margaret would go home and Nicolai would take Bobby to his car in Long Beach.

"How's the old Champ running?" Nicolai said.

"Like Gene Autry's horse Champ—never quits."

Bobby stared out the window at the passing scenery thinking about how much his life had changed in the past few days.

"We're getting close, I can feel it." Bobby filled Nicolai in with the relevant details of his and Wilde's experiences at the warehouse and in the truck. Then, "I saw the crates at the warehouse. IBM was stenciled on them. Right below that in smaller letters *Hollerith*. We still don't know what exactly a Hollerith machine does."

"That should be easy enough to find out."

"How?"

"Just call IBM. Ask them. Make up some BS about having heard about it and how maybe you can use one in your business."

"I'm never going to be a good detective."

"It takes practice."

"It also takes instinct. I don't think I have that." Maybe I have women's intuition, he thought, remembering how he'd blurted that out to Margaret.

"You can hone it," Nicolai said. "It's not necessarily something that comes naturally."

Bobby watched the buildings fly by, waiting till they hit the truck farms farther south. He liked the open feeling there.

"You think this Stinson guy had you beat up a few days ago, it was his thugs outside the joint in Hollywood?"

Bobby stared out the window. The buildings became sporadic. Building, field. Field, building, until there were more fields than buildings.

"Don't overlook the obvious, kid." Nicolai sucked in the fresh air.

Bobby nodded.

They hit Long Beach; Nicolai pulled in next to the Studebaker.

"Thanks for the lift, Sarge. For the advice too."

Nicolai grinned. Bobby started to get out of the car. "Hold up. I got a present for you."

"Present?"

Nicolai retrieved a small scrap of paper from his pocket, handed it to Bobby. A mix of numbers and letters. "The license plate to the big car at the cemetery."

"I thought it belonged to Stinson."

"Nope. He drives a Packard like you said. Belongs to a David Chambers."

Bobby thought he should have known this as he'd—she'd—gone for a ride in that black Caddy—though there are lot of big black Caddies. Besides, it was something he didn't want Nicolai to know because telling him about Bobbie would just be too damn complicated.

"And guess what," Nicolai said. "Chambers came up with a second car registered in his name. A maroon Merc."

"Mercury? Like the one with the two men—"

"Yup." Nicolai looked more than pleased with himself.

"But I only gave you a partial license. Maybe it's not his."

"And maybe it is. I don't believe in coincidences, kid."

* * *

David Chambers. That must have been who was sitting in the car at the cemetery. *Criminy!*

Bobby waved as Nicolai drove off. He hadn't said anything to him about Chambers. He wanted to handle his high school chum himself. He circled the Champion, running his fingers along the smooth, polished finish. Fished the keys from his pocket. Changed his mind and stuffed them back. He walked down the midway to the Mirror Maze. It was open for business now. Kids and their parents running in and out, giggling. He'd thought he might pay a visit to Jerry. Decided against it. If he got into it with Jerry now it would put Stinson and Chambers—*Chambers!*—on alert. Jerry's time would come. It was probably better this way anyhow. Much as he liked to think of himself as a tough guy, he wasn't a man. He didn't think he could fight Jerry *mano-a-mano*. A feeling of melancholy swept over him as he climbed into the Champ for the ride home. He held back a tear—damn, men don't cry. But he felt betrayed by David Chambers. He'd thought they were friends.

CHAPTER FORTY

Bobby hit the Alabam instead of going next door to the Dunbar. He didn't have a phone in his room and maybe Lawrence would let him use the bar phone. The place was empty and spooky in the off-hours gloom. He gravitated to the piano as Lawrence brought the phone on a long cord. Bobby absent-mindedly noodled on an arrangement for "La Tempesta" without really thinking about it. Bobby dialed information, while still hitting the keys with the other hand. Called the local IBM office in the Bradbury Building. He talked to Gwen Cooke, Stinson's secretary. A short conversation. Just long enough to find out that Holleriths were tabulating machines that used punch cards to catalog millions of pieces of data. Keep track of anything and everything.

"People?" Bobby asked.

"Yes, of course," Gwen said. "They use them in the census."

"In Germany?"

"Who is this?"

Bobby slammed the phone down, walked back out to the bar. Lawrence grabbed a Bubble Up.

"Belay that, Lawrence. Give me a whiskey."

Bobby made a quick stop at Margaret's duplex before heading to his destination.

"What're you telling me?" he said, after Margaret had asked

her father to fill Bobby in on what he had told her.

"The film—" Mr. Lane hesitated.

"—The concentration camp photos?"

Mr. Lane nodded. "One of the refugees we were trying to help gave me the roll of undeveloped film. He thought maybe I could do something with it. I gave it to Thomas, he was an amateur photographer, developed it in his house."

"So you saw the camps, the Holleriths?"

"Yes, but Thomas and Dietrich never told me what they were planning to do. They never told me about the Holleriths."

"So they set about going after IBM on their own?"

Mr. Lane nodded. "When Dietrich and then Thomas were killed, I began to suspect, but I never dreamed they would—"

"Why didn't you tell me this before?" Margaret said.

"I wanted to protect you. I don't know how deep this goes, who's involved."

"We're all involved," Margaret said.

Bobby arrived at Leach's hotel. The bartender recognized him, knew he was a *friend* of Leach. Steered him to the Apollo.

As soon as he hit the border with Santa Monica, a cold fog enveloped the Champ. Bobby turned up his collar. He drove down Olympic, studiously avoiding any streets near Clover Field. The wooden planks of the pier rattled the Champ's chassis. Bobby parked, trotted to the end of the wharf. The railings had been roped where Bobby's Olds had blasted through them. He wondered if he'd ever get it back—if they could even pull it from the water—and if he did, could he make it run again?

No water taxis were running. Two men in overcoats and Dick Tracy hats, with cigarettes dangling, stood near the end of the pier. But, Bobby knew, they weren't cops.

"You?" one of them said.

"Can you take me to Leach?"

The men talked among themselves. In a few minutes, Bobby

was in a launch heading out to sea.

On deck, Leach's men frisked Bobby. Found nothing. With one man grabbing each of Bobby's arms, they escorted him to the fantail of the Apollo. Leach sat under a heat lamp, like a royal poobah, attended to by various servants, including a barber and a wine steward.

"Welcome aboard," Leach said, as if to a long-lost friend. He signaled for Bobby to sit. Saw him shiver. "Bring my friend a coat."

One of the lackeys ran off. Leach dismissed everyone else, except the steward.

"Scotch-rocks, my friend?"

"Just a Bubble Up."

"Seven-Up okay?" the steward said. Bobby nodded.

"You're not much of a drinker for a musician. Maybe you smoke the reefer?"

"Nope."

"You're a paragon of virtue, my friend."

"I'm not sure about that. I'm a paragon of something; I'm not sure it's virtue."

Leach grinned. His lackey brought Bobby a pea coat. Bobby swam in it like he might in the ocean, it was that large. But it kept him warm. The steward brought the drinks and appetizers. Laid the spread out. Leach nodded, the steward disappeared.

"What can I do for you, my friend? It seems you aren't going to let this Dietrich business drop."

"James Christmas did not kill Hans Dietrich."

"I know this."

"Then why don't you help? You've offered your help. When do I get it?"

"You're very cheeky, young man." Leach stuffed a caviar-topped canapé in his mouth. "You know you're sticking your nose in places where it shouldn't go, like a dog." He laughed at his own joke. "What can I do for you, young man?"

"I need a gun."

Leach grinned thinly. "A gun? What kind of a gun?"

"I, I don't know. A pistol."

"Have you ever fired a pistol?"

"No."

"And you think you can do that and shoot a man? I'm assuming it's a man you want to shoot—"

"Why are you giving me such a hard time?"

"Tell me what you know," Leach said.

Bobby had only a split-second to decide how much to tell Leach. He decided to spill everything, Dietrich, Thomas, the house of mirrors, and the warehouse. IBM, Stinson, the Holleriths. The concentration camp pictures. Chambers. Everything. He'd come here for the man's help. He would get it or not.

"Dietrich wasn't a Nazi."

"And you're wondering why he sounded like one when you heard him on the boat here?"

Bobby nodded.

"You're also wondering about my relationship with him."

"Yes."

"As you know," Leach went on, "along with Bugsy Siegel, Jack Dragna, and Mickey Cohen, I'm the top—"

"—I know, like in *Casablanca*, where the Fat Man tells Bogey, 'As the leader of all illegal activities in Casablanca, *you* are an influential and respected man.'"

"Most people wouldn't dare interrupt me, kid. But yes, I am, indeed, such a man—though not fat—and my domain is Los Angeles. As such, I have my ear to the ground, so to speak. You seem like a good kid, Bobby Saxon, so let me tell you about the Chosen People."

Where was Leach going with this? Bobby didn't know what the hell he was talking about. Maybe he'd made the wrong decision coming here and time was wasting. "The Chosen People?"

"The Jews."

"What about them?"

"Everyone *chooses* the Jews to grind under their heels. Today it is Hitler and the Germans. Hans Dietrich was trying to help the Jews of Germany. As you might be aware, things are not good for them there." Leach sipped his scotch. "Dietrich was murdered because he was going to expose a giant scandal. You are on the right track with this IBM business, son."

To being murdered, Bobby couldn't help thinking.

"I know IBM's involved," he said. "We have those pictures of the camps, with the IBM Holleriths in almost every one. The Holleriths are tabulating machines—counting machines, and what are they counting—"

"—Jews. Yes, the camps that our illustrious president will not bomb the train tracks to, but I get off course. So, this IBM company is selling computational tabulating machines—"

"—the Holleriths—"

"—to the Germans to help them keep track of the Jews of Europe, so they know where to find them, down to the apartment, to make their disposal more efficient."

"Isn't that illegal, to be selling to the Germans? I thought there was no more exporting to Germany."

"There isn't. They, IBM, claim it is being done through their European subsidiaries, over which IBM no longer has control due to the war."

"But if there's no more exporting, then where are IBM's subsidiaries getting the machines?"

"Precisely. That is why they're doing it clandestinely."

"So Dietrich found out," Bobby said.

"Stinson and your friends, Dietrich and Thomas, had been doing business a long time. Since before the war. But after war broke out, Stinson could no longer ship the machines through IBM's normal channels, *as IBM is an upstanding and patriotic American company*. So he hired Dietrich and Thomas' firm as the transshipper as they were in the import-export business and had experience with this and contacts with the Germans from before the war. They didn't know what was really happening at first, but figured it out eventually. Hans Dietrich was trying to gather hard proof to show Stinson and IBM's total complicity, which is why he was acting the faithful Nazi, so Stinson would trust him."

"How do you know all this?"

"I knew a little. Mostly I'm putting it together as we speak. But let me tell you something, my friend. Regimes come and go. But the underworld is always here. I did business in Europe; I have contacts there." Leach ran his hand over his freshly cut hair.

"Why wouldn't Dietrich just turn Stinson in to the authorities and end it all?"

"You're missing the point. The point wasn't to stop Stinson, but to find out who else was involved all along the way. Besides, if Dietrich turned Stinson in IBM would just have replaced him with another lackey."

"But why? Why were they doing it in the first place?"

"You're very naive, my friend. They are in business."

"Just to make money?"

"And maybe because they don't like Jews so much either."

"And Stinson had Dietrich killed—"

"—Because he found out Dietrich was onto him, that Dietrich was only pretending to have Nazi sympathies and was trying to expose him."

Bobby's breath quickened. He felt like he'd been climbing a mountain and had just reached the summit. It was all starting to come together and the trip down should be a lot easier than the climb to the top—he hoped.

Bobby's mouth dropped. "So Dietrich and Thomas were killed to keep from exposing IBM's involvement with this? What's your stake in this?"

"You mean, where am I making my money from by helping Dietrich?" Leach said.

Bobby nodded.

"I'm not. But I am Jewish and I wanted to help my people. And like you, Dietrich came to me for information and arms."

"To kill Stinson?"

"No. For the Resistance. He was planning to smuggle them to Europe. Mostly I was helping from the sidelines and Dietrich kept me in the dark on the specifics." Leach sipped his drink. "It wouldn't look good for such a patriotic and upstanding company, not to mention the charges that might be laid on them. And Stinson, or whoever he hired, had the job done on Dietrich on my boat. And now my gambling is closed down and I'm losing money."

"Why doesn't the government do anything about it?"

"I guess they have more important things to do than to save the Jews. That son of a bitch Roosevelt smiles and smokes his cigarettes in those fancy-schmancy holders, all the while Hitler is killing thousands of Jews every day and no one gives a damn." Leach grabbed his scotch tumbler, wound up, hurled it into the deck.

"You knew all this. Why didn't you tell me? I had to go through hell."

"Like I said, I knew some, but not all. I needed someone on the ground to—"

"—So you used me as bait!"

"Trial by fire, kid. You needed to learn by doing."

"A man's rotting in jail."

"I have a business to run. It's not quite above-board and I can't be calling attention to it. I already got enough *tsuris*. I had faith in you."

"You used me. I could have been killed." Bobby jumped up. Carnie appeared as if from nowhere.

Leach signaled him to back off.

"You still can. It's not over yet." Leach gestured for Bobby to sit back down. "You need anything, any muscle, any help of any kind, you come to me."

"I still want a gun."

Leach nodded toward Carnie. Carnie pulled a .32 automatic pistol from his coat. He showed Bobby how to use it, shooting at a buoy in the ocean. Bobby wasn't a bad shot for a beginner.

"Keep the coat," Leach said, walking off.

Carnie rode the launch back to the pier with Bobby.

"Kid, you do a good job, the boss'll be grateful. He wants to get that Stinson slob. You need any muscle?"

"I do need one thing," Bobby said.

CHAPTER FORTY-ONE

Bobby splashed water on his face. Examined himself in the mirror carefully.

He still hadn't really answered the question: who was he? Bobby, Roberta-Bobbie? He might never fully answer it. But he knew he was happy in Bobby's skin and clothes. As content as he'd ever been. He wondered if Margaret would be happy if she knew the real Bobby.

He had just come from the hospital. Wilde was doing better, but he was out of the fight, at least for now, and Bobby had things to do, couldn't wait for his friend to wake, even though he would have liked to run his plan by Wilde. He plopped his fedora on his head, closed the door to James' room at the Dunbar behind him.

Bobby and Margaret sat in the back of her car on Broadway, a couple buildings up from Stinson's office. It was only seven p.m., early enough that the buildings weren't completely deserted so they wouldn't look out of place.

Bobby needed someone to help him on this assignment. He would have preferred Wilde for a lot of reasons. Margaret was who he had. He'd filled her in on what he'd learned, including about David Chambers, though he wasn't one hundred percent sure of Chambers' involvement. He just didn't want to believe that about his friend. Still, there was Stinson in Chambers' car at the funeral and Bobby's possible sighting of him with Stinson at the Brown Derby. And what about Chambers having been on the Apollo the night Dietrich was killed? All these things were pretty innocent on their own, until he added in Chambers owning a Mercury. If his plan worked, he'd know for sure about Chambers, one way or the other.

"You're sure you never heard Dietrich mention David Chambers?"

"No, never," Margaret said.

"And you've never been here before?"

"I would have remembered that."

"Are you sure you want to do this?" Bobby said.

"I want to nail Hans' killer."

On the seat between them sat a breadbox-sized brown case— a wire recorder. Bobby had taken Leach up on his offer of help. He had asked Carnie to supply him with the machine.

"You know how to use this thing?" Margaret said.

"Carnie showed me. I think I remember." He patted the brown box, then patted the .32 in his pocket, pulled it out. "Showed me how to use this too."

"Jesus, Bobby, be careful."

"I will." Bobby grabbed the case, exited the car.

Bobby and Margaret walked into the Bradbury Building as Pop was closing up his newsstand, their footfalls clacking on the tile floor. Bobby told him that Stinson was committing treason. Pop joined their cause—what the hell, he hated Stinson anyway.

While Pop occupied the security guard with idle conversation, Margaret followed Bobby to Stinson's office door. They were in luck, the lights were out. Bobby handed off the case to Margaret, fished in his pockets for Wilde's lock picking set.

"Now this I'm not so sure about. Hopefully practice makes perfect." He fiddled with the lock picks in the keyhole while Margaret kept an eye out. After what felt like an hour but must only have been a couple minutes, they were in Stinson's office.

Making sure not to disturb anything, Bobby hid the wire recorder under Stinson's desk, in a spot where his feet wouldn't kick it and give it away. He ran the microphone cord up the inside of the desk, placed the mic in the leaves of a green plant. He'd seen that done in a movie. Turned to Margaret, "The hardest part will be turning on the damn thing without him noticing, but Carnie gave me this wire and gadget to do it remotely. I don't have to be where the unit is, just run this wire and press this button on the end."

"You just have to hope he doesn't find it before you're ready."

Bobby crossed his fingers behind his back.

They returned to Margaret's duplex so Bobby could get his car. It wouldn't start.

"Do you belong to the Automobile Club?" she asked.

"Can't afford to. I'll get some tools and try to start it tomorrow. Do you mind giving me a lift?"

The hum of Margaret's engine was the only thing that filled the car for most of the trip back to the Dunbar. The little conversation they did have revolved around FDR's latest fireside chat and the Goldbergs' radio adventures. Nothing of any substance, which didn't mean that Bobby wasn't thinking about the course of events.

As they drove farther south there were few white faces on the street and in cars. Many black ones.

"You live down here? I knew you hung out at the Alabam but I didn't know you lived near here too?" Margaret said.

"Ever since I got evicted, Booker put me up in the Dunbar Hotel."

"I don't know it."

"It's the place where all the colored stars stay when they're in L.A. They aren't allowed anywhere else. Cab Calloway, Duke Ellington. Billie Holiday. All of them."

"So it's segregated, but in the opposite way."

"They have no choice. But they're letting me stay there, I wouldn't call that segregation." Bobby lit up a Viceroy.

Crowds from the Alabam thronged the sidewalk in front of the Dunbar. Margaret pulled to the curb around the corner from the hotel. Bobby's heart pounded. He wanted to lean over and kiss her good night. He'd grown up a lot over the last couple weeks, but he didn't have what it took to do it. They said their good nights, his hand went to the door handle. Click. The door opened. Before he could step out, Margaret leaned over, kissed him on the cheek. He turned his face to hers. Their lips met, just like Gable and Crawford might on the silver screen. After he'd gone up to his room he couldn't have said if the kiss lasted ten seconds or ten minutes. Either way, he could still taste it. He always would.

He started the night in bed, on his back, eyes open, staring at the ceiling. Listening to the music drift in from the band at the Alabam next door. Sleep wouldn't come. Too many things to consider. Should he call David Chambers in the morning and make an appointment? What if he dressed up as Roberta—Bobbie—went to Chambers' office without an appointment and then he wasn't there? What if Stinson found the wire recorder?

He thought Stinson was the real bad guy. And despite the Mercury, he still didn't want to believe that Chambers was involved. Maybe there was another explanation? But if he was, maybe Chambers could give him the info he needed to get Stinson. *Oh the tangled webs we weave.*

Criminy!

No wonder he couldn't sleep.

He grabbed his tools, caught a bus, and made his way back to his car at Margaret's. Finally got it running before the sun came up. He looked at Margaret's window, dark. Thought about her sleeping just on the other side. He headed back to the Dunbar to catch a little shuteye before heading out again.

* * *

He—*she*—had to start putting himself into a feminine frame of mind. She had done a damn fine job on her hair and makeup, easily disguising the small cuts on her face. It got easier every time. She slipped into her slinky dress and heels, looked at herself in James' mirror. Not bad. Bobbie grabbed her purse and was ready to go. All except for one thing. She was paralyzed with fear, hands cold, clammy. Heart racing. Breath coming fast and furious, she worried that she would hyperventilate. The ringing in her ears didn't help. She glanced at the clock in anticipation. She had worked a script out in her head last night as she lay staring up at the ceiling. Now she had to give the performance of her life and her mind was blank.

Her fear didn't extend to leaving the Dunbar anymore. She breezed out of the hotel to her car.

She hadn't called Chambers to set up an appointment. She still could, decided not to. She pointed the car north and gripped the steering wheel.

"Break a leg," she said out loud.

Getting past Renata Wallace, Chambers' secretary, was a lead pipe cinch. David was eager to see Bobbie, not knowing, of course, her real reason for coming.

"Bobbie, I'm glad you came back." He nodded to Renata, who quickly departed his private office. "I've been thinking about you. Didn't know how to reach you."

"I've been thinking about you, too." Bobbie was on autopilot—an autopilot based on a thousand movies she'd seen over the years.

The small talk didn't last long, as David's eyes drank in the very feminine Bobbie in her heels, dress, and makeup.

Renata returned quickly, with a bottle of scotch, water, and two cut crystal glasses on a silver tray. She left the setup on the desk. Chambers told her to hold his calls and she left again.

He came round the front of his desk. She smiled seductively, she hoped.

"It's good to see you." His smile was broad, his words pregnant with meaning.

She sat on the edge of the desk, subtly hiking her skirt up. He seemed to like what he saw.

He moved toward her, resting his hand on her thigh, giving it a little squeeze. She recoiled, on the inside only, she hoped. He put his lips on her neck. Kissed softly. Her skin crawled with things she'd rather not imagine.

She backed away from him, trying not to show how repulsive she found him, movie star looks or not.

"David, I did want to see you. But I came here for another purpose too."

"Hmm." He closed in on her again, spread his large hands across her back. Leaned in tight.

"I have a friend who works for the FBI."

That got his attention. He backed off, stood up soldier-straight. "What does that have to do with me?"

"She was talking out of school, I guess you'd call it. She was talking about IBM—"

"—IBM?"

"And I thought of you, since we had talked about it before."

"I'm not sure what that has to do with me." He was cool as a cucumber.

"I'm not sure either. She'd had a couple of drinks, blurted it out. Something about J. Edgar Hoover wanting to bring them down. They're doing something they shouldn't be, I guess." Bobbie was playing a dangerous game, trying to tease information out of Chambers, make him nervous. She hoped it wouldn't backfire on her.

"Why're you telling me this?"

"I'm not really sure." Vamping. "But since we'd talked about it last time, I wanted to warn you—in case you had any dealings with them."

"My dealings with them are peripheral."

"Well, I thought since you'd done some work for them you might still be representing them. I just didn't want to see you get in any trouble. She said they're going after a man named Stinson."

"I've met the guy a few times. Never liked him. He wanted me to do some contracts for him 'cause I did a couple small deals for IBM, but I turned him down."

"That's good, 'cause I think it's going to get ugly. Especially with the war and all. I think he's a bad man, does bad things."

"I had no idea."

"Someone told me he, IBM, they're helping the Nazis. Something about Hollerith machines, whatever they are."

"Never heard of them." But the color washed completely out of Chambers' face. That didn't keep him from putting on the hundred-watt smile. Underneath all that wattage he seemed to have lost his confidence, as if he didn't know how much Bobbie knew about the operation. His response told her that he was more involved than he was letting on. The conversation came to a total standstill. Chambers changed tack, tried turning on the charm with small talk of getting together for another date. That made Bobbie sick inside. Of course, she agreed enthusiastically.

She knew she'd rattled his cage. Just didn't know how to get him to fess up with any more info. He told her he had a meeting he couldn't get out of and had to go. She didn't believe it; he just wanted to get rid of her.

He blew back on her, grabbing her in his arms. Yanking her close. She could smell the treacly mints on his breath under the scotch. He stabbed his tongue down her throat as if shoving a battering ram into her. He ground his groin on her, she felt his excitement. He slid his hand inside her dress, sliding the dress down at the same time.

"Renata," Bobbie said. "Your secretary, she might—"

"Oh, she knows not to disturb us."

She pushed off him. He came back at her. She danced aside.

He gave her a deep, soulful kiss—it felt like a vampire's last kiss—before almost literally shoving her out the door. As she walked, her back to him, she couldn't hide the Cheshire Cat grin on her face from the secretary. Renata probably thought it was the cat-that-ate-the-canary look of someone who'd just had sex in the office with her boss.

Bobbie parked her car around the corner from David's office and waited. At four- thirty David's Caddie pulled out of his parking space. Bobbie followed at a distance, glad in some ways that she didn't have the magenta Olds anymore. It would have stood out like a sore thumb and David would have remembered it. The black Caddie pulled in front of the Hollywood Athletic Club on Sunset. He went inside. It didn't seem as if David was concerned about the warning she'd given him. After another hour, she decided nothing was going to happen tonight and turned her car around, headed back to the Dunbar.

Even though he'd felt comfortable leaving earlier, Bobby couldn't face going back to the Dunbar and working her way upstairs. She stopped at a thrift store, bought a cheap pair of coveralls and tennis shoes. She hit a Shell gas station restroom, peeled off her makeup with soap and water and combed her hair in the mannish fashion that Bobby, not Bobbie, would. Slipped into the coveralls and soft shoes. She was a man again. Or man enough to walk through the Dunbar lobby. Before leaving he rinsed his mouth to get rid of the taste of Chambers' kiss.

He called Pop from a pay phone. No sign of Chambers at Stinson's office and Stinson had left at six p.m. Maybe they were both trying to play it cool? Maybe there was nothing going on between Chambers and Stinson and it was all Bobby's overactive imagination? But then why were those thugs driving Chambers' Mercury when they shot Thomas? Why did they payoff Mrs. Hazelton to evict him? And why did they beat up Bobby? Maybe Bobby's plan was a waste of time. He decided to head back to the Dunbar and call it a day.

At seven thirty the next morning Bobby picked up Margaret

at her house. They bought doughnuts and coffee at a diner kitty-corner from the Bradbury. At seven forty-five, Bobby was in the lobby. Pop was already there. Pop nodded to Bobby, but that was all the acknowledgement there was. Stinson entered, looking like he was in a hurry today. Went up the elevator with several other people who worked in the building.

Seven fifty-eight, Chambers walked toward the elevators. Maybe his little act yesterday had worked after all? Bobby, on the far side of the lobby where he couldn't be seen by Chambers, doffed his hat. Pop saw.

Chambers went up.

Pop looked at his watch. He waited exactly five minutes, walked to the elevators and rode up. Bobby's feet tapped a nervous Krupa beat on the Bradbury floor. He felt outside the action. He wanted to be the one going upstairs instead of Pop, going into the lion's den of Stinson's office. But he couldn't take the chance of being seen and recognized by Chambers, even as a boy. And Stinson would probably remember him as well. Margaret waited in the car.

If everything went according to Hoyle, Pop would just be entering the outer office. If Stinson's secretary was there he'd ask to see her boss. If not, he'd just knock on the private office's door. He'd give Stinson his morning snack and paper. Stinson would say something like "I haven't even put my order in yet." Pop would come back with, "I have a dentist appointment. Wanted to make sure you got your paper and cruller." On his way out, Pop would hit the remote button for the wire recorder.

If all went according to Hoyle.

Bobby drove Margaret home. The plan was to come back later that night and get the recorder while Pop played lookout.

Bobby waited in his room until six p.m., then drove back to Stinson's office. Pop was waiting for him and gave him the all clear to head up to Stinson's office. Using Wilde's picks he got in easily this time—practice. Grabbed the recorder and split.

* * *

He and Margaret sat in her kitchen, eating sardine sandwiches on rye, listening to the wire recording. They heard Stinson yell to Gwen to hold his calls while he met with Chambers.

"We've got trouble," Chambers said excitedly.

There was a short pause, then Chambers responded to something Stinson said. "No. It's about IBM. The Holleriths."

"It's your game, you run with it." David's voice was clear and strong on the wire.

"Don't worry about it, they don't have anything on us," Stinson said. "Our tracks are covered and the warehouse isn't in our names or IBM's. We can just say the Holleriths were stolen."

"Do you know how many Jews we've helped to kill?"

"Nobody gives a damn about Jews. All we're doing is selling machines to the Germans, what they do with them is their business—we're not killing any lousy Jews," Stinson shouted. "Do you see Roosevelt bombing the tracks to the camps? Hell, we're doing the world a favor and making a ton of money at it. The Germans are paying ten times what those machines are worth and you're getting your share."

"Besides, exporting the machines to Switzerland isn't illegal." But David didn't sound so sure of himself.

"As long as they don't know they're ultimately bound for Germany."

"We've got that covered." David sounded more confident now. "There's so many layers of legal paperwork, dummy corporate entities, so many transshipment points that nobody will find the trail. And even if they do, it will take them till the year 2000 to figure it all out."

Bobby turned to Margaret. "If that doesn't put them in Leavenworth, I don't know what will."

He was about to turn the machine off when he heard a cough on the recorder wire. Then Chambers' voice again. "We have another problem."

"Well, this is turning out to be a red-letter day. What is it?"

"My pesky little friend, Bobbie Saxon, is trying to worm information out of me."

Margaret looked puzzled. "You and Chambers are friends?"

"I'll fill you in later," Bobby said.

"Make the problem go away," Stinson said.

"I'll deal with it," Chambers said. Bobby shut the machine off. Shivered.

"What does that mean?"

"Don't worry. It's all coming together."

Margaret gave Bobby a warm kiss on the lips. He was in heaven.

But one man's heaven is another man's hell.

Bobby and Margaret brought the recordings to Nicolai. Through him they got to Sergeant Duff, of the Santa Monica Police—Bobby wanted to include him. Duff was a good guy and Bobby thought he would get some glory.

Nicolai arranged for them to meet with FBI agent Gene Pallette. Pallette agreed to meet them at the FBI offices in downtown L.A.

They sat in a small, windowless room in the Federal building. The quarters were close, the room stifling. Pallette and two other agents jammed in there, along with Bobby, Margaret, Nicolai, and Duff. Bobby watched the wire spools spin round and round and spin out their tale. Their confessions and guilt. Mesmerized by the spinning wheels, he shook himself out of it. His eyes drifted down to the IBM name and logo on the brown wire recorder box. He smiled inwardly.

"What do you want me to do with these?" Pallette said, after listening.

Bobby filled him in on the beat-down, Stinson, Chambers, Dietrich, the Hollerith machines. Agent Pallette listened attentively.

"You shouldn't be playing detective, Mr. Saxon. Leave that to us and the real detectives." Pallette nodded toward Nicolai and Duff.

"Nobody wants to do anything."

"And I'm afraid I'm not going to spoil that batting average. You haven't really given me any evidence. Merely supposition."

A word Bobby had heard recently.

"Don't you care about espionage?"

"Of course we do and I don't appreciate your implication. But you haven't given me anything about espionage."

"Well, maybe it's not that per se. But if it's true, it's giving aid and comfort to the enemy. Isn't that the definition of treason? The Nazis are using the Holleriths in the war effort."

"To do what?"

"To find, count, and keep track of Jews—to send them to concentration camps."

"And you have no proof, Mr. Saxon."

"How much proof did you have when you rounded up every Japanese on the West Coast?"

Pallette scowled. "We appreciate that you want to help your country."

"But my country doesn't want my help."

"Your country does want your help. Just not in this way, not at this time. If you want to help out, join the marines."

The brick wall Bobby just hit hurt more than the beating or falling out of the truck had. He didn't know if Pallette was giving him a line of BS or if he really thought there wasn't enough evidence. He was determined to get the evidence the FBI needed, though he wondered why they weren't doing it themselves. Wasn't that their job?

Nicolai's and Duff's faces were impassive. Margaret looked from one to the other.

"Arrest them. For treason," Bobby said.

"All they're guilty of is maybe violating some trade restrictions. Besides, they're just tabulating machines. It's not like it's war materiel, machine guns, bombs."

"Just tabulating machines, which the Germans use to find and keep track of Jews so they can send them to the ovens. Oh, and they had three people murdered, Hans Dietrich, Harlan Thomas, and probably Lois Templeton, but what's three people when millions are dying." Bobby dug his nails deep into his palms, until it hurt. Until he focused on that instead of the rage welling up inside him.

"You're right, this is just a little blip," Pallette said. "We need IBM. They're too important to our own war effort."

"They're playing both sides. And you don't need Stinson."

"We do need him. IBM is—"

"Stinson's not IBM."

"I might be able to make a case against Chambers," Pallette said. "We'll compromise."

"During war?"

"War—everything—is the art of compromise. Hell, we're in bed with Stalin, that's compromise."

Bobby wanted to jam his fist straight, fast, and hard into Pallette's jaw. Margaret saw this, as did Nicolai. They each took an arm, walked him outside, followed by Duff.

"All of this. And for what?"

"You're learning how the game is played, kid." Nicolai jammed a soggy, half-smoked, half-chewed cigar in his mouth, fired it up.

"It's a great game." Bobby scratched his finger on a match, lit a Viceroy. Sucked in a deep breath.

CHAPTER FORTY-TWO

Bobby parked around the corner from the Dunbar. Lit up another Viceroy. He was glad to be home, such as home was these days. James was still in jail; Nicolai and Duff were working on that. He was disappointed that Pallette wasn't going to go after Stinson, but he said he'd look at Chambers. Lot of good that would do. Chambers would probably just get a slap on the wrist.

He opened the Champ's door, slammed it. As soon as he stepped onto the curb, two men with fedoras chucked low over their eyes jumped out of a car, came up on either side of him. They were each a head taller than him. In the dark, he thought they might be the men from the maroon Mercury. In the night shadows, he couldn't tell what their car was. He hoped it wasn't a Merc.

"Boss wants to see you."

"Why? What's going on?"

Silence. They stopped him in his tracks, frisked him, took the .32 Leach had given him, walked him to their car. One man drove, the other sat in back with Bobby. Nobody said a word. The radio blared war news and swing tunes. Nobody tapped their feet; nobody seemed to pay attention to any of it; it was just background noise.

As they'd picked Bobby up at the Dunbar, they took a southerly route toward the ocean. He had never seen as much of the ocean as he'd seen in the last couple of weeks. He hoped this wouldn't be his last trip there. He'd finally come to believe he could trust Leach—now he was having second thoughts. They drove through Venice, a part of Los Angeles that had begun as a USA version of its famous Italian counterpart; now it was only a shadow of what its founder Abbott Kinney had envisioned. The smell of tar and oil coated Bobby's nostrils. Venice was a pool of oil and derricks.

Bobby still wasn't sure if the car was a Mercury and he didn't recognize the men as being the ones from the car who had beat him outside of Musso's. But it couldn't be a good sign that they were heading for the Apollo. He'd thought Leach was his friend; now Bobby wondered if he'd turned on him—what if he was working with Chambers after all? If Leach was on his side, why have these torpedoes come for him, frisk him, and not tell him anything about what was going on?

The ocean chop nearly made him lose his lunch. Or maybe it was fear. His stomach was churning like it never had before.

The men led Bobby down a familiar passage on the Apollo. Opened a door and gave Bobby a gentle push inside, closing the door behind him. He'd been here before, the band room. No band now. Just one person besides himself.

"Hello, David."

Chambers sat in a comfortable easy chair, a half grin on his face.

"You. You're the one who brought everything down," Chambers said.

Bobby smiled.

"And don't you look silly, dressed up like a man. You always did like playing dress up. And you always did look silly."

"You knew all along," Bobby said.

"Right from the start. But I wanted to see what you knew."

"Did you kill Dietrich?"

"I had some help. It was a little tricky getting his body up there, but I always did like the theatrical."

Something clicked in Bobby's head. "Was that before or after you hired the thugs in the maroon Mercury?"

"Those goons? They were out of town boys. Boy did I get rooked on that deal."

"Looks like you got rooked all around."

"Thanks to you, you faggot-sissy or whatever the hell you are."

"Hazelton? The beat-down outside Musso's? Thomas?"

Chambers grinned like a sadist.

"Why did they finish off Thomas?"

"Might as well tell you: just tying up loose ends," Chambers said. "Him and Dietrich got in the way. They were both Jew lovers."

"And then I got in the way."

"Yeah, but you were too slippery. I didn't realize at first you were playing both sides of the coin. I got suspicious when you came to me asking about IBM. But even that wasn't the clincher—that was when you were all dolled up. You've always hated being a girl."

"What about Lois?"

"I got rid of everything in Dietrich's office, cleaned it out. And I took care of her personally. She was easy."

"I'll tell my friend Sam Wilde about that. He'll want to know."

"I don't think you're going to be telling anybody anything. I'm not dead yet. I cut a deal with Leach. He's just another Jew businessman who likes a good deal."

Bobby hoped it wasn't so, but he wasn't sure.

"Watch," Chambers said. "You think Leach is your friend. I know him—know how he operates. Watch your back."

"—Watch my back, the nig—the Jew's playing me," Bobby said, echoing the wording of the note he'd received. Shaky hands lit up another Viceroy. He tried to hide the shakes as best he could. "I didn't want to think you were a murderer and a traitor, David. I liked you. I thought we were friends."

"I have no friends, only business associates. And enemies."

"All this for money, surely you don't believe in the Nazi cause."

"You know, the Jews control everything. I don't believe in Nazism, but Hitler's not wrong about everything. All those Jews moving into our neighborhood—"

The "No dogs. No Jews" sign on North Edinburgh popped into Bobby's head.

The door opened. Carnie entered, followed by Leach.

"You two enjoying a nice reunion?"

Chambers glanced at Leach—for what, approval? Bobby couldn't read Leach's face.

"Well, Bobby," Leach said. "If you'll excuse David and me for a minute, we have some business to discuss."

Chambers brushed himself off, smiled at Bobby on the way out. Carnie stayed with Bobby. He didn't have a good feeling about this. Maybe Chambers and Leach had cut a deal?

"Let's go," Carnie said, nodding to Bobby.

Bobby, the two men who'd brought him here, and Carnie sat in a small motor launch. After a few minutes they heard laughing and backslapping.

"We have a deal then?" Chambers' voice carried down to the launch.

"My hand," Leach said.

Bobby looked up to see Chambers and Leach shaking hands. What the hell was going on?

Chambers joined them in the boat for the ride back to the pier. He said nothing to Bobby, though his eyes were smiling triumphantly the whole time. The five of them found themselves in the car, which Bobby now saw wasn't a Mercury. Chambers sat in front with one of the men who had picked Bobby up. He bopped his hand on the dash to the music coming from the radio. Bobby sat in the back seat, crammed between the other man in the fedora and Carnie. The ride back into town was almost as bumpy as the boat ride to and from the Apollo.

"Let's check out this park," Carnie said as they cruised Sixth Street by the La Brea Tar Pits. The main entrance was on Wilshire, so they came on the park from the back side. It was late and dark and none of this looked good to Bobby.

Bobby and Chambers walked across the grass, ahead of Carnie and the two men, toward the oozing black pits. Chambers didn't need to talk to gloat, it was in his step, his eyes. The turn of his mouth.

"I told you, Bobby, no sweat. This is the last stop for you," Chambers said. "You know what happens when you sink down in that tar. Just look at the bones of the mammoths and saber-toothed tigers they have here. We grew up in this neighborhood, we know all about the tar pits, don't we?"

"You have no conscience, do you?"

"This is war."

"Don't you mean business?"

"It's all the same thing, isn't it? Well, at least you'll die like a man." Chambers couldn't contain his laughter.

They came to the edge of the small lake of tar and oil, blocked only by a three-foot-tall split-rail fence.

Bobby and Chambers stood by the fence. Behind them Carnie was flanked by the other two hoods. Carnie fished in his pocket, pulled out Bobby's .32. Hefted it. He tossed it to Bobby. Surprised, Bobby wasn't ready to catch it and it landed on the grass. Chambers dived for it, but Bobby was too fast. Bobby backed away from Chambers.

"What—what's going on here, Carnie? I thought we had a deal." Chambers' eyes opened wide—not because of the darkness in the park.

"Got no deal with me."

"Leach won't like this."

Carnie turned to Bobby. "You remember how I showed you?"

"You want me to kill him?"

"You know at best the government'll give him a slap on the wrist," Carnie said. "Look at the trouble he's caused you—and us."

"Do you know who Bobby Saxon really is, let me—" Chambers shouted.

"Shut up," Carnie said in a voice softer than Bobby could imagine. Chambers did shut up. Bobby guessed when a man like Carnie tells you to do something, you do it, even if you're going to die.

"Step over the fence, Mr. Chambers," Carnie said.

Chambers hesitated. Bobby racked the slide on the .32. Chambers clambered over the fence. He knew Bobby had reason to kill him.

Chambers stood on the edge of the tar lake. Carnie nodded to one of the hoods. He tossed a suitcase he'd carried from the car to Chambers. Chambers caught it automatically, without thinking. He almost stumbled under the weight. The hood stepped over the fence, retrieved a pair of handcuffs from his pocket. Clicked one cuff to Chambers' wrist, the other to the suitcase handle. The cuffs glinted in the moonlight.

"Whyn't you go for a dip?" Carnie said.

Chambers stood his ground. The hood gave him a hard shove. He stumbled into the tar, farther than Bobby thought he would. He began to sink slowly.

"Put one in him for good measure," Carnie said.

"Bobby, please," Chambers pleaded.

Bobby aimed the pistol. Squeezed on the trigger. Couldn't pull it all the way. "Maybe we should just let him rot in jail."

Carnie grabbed the little gun from him, aimed—tapped the trigger twice. The sound of the shots caromed off the sky. Chambers fell into the ooze. After less than a minute he disappeared from view.

"When they finally find him in a hundred years, he'll just be another fossil," one of the hoods said. "They'll think he was a caveman." Everybody laughed—everybody except Bobby.

Carnie turned to him, "Boss figured you might not be able to pull the trigger."

Bobby was stunned into silence. What made Leach and Carnie think he wouldn't turn them in? But he wouldn't. He knew that and he guessed they did too, just like they knew he wouldn't be able to pull the trigger.

"I thought Mr. Leach had a deal with Chambers?"

"Chambers screwed up the boss' life. His business. The deal was just a ruse."

"Scared me half to death. I thought I was going to—" Bobby was more than glad that he hadn't had to pull the trigger. And he thought Chambers got what he deserved. Still, he felt a twinge of remorse.

"We wanted him to be calm. Could've killed him on the boat, but the boss didn't want that."

They headed back to the car.

"What was in the suitcase?" Bobby said, unsuccessfully trying to light a Viceroy in the wind. He used the trick Nicolai had taught him and the cigarette took the double-match easily.

"Lead weight and the busted-up pieces-a one-a them IBM machines."

"A Hollerith?"

"Yeah, that's it. Boss thought it was, what did he call it? Oh yeah, poetic justice."

The two hoods sat in the front seat on the way back to the Dunbar, Bobby and Carnie in back. Nobody said a word, nobody tapped the dash to the music. They pulled up in front of the Dunbar. Carnie handed Bobby the .32.

"No thanks. I don't need it now."

"Right, it has a murder on it. I'll tell the boss you want a clean one."

Bobby started to get out. "Do you know what happened to Stinson?"

"The IBM guy? He fled the country before we could get to him. We heard he's in Germany. Don't know if it's so."

Bobby nodded. "Tell Mr. Leach thanks."

"He said to tell you he's your friend, Mr. Saxon."

"Tell him I appreciate his friendship."

"That'll mean a lot to him."

Bobby closed the door, waved. The car took off.

Bobby walked into the Dunbar a different man than when he'd first set foot here a few days ago. He'd grown a lifetime in those few days. Learned a lot, about being a man, about being a detective, but mostly about himself. He liked what he'd learned about the young man he'd become.

CHAPTER FORTY-THREE

The drive to Long Beach was becoming second nature to Bobby. He could almost do it with his eyes closed. He and Margaret rolled down Western, past the buildings, through the fields of tall grass and the truck farms. Nearing the coast the tangy scent of the ocean filled the Champ.

"You're awfully quiet today," Margaret said.

"Lotta things boiling around my mind. Nicolai called me. They caught the guys in the maroon Mercury. They confessed. Said Chambers hired them to hit Dietrich and Thomas and to scare me."

"I know you're upset that Stinson got away with it. At least they'll be going after Chambers. He'll be going away for a long time."

Bobby winced at the mention of Chambers' name. Knew he could never tell anyone what happened at the Tar Pits. "He's a lawyer and he'll hire a good, expensive lawyer. He might not go away for long, if at all. Maybe he's also needed for the war effort." His acidic sarcasm almost ate a hole in Bobby's stomach.

"Well, let's try to forget all that today. We're going to have fun."

For now, Bobby would have to be satisfied. He'd done what he could. If the government didn't care, what could he do?

Bobby peered out the window at the brick warehouse that might have been the last place he and Wilde saw. There was no truck at the loading dock; the building appeared locked up tight. That didn't mean there wouldn't be a truck there in an hour or a day, offloading or picking up Hollerith machines. Even if the government went after Stinson it didn't mean IBM couldn't continue with the operation.

He said nothing about the warehouse to Margaret, just reached over and patted her thigh.

A few minutes later they were walking down the Pike's midway, among civilian visitors, sailors, soldiers, and an overabundance of noise from joyful, shouting children and screaming coasters and other rides. They passed the cotton candy kiosk and the Mirror Maze.

Bobby's mind whirled faster than the fastest spinning ride there.

Margaret looked sleek and sexy in shorts and a modified sailor top. It showed off her figure to her advantage. He took her hand as they cruised the midway, held her tight as they waited for the Cyclone to roar out of the station.

"What's that?" Margaret asked.

"What?"

She reached for his coat pocket. "This."

She nudged the .32.

"Protection."

"Here?"

"Everywhere."

The Coaster took off. He took her hand in his. But he was waiting; the whole time waiting.

After the ride, she said she had to go to the ladies' room—he'd been anticipating this. He said he also had to use the restroom; not to worry if it took him a little time. That was embarrassing, but he didn't know what else to say. He escorted her to the nearest ladies' room, then jogged half the midway, back to the Mirror Maze.

His plan was only half-formulated; he would ad-lib as needed. However it went down he knew he would enjoy it. He paid his ticket. Esmeralda-Katherine was at her post at the front, telling fortunes, gazing at her crystal ball. Bobby tucked his head into his shoulder, pulled his fedora down, walked past her with ease, into the maze.

He looked at himself in the mirror that made him tall and skinny. Next the one that made him short and fat. Where was the mirror that made him really look like a man? He found one in which he looked *normal*, though he wondered what that meant. He saw himself as a man, inside and out, unlike when he'd gone as Roberta to see Chambers. Then he'd felt like a phony, an actor playing a part—he'd felt like a man in drag. He thought of himself as a man and, as far as he knew, others did too. He moved on down the maze, trying to figure out which panel of mirrors and tiny little lights Wilde had opened before.

He tried one panel. No go.

Another. This was it. He looked around, made sure no one was in his line of sight and went in. He reached in his left coat pocket, felt the heavy .32 there, which was why he'd tried to keep Margaret on his right side the whole time they were at the Pike. Unfortunately, the coaster operator had sat her on his left. Oh well, it's better she know what kind of man he was.

Jerry sat at a beat-up old wooden desk, doing paperwork, chomping on a cigar. Maybe selling-out-his-country paperwork. Several suitcases and trunks were in various stages of packing. Looked like he and Esmeralda were getting out.

With all the noise from the rides and the midway and the music playing in the maze itself, he hadn't heard Bobby enter. Bobby swept up behind him, raising the .32, butt end high. His arm cocked back, then slashed forward with every ounce of strength he had. He belted Jerry hard enough to knock him to the floor. Bobby imagined Jerry seeing stars like in the cartoons they ran before the movies. Bobby pounced on him, flailing the pistol into Jerry's head again. Blood sprang from Jerry's forehead, his cheek. His mouth. A bloody tooth popped out onto the floor. He was clearly dazed, his eyes unable to focus.

Bobby wanted to keep sapping him, but he also wanted to

get information from him and let him know who his attacker was. He stood over the groaning man.

"It's kind of fun," Bobby said.

"Who? What?"

Bobby waited a moment until Jerry could focus his eyes.

"You? I thought you were dead," Jerry mumbled.

"You guys need to communicate better. Or maybe Stinson and Chambers are letting you twist in the wind."

Jerry tried to get up on wobbly legs that wouldn't support his weight. He wiped a ribbon of blood from his cheek with the back of his hand. "All right, you got your revenge, had your fun—"

Jerry was right. Bobby wanted revenge on him—on someone for all the hell that he and Wilde and Margaret and James and everyone else had been put through. "I'm not done with you."

"Then get it over with."

"Now that wouldn't be any fun, would it?" Bobby lit up. "Tell me about your setup. How does it work?" He already knew a lot about the operation, but he needed someone on the inside to pull it all together for him. Coming here was the only thing Bobby could think of and he was more than glad to find Jerry and Esmeralda still at home, so to speak.

Jerry leaned back on the palms of his hands. Spat out blood and maybe another tooth, Bobby couldn't tell for sure. He coughed, said nothing.

Bobby moved in on him, pistol held high, ready for action. "Tell me how it works."

"All right, all right." He spit up more blood. "I'm just the middleman."

"For?"

"Stinson. IBM. They, we, ship their machines—"

"Holleriths."

Jerry nodded. "We ship 'em to Switzerland. From there they go to Germany."

"What for?"

"What for? You know what for."

"Tell me anyway."

"Soes the Krauts can keep track of the Jews. Find 'em and—"

"Say it."

"Goddamn it."

"Say it!"

"Slaughter 'em. And good riddance I say."

Bobby sapped him upside the head with the pistol. Jerry's hands gave out under him and he landed flat on his back.

"Sit up."

Jerry struggled but did as ordered.

"So you get them from IBM?"

"Yeah, they send 'em to the warehouse on Pine. Then I move 'em to ships in the harbor."

Bobby pulled the pistol's hammer back. He didn't know if he could actually fire the gun, but he hoped it would make Jerry take notice. "Keep talking."

"We were gonna ship the Holleriths out on that boat, the Seven Seas, till you stumbled into the warehouse."

Bobby remembered the Seven Seas—7 Seas—from Thomas' notes. "What about Chambers? Where does he fit?" Bobby thought he knew the answer, just wanted to hear Jerry say it.

"Chambers is a shyster. He prepared all the phony paperwork. Made it all look legit. Created phony corporations to receive orders, do the shipping."

That made sense.

"And where is Stinson now?" If the government wouldn't take care of him Bobby could try a little vigilante justice like he'd done here with Jerry.

"Hell if I know? All's I know is he was packing up to leave just like we are."

Bobby turned to go. Decided he wasn't quite done yet. He walked back to Jerry, stared down at the man groaning on the floor. Bobby raised his right foot, kicked it between Jerry's legs, then sapped his head one more time, "That's for Lois Templeton and Sam Wilde." Bobby saluted his pal Wilde, even if he wasn't there to see it. He grabbed Jerry's lighter off the desk—a souvenir. It was engraved with the *Kilroy Was Here* picture. Bobby smiled, slipped the lighter in his pocket.

He left Jerry in a pool of blood and groans. The vivid colors of the midway and its harsh sounds made Bobby's head spin. He leaned against the outside of the maze building to catch his balance and used Wilde's trick about listening for the sound of the ocean to orient himself. He joined Margaret after hitting the restroom, dabbing off the blood splatter from his coat and ditching his bloody handkerchief in the trash can.

"I thought I'd lost you," Margaret said. "I was about to go to the Lost and Found to see if you were there."

Bobby smiled at her. She returned it. His arm felt sore from the pistol whipping he'd given Jerry. It was a good sore, the kind you get after exercising, which he vowed to do more of. Get in shape. Be a man.

Bobby would tell Nicolai and Duff, though not Pallette and the FBI, what he'd learned from Jerry. They could do with it what they might. Though Bobby knew that wouldn't be much, if anything. He was learning.

He and Margaret walked hand in hand down the midway until they came to the Tunnel of Love. They climbed in the boat. Bobby made sure she was on his right side, even though she already knew the gun was in his other pocket. They snuggled close. Once the ride took off, he kissed her hard in the dark, scary ride. She clung to him; he to her. There was a war on and they'd just survived a small skirmish in that war. There were casualties, but they were alive. And in love, maybe?

He relished making out with Margaret in the dark ride. Looked forward to more of that. Did that make him—*her*—a lesbian? He wasn't sure. She rested her head on his shoulder. He started to speak. Bit it back. He had to though. He knew it. Better sooner than later. It was only fair.

"There's something I need to tell you."

"I like you too," she said softly.

"It's, it's more than that. Something I need to tell you about me."

"You're married?"

"If it were only that simple."

"Jeez, what can it be?"

"You and I have something in common."

"I think we have a lot in common."

"More, deeper than what you may think."

"I'm intrigued now."

"I, I don't know how to say this—"

They came out of the tunnel into the bright seaside sun. It was almost like being saved by the bell, only Bobby knew he had to finish what he'd started. They rode the ride again. It took him a minute to restoke his courage.

"Margaret, I like you. I'd like to see more of you."

"I'd like that, Bobby."

"But there's something I need to tell you. I'm not a man."

"I know you're young, but I think you've grown a lot just in the time I've known you. You're harder. Not so much a boy anymore."

Bobby hesitated, still debating whether to tell her everything. "No, you don't understand. I'm not a man—I was born Roberta."

Margaret's expression didn't change. Bobby thought she must be trying awfully hard not to show any surprise.

Silence followed. Finally, Margaret spoke, "I thought there was something soft about you."

"Well, you haven't jumped overboard. Can I take that as a good sign?"

"I, I don't know, Bobby. I'm not a lesbian, that's the word, isn't it? I don't like women in that way."

"Maybe we—"

"Maybe. I need time to think about it."

The ride back to L.A. was long and silent. Every once in a while Bobby glanced at Margaret. Her gaze was far off. He didn't know how to interpret that. It didn't matter though. He'd come clean. He was glad. No more games, at least not with Margaret.

He pulled up to the duplex on Edinburgh. She turned to him.

"I know you want an answer, Bobby, but I can't give you one right now. What I can say is that we can be friends."

"That's a start." She hadn't closed the door and that's as good as he could hope for. Who knew what the future held? He wanted to kiss her goodbye, instead she took his hands. Held them warmly. But no kiss.

CHAPTER FORTY-FOUR

"La Tempesta" raged across the Alabam. Two grand pianos and Booker's whole band wailing away. Booker had brought in a second piano just so Bobby—and James, who had been released from custody—could strut their stuff across the keyboards. James looked across his piano to Bobby, nodded. That nod said more than a million words could have. Bobby nodded back.

He looked over at Booker. Bobby had thought about asking him if he'd really killed a man, but thought some things were better left unsaid. Booker flashed him the victory sign. Bobby looked out at the crowd; man, this place was packed, the joint jumpin'. And Bobby was on Cloud Nine. He had a place in the band and Booker had told him, "You're not just a reet musician, you're a damn fine private eye too."

Wilde had insisted the hospital let him out for the night. The doctors had argued. He'd said he would jump ship. They sent him with a nurse. She was pretty. And Wilde, banged up as he was, couldn't take his eyes off her when he wasn't looking up at the stage. Marion, Pop, and Margaret's father, but no Margaret, sat at Wilde's table—the best table in the joint. Between numbers, Bobby snapped them a little wave. Feeling victorious, he fired up a Viceroy with Jerry's Kilroy lighter. Still, a wistful breeze of regret shot through him: his parents and brothers were nowhere to be seen, even though he'd invited them all. He hadn't really expected them to show, but there was always that slight glimmer of hope. Having the others there made up for his missing family to some degree.

Nicolai sat with Duff, drinking beer and cheering Bobby on. Squeezed in at their table, chatting gaily with the cops, Leach and Carnie enjoyed themselves, the comped booze and the babes.

Booker led the band, but this was Bobby's and James' moment to shine. Booker had loved the chart Bobby did for "La Tempesta." James had too, and though his main axe was the sax, he was also a damned fine piano man. Booker wanted Bobby in the band permanently, even wanted him to do some arranging. Told him that if they went on the road Bobby could have his own room—Booker knew. Nurse Landers also knew Bobby's secret. Bobby had talked with her one day while visiting Wilde in the hospital. She was good with keeping his secret and he'd invited her to come tonight. She walked in a little after the set started, joining Wilde and the other nurse at their table.

Only Stinson, Chambers, and Jerry and Esmeralda were missing. Chambers was drinking tar cocktails. Jerry was probably nursing his wounds in some dirty hole, plotting revenge on Bobby. And Stinson—he was probably wearing a thousand-dollar suit or maybe a striking black SS uniform, smoking a huge Cuban cigar, hobnobbing with German movie stars and Eva Braun.

Bobby's fingers flew across the eighty-eights in an encore of "La Tempesta." He looked down at the empty chair where Margaret should have been. She still hadn't given him an answer. He knew that he would always have a difficult life. He was happy with his new gig and having solved the crime, but that wasn't everything. He hoped to see Margaret again. Maybe she just needed time. Did they have a future?—he hoped so. But right now he was having too good a time to give it too much thought. Like Scarlett in *Gone with the Wind*, he would think about it tomorrow.

And that's just the way it was in those days, the *good old days* to some.

EPILOGUE

"And that's how Bobby and I met," Booker said, grabbing for a gulp of air.

Diane's mouth hung open, her eyes wide. She caught a glimpse of her astonished look in the mirror and tried to put on a normal face. She pulled a cigarette from her purse. She'd been trying to quit, but now wasn't the time. She fumbled for her lighter, pulled out Bobby's Kilroy lighter instead, gave it a flick. It lit up the first time. Dr. Takamura looked at her askance, then nodded it was okay.

What a story. And how could she not have known that about Bobby—about her father? Booker's story certainly cleared up a lot of things, including maybe why her and Mindy's moms had *divorced* Bobby. Divorced—is that even the right word? But they were married, weren't they? Bobby was really something to pull all this off.

"That's some story," Dr. Takamura said. He turned to Diane.

"I think I have to catch my breath." She sat on a chair in the corner. "I knew my father had some interesting times in his—her—life. But he kept it a big secret. I wish he'd have shared it with me."

Booker put his hand on her shoulder. "He was afraid you'd reject him."

"My older sister Mindy did. I wonder if she knew?" Diane

took a Kleenex from her purse. "My dad was a man. All man."

"Bobby never had a sex change," Booker said. "But I'm afraid he wasn't all man either."

Booker looked at Dr. Takamura, who nodded. Diane stepped closer to the body, as did the Times' reporter, Irvin Hernandez.

"I take that back," Booker said. "Your father was all man— the best man I ever knew."

"You had no idea, Ms. Saxon?" Dr. Takamura said.

"None whatsoever. Though he—she—was always a very private person. Very reserved. I thought he was shy the way he liked to change in the bathroom or in the locked bedroom." Diane thought a moment. "So what do I call him now?"

Booker looked her in the eye, "Call him Dad. And keep groovin' to his music."

Booker walked off, a little unsteady on his feet, but steadied by his cane. Diane pulled out her cell phone. Hit speed dial. "Hello, Mindy."

READER'S GUIDE AND DISCUSSION QUESTIONS

The novel *The Blues Don't Care* takes place on the Los Angeles homefront during World War II. While the war rages in the Pacific and European theaters the book gives us a glimpse of what's happening back home, at least one slice of the homefront in the context of a mystery-crime novel. Here are some things to think about:

1. What main ideas or themes does the author explore? Does the title give any hint as to what the story is about?

2. In the book, the character of Bobby is exploring who he wants to be. He uses 'B' movie cowboy star Gene Autry's code as a guide. Does it help Bobby? And do you think that code still works today?

3. Bobby has to disguise who he really is in order to get a gig with Booker's band. He also has to deal with issues of identity. Discuss how our attitudes as a society have changed.

4. How would you have reacted if you were Diane, Bobby's daughter, discovering things about him for the first time, when you had thought one way about him all your life?

5. Did certain parts of the book make you uncomfortable? If so, why did you feel that way? Did this lead to a new understanding or awareness of some aspect of your life you might not have thought about before?

6. Is it okay for an author to use offensive language from the era in which the story is set in order to accurately portray the times?

7. Did the author's note/trigger warning help you? Do you think trigger warnings are necessary?

8. How well do you think the author built the world in the book? Do you think he portrayed Los Angeles in the 1940s realistically?

9. How do the characters change or evolve throughout the course of the story? What events trigger such changes? How did Bobby change by the end of the story?

10. How does Bobby navigate the masculine world of the 1940s? What problems does that cause him?

11. What moral/ethical choices did the characters make? What did you think of those choices? How would you have chosen? Did Bobby make the right choices for himself?

12. How does the setting figure as a character in the story?

13. Does reading the book make you want to explore the history, music and/or movies of the 1940s?

14. If you were casting a movie who would you cast in the roles of Bobby, Booker, Margaret, Sam, Leach and James Christmas?

ACKNOWLEDGMENTS

I think I have to acknowledge Los Angeles for being the city that it was back in the day. It wasn't perfect, flawed in many ways, and certainly better for some than for others. In order to know about that city, I had to do a lot of research. Some things I remembered from when I was a kid as L.A. hadn't started its growing boom yet. Other things I researched in books, on the internet and by listening to music and watching movies from the 1940s.

But mostly I have to acknowledge my mom and her friends, who were in L.A. at the time and were first-person sources to find things out that you can't find in books or on the net or any other way. They were an invaluable resource. As was my friend Clyde Williams, African-American artist and cowboy, who had exhibited at the Dunbar Hotel.

Photo by Linda Campanelli

PAUL D. MARKS is the author of the Shamus Award-winning mystery-thriller *White Heat. Publishers Weekly* calls *White Heat* a "taut crime yarn." Betty Webb of *Mystery Scene Magazine* calls its sequel *Broken Windows* "Extraordinary". His short story "Ghosts of Bunker Hill" was voted #1 in the 2016 *Ellery Queen Mystery Magazine* Readers Award. "Windward" was selected for the *Best American Mystery Stories of 2018*, and won the 2018 Macavity Award for Best Short Story. He has written four novels, co-edited two anthologies and written countless short stories, including many award winners and nominees. His short fiction has been published in *Ellery Queen Mystery Magazine*, Akashic's Noir series (St. Louis), *Alfred Hitchcock Mystery Magazine*, *Hardboiled*, and many others. He has served on the boards of the Los Angeles chapters of Sisters in Crime and Mystery Writers of America.

BOOKS

On the following pages are a few
more great titles from the
Down & Out Books publishing family.

For a complete list of books and to
sign up for our newsletter,
go to DownAndOutBooks.com.

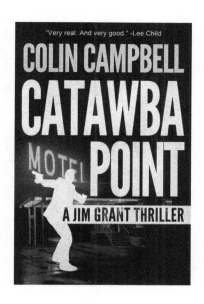

Catawba Point
A Jim Grant Thriller
Colin Campbell

Down & Out Books
June 2020
978-1-64396-105-7

When Jim Grant's flight home to give evidence about Snake Pass is cancelled he is diverted via Charlotte NC where he is forced to spend a 3-day layover at a seedy motel on the outskirts of town.

All Grant wants is a good night's sleep, but with a skinny hooker and her pimp causing trouble along the hall that isn't going to happen. Maybe throwing the pimp over the balcony wasn't such a good idea but that's just the start of Grant's problems, which lead him to a gang of white supremacists and their training camp at Catawba Point.

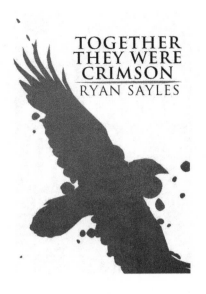

Together They Were Crimson
Ryan Sayles

Down & Out Books
July 2020
978-1-64396-037-1

An Angel of Mercy serial killer targets the elderly, but when a visitor catches her in the act, the Angel is forced to murder her.

Norm Braden, the victim's widower, is grieving for his lost wife and struggling to hold his family together. The killer visits Norm, claims she hasn't been feeling right since, Norm says, "It's guilt. "You feel guilty for what you did."

Norm seeks revenge. The Angel seeks some form of completion she sees in him. And their cat-and-mouse game begins.

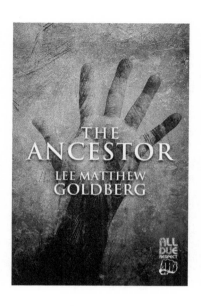

The Ancestor
Lee Matthew Goldberg

All Due Respect, an imprint of
Down & Out Books
August 2020
978-1-64396-114-9

A man wakes up in the Alaskan wilderness with no memory of who he is, except for the belief that he's was a prospector from the Gold Rush and has been frozen in ice for over a hundred years.

A meditation on love lost and unfulfilled dreams, *The Ancestor* is a thrilling page-turner in present day Alaska and a historical adventure about the perilous Gold Rush expeditions where prospectors left behind their lives for the promise of hope and a better future.

Shotgun Honey Presents Volume 4: RECOIL
Ron Earl Phillips, editor

Shotgun Honey, an imprint of
Down & Out Books
May 2020
978-1-64396-138-5

With new and established authors from around the world, Shotgun Honey Presents Volume 4: RECOIL delivers stories that explore a darker side of remorse, revenge, circumstance, and humanity.

Contributors: Rusty Barnes, Susan Benson, Sarah M. Chen, Kristy Claxton, Jen Conley, Brandon Daily, Barbara DeMarco-Barrett, Hector Duarte Jr., Danny Gardner, Tia Ja'nae, Carmen Jaramillo, Nick Kolakowski, JJ Landry, Bethany Maines, Tess Makovesky, Alexander Nachaj, David Nemeth, Cindy O'Quinn, Brandon Sears, Johnny Shaw, Kieran Shea, Gigi Vernon, Patrick Whitehurst.